Vol. XCI

D1577845

No. 4

Bible Expositor and Illuminator

FALL QUARTER
September, October, November 2019

Editor in Chief: Todd Williams

"CHRISTIAN LIFE SERIES"

UGP

UNION GOSPEL PRESS

Edited and published quarterly by
THE INCORPORATED TRUSTEES OF THE
GOSPEL WORKER SOCIETY
UNION GOSPEL PRESS DIVISION

Rev. W. B. Musselman, Founder

Price: $5.00 per quarter*
$20.00 per year*

*shipping and handling extra

ISBN 978-1-59843-827-7

LOOKING AHEAD

The Exodus, God's deliverance of Israel from Egyptian bondage, is one of the central events in Old Testament history. It is remembered annually even today by Jewish people throughout the world in the Passover celebration. Our studies this quarter look at this crucial event and how God, through both providence and miracles, brought it about.

The circumstances of Israel's bondage in Egypt is the subject of the first lesson. Even though greatly oppressed, God multiplied the people and protected them from the pharaoh's plan to murder their male children.

The next three lessons recount God's unique call and preparation of the deliverer, Moses. Lesson 2 tells of the birth of Moses, his preservation through his parents' faith, and the compassion of Pharaoh's daughter. Lesson 3 then tells of the grown Moses' identification with his own people and the rash act that led to his exile. We meet the now aged Moses in lesson 4, where we witness God's dramatic call of him to return to Egypt to lead his people out of slavery.

The second unit of lessons (lessons 5 through 9) focuses on Moses' confrontation with Pharaoh, as well as the Egyptian gods, as he presented God's demand that the Israelites be set free. Lesson 5 describes the initial meeting with Pharaoh and the negative results. The sixth lesson brings us to the beginning of the divine plagues God brought upon Egypt, as the waters were turned to blood. Lesson 7 reviews the aftermath of the devastating plague of hail and Pharaoh's failure to keep his promise to release the Israelites. The following lesson is on the plague of darkness and another refusal by Pharaoh to follow through on his promise to release the people.

God's instructions to Israel about preparing for the final plague—the death of the firstborn—are found in lesson 9. Lesson 10 recounts the plague itself, which finally led to freedom for Israel. Lessons 10 through 13 describe the final deliverance of Israel from Egypt and then from the pursuing Egyptian army—which God destroyed in the sea through which Israel passed safely.

Through the lessons for this quarter, we gain a greater understanding and appreciation for God's holiness, power, justice, and grace.

—*Jarl K. Waggoner.*

EDITORIALS

Between "Ask" and "Receive"

JEFFERY J. VANGOETHEM

We have before us in this issue of the *Bible Expositor and Illuminator* a lesson series entitled "Deliverance," based on the powerful narrative of the Exodus. How wonderful it is when God intervenes in our lives and brings a mighty deliverance. We pray for such things frequently.

Sometimes God delivers us in an instant. The church I pastor is named after C. I. Scofield, author of the well-known *Scofield Reference Bible*. It is said that when he came to Christ, he was wonderfully and instantaneously delivered from a terrible addiction to alcohol that was destroying his life. Sometimes God works in that fashion.

I think also of Abraham's servant in Genesis 24 in his mission to find a bride for Isaac. The Bible states that even before he was done praying, Rebekah appeared on the scene (vs. 15). God immediately answered the prayer of Abraham's servant.

There are other occasions, however, in which we seek the Lord with earnest prayer, but deliverance does not come quickly. God's answer is not immediate. This was the case with the Israelites during the period of the Exodus. Things came along step by step, but there were many challenges and delays. The people often cried out to God, but there was no immediate answer.

Despite wonderful promises like John 16:24, "Hitherto have ye asked nothing in my name: ask and ye shall receive, that your joy many be full," we often find ourselves between "ask" and "receive." We have prayed, we have asked, we have sought the Lord, but we do not see the answer yet.

We find this period of waiting difficult, and such verses as John 16:24 can make us think that every answer should come as soon as we pray. A young woman in church prays for a godly husband and wants to find him in the foyer of the church that very day. A businessman prays for the success of a new business and expects a hundred new customers within the first week. But it does not always happen like that.

What are we to think about our lives when we are stuck between "ask" and "receive"? We have prayed and are praying, but the answer, the deliverance, has not yet come.

First let's remember that all prayer has conditions. John 16:24 and verses like it are given in the context of all the rest of biblical teaching on prayer. And prayer has many conditions.

First, we have to confess all known sin and seek to be in a right relationship with God as we pray (Ps. 66:18). Similarly, God also asks us to be in a right relationship with the other people in our lives. We need to be living and abiding in forgiving, honest, and loving relationships (Matt. 5:23-24).

Of course, the Bible also strongly cautions us about praying with bad or selfish motives (Jas. 4:3). Moreover, God's Word teaches us to pray perseveringly in faith and that we are not to give up in prayer (Luke 18:1-8). These are some of the general conditions of prayer.

However, even when we have met these conditions, we can still find ourselves between "ask" and "receive." So

(Editorials continued on page 186)

SCRIPTURE LESSON TEXT

EXOD. 1:7 And the children of Israel were fruitful, and increased abundantly, and multiplied, and waxed exceeding mighty; and the land was filled with them.

8 Now there arose up a new king over Egypt, which knew not Joseph.

9 And he said unto his people, Behold, the people of the children of Israel *are* more and mightier than we:

10 Come on, let us deal wisely with them; lest they multiply, and it come to pass, that, when there falleth out any war, they join also unto our enemies, and fight against us, and *so* get them up out of the land.

11 Therefore they did set over them taskmasters to afflict them with their burdens. And they built for Pharaoh treasure cities, Pithom and Raamses.

12 But the more they afflicted them, the more they multiplied and grew. And they were grieved because of the children of Israel.

13 And the Egyptians made the children of Israel to serve with rigour:

14 And they made their lives bitter with hard bondage, in morter, and in brick, and in all manner of service in the field: all their service, wherein they made them serve, *was* with rigour.

15 And the king of Egypt spake to the Hebrew midwives, of which the name of the one *was* Shiphrah, and the name of the other Puah:

16 And he said, When ye do the office of a midwife to the Hebrew women, and see *them* upon the stools; if it *be* a son, then ye shall kill him: but if it *be* a daughter, then she shall live.

17 But the midwives feared God, and did not as the king of Egypt commanded them, but saved the men children alive.

18 And the king of Egypt called for the midwives, and said unto them, Why have ye done this thing, and have saved the men children alive?

19 And the midwives said unto Pharaoh, Because the Hebrew women *are* not as the Egyptian women; for they *are* lively, and are delivered ere the midwives come in unto them.

20 Therefore God dealt well with the midwives: and the people multiplied, and waxed very mighty.

21 And it came to pass, because the midwives feared God, that he made them houses.

22 And Pharaoh charged all his people, saying, Every son that is born ye shall cast into the river, and every daughter ye shall save alive.

NOTES

4

A Long, Hard Oppression

Lesson Text: Exodus 1:7-22

Related Scriptures: Acts 7:17-19; Psalm 105:23-25

TIME: around 1528 B.C.   PLACE: Egypt

GOLDEN TEXT—"The Egyptians made the children of Israel to serve with rigour: and they made their lives bitter with hard bondage" (Exodus 1:13-14).

Introduction

Golda Meir was prime minister of Israel from 1969 to 1974, serving her country during a critical period that included the Yom Kippur War in 1973. Meir's rise to the most powerful position in Israel followed a long, circuitous, and unexpected route. She was born in Ukraine but moved to Wisconsin at an early age. She became a schoolteacher, but after marrying, she and her husband immigrated to Israel, where Golda worked on a kibbutz doing simple agricultural work. Forty-eight years later, she became the fourth person to serve as Israel's prime minister. Who could have imagined it?

Golda's ancestors, the people of Israel, also took a long and winding course to becoming the "great nation" God promised to make of Abraham's

descendants (cf. Gen. 12:2). It was not what they expected or even wanted, but through it all, God was working out His plan for them.

Our plans often change; God's plans do not. He is present and at work, leading us, teaching us, and molding us through all our experiences to make us who He wants us to be. He asks only for our faith in Him and faithfulness to Him.

LESSON OUTLINE

I. ISRAEL PROSPERS IN EGYPT— Exod. 1:7

II. ISRAEL SUFFERS IN EGYPT— Exod. 1:8-14

III. ISRAEL SURVIVES IN EGYPT— Exod. 1:15-22

Exposition: Verse by Verse

ISRAEL PROSPERS IN EGYPT

EXOD. 1:7 And the children of Israel were fruitful, and increased abundantly, and multiplied, and waxed exceeding mighty; and the land was filled with them.

Abraham's grandson Jacob (also known as Israel) and his family were spared from famine when, in God's providence, Jacob's son Joseph rose to power in Egypt and settled the entire family there (Gen. 41—50). They were welcomed there, though they lived apart from the Egyptians. However, they were still not in the land God had promised them.

Exodus 1:6 reminds us that Joseph died in the land of Egypt, along with all his generation. Verse 7 tells us that the Israelites prospered greatly in the time following Joseph's death. This was perhaps a considerable period, for as we shall see, a lot of time is compressed into Exodus 1. The description of the Hebrew people focuses on their phenomenal growth, as they "increased," "multiplied," grew "mighty," and filled the land (cf. Gen. 1:28). The fruitfulness of the Israelites is an indication that God was fulfilling His promise to make them a great nation.

ISRAEL SUFFERS IN EGYPT

8 Now there arose up a new king over Egypt, which knew not Joseph.

9 And he said unto his people, Behold, the people of the children of Israel are more and mightier than we:

10 Come on, let us deal wisely with them; lest they multiply, and it come to pass, that, when there falleth out any war, they join also unto our enemies, and fight against us, and so get them up out of the land.

11 Therefore they did set over them taskmasters to afflict them with their burdens. And they built for Pharaoh treasure cities, Pithom and Raamses.

12 But the more they afflicted them, the more they multiplied and grew. And they were grieved because of the children of Israel.

13 And the Egyptians made the children of Israel to serve with rigour:

14 And they made their lives bitter with hard bondage, in morter, and in brick, and in all manner of service in the field: all their service, wherein they made them serve, was with rigour.

A new king (Exod. 1:8-10). A dramatic change is noted with the rise of a new king over Egypt who did not know Joseph (vs. 8). Given the prominence of Joseph and the presence of the Israelites, it seems surprising that a new king would not know of Joseph. However, there are several indicators that this king was not, in fact, a native Egyptian.

First, historically, we know that a foreign people known as the Hyksos gradually infiltrated Egypt, grew in power, and eventually displaced the Egyptian ruler and took control of Egypt. "The Hyksos were not really numerous during these years, but remained dominant by holding key positions" (Wood, *A Survey of Israel's History,* Zondervan). It seems that biblical chronology (cf. Exod. 12:40; I Kings 6:1) would place the Hyksos takeover around this time.

Second, this new king was concerned that the Israelites were "more and mightier" (Exod. 1:9) than his own people. It would seem unlikely that a native Egyptian king would have such a concern, even with the large increase in Israelites.

Third, the king's real concern was that the Israelites might join with his enemies to fight against him (vs. 10). This would make more sense if the king was a Hyksos, in which case he was expressing his fear that the Israelites might join the native Egyptians and expel him and his people.

Whoever this new ruler of Egypt was, he saw the increase of the Israelites in the land as a threat to his rule. This was his justification for the actions he was about to take.

New circumstances (Exod. 1:11-12). The king of Egypt "set over [the Israelites] taskmasters to afflict them with their burdens" (vs. 11). This marked the beginning of Israel's oppression in Egypt. They were assigned to slave labor under officers of labor gangs. "By placing large numbers of the Israelites in labor gangs, it would break down their will to become independent, and prevent any security threat to the Hyksos" (Davis, *Moses and the Gods of Egypt,* Baker).

Slave labor also enabled Egypt's rulers to build "treasure cities" (vs. 11), namely Pithom and Raamses. These cities were built to store various goods. The exact sites of these cities have not been positively identified to everyone's satisfaction, but they were located in the eastern Nile delta region.

The oppression of the Israelites did not stop their growth, however. In fact, the more they were afflicted, "the more they multiplied and grew" (vs. 12). A divine work is probably implied here (cf. Gen. 15:5). Years later, when the Israelites left Egypt, they probably numbered over two million (cf. Exod. 12:37; Num. 1:45-46).

God's unique blessing in multiplying the Israelites in spite of their affliction was not welcomed by their oppressors, who "grieved" (Exod. 1:12) over the situation. The word indicates that they deeply detested the Israelite people. The intensity of this attitude only seemed to grow with time.

New taskmasters (Exod. 1:13-14). At first glance, it might appear that verse 13 adds nothing new to what the text has already told us. However, here we learn that the Israelites were made to "serve with rigour." This seems to be a harsher situation, and it seems it was instigated by the Egyptian people, not just the pharaoh.

The Hyksos, who apparently initiated the enslavement of Israel (Exod. 1:8), were driven out of the land around 1570 B.C. by Ahmose I, who reestablished Egyptian rule. Seeing the advantage of the enslavement of the Hebrews, the Egyptians continued the oppression. If this is correct—and there is some debate about it—there is a time gap between verses 12 and 13. Between these verses the Egyptians

drove out the Hyksos but decided to continue with even greater rigor the harsh treatment of the Hebrew slaves.

The Israelites' lives were embittered by hard labor in the making and use of "morter" (i.e. mortar, or cement) and bricks for Egypt's building projects. They were also forced to work in the fields. Their work is again described as rigorous (Exod. 1:14), emphasizing that whatever they did was beyond what would normally be expected.

ISRAEL SURVIVES IN EGYPT

15 And the king of Egypt spake to the Hebrew midwives, of which the name of the one was Shiphrah, and the name of the other Puah:

16 And he said, When ye do the office of a midwife to the Hebrew women, and see them upon the stools; if it be a son, then ye shall kill him: but if it be a daughter, then she shall live.

17 But the midwives feared God, and did not as the king of Egypt commanded them, but saved the men children alive.

18 And the king of Egypt called for the midwives, and said unto them, Why have ye done this thing, and have saved the men children alive?

19 And the midwives said unto Pharaoh, Because the Hebrew women are not as the Egyptian women; for they are lively, and are delivered ere the midwives come in unto them.

20 Therefore God dealt well with the midwives: and the people multiplied, and waxed very mighty.

21 And it came to pass, because the midwives feared God, that he made them houses.

22 And Pharaoh charged all his people, saying, Every son that is born ye shall cast into the river, and every daughter ye shall save alive.

A new plan (Exod. 1:15-16). The plan to totally subject the Israelites and restrain their growth was at best only partly successful. So the king proposed a new plan.

The Egyptian king mentioned here appears to be the same king who was ruling when Moses was born (Exod. 2). A careful study of biblical chronology places Moses' birth at 1525 B.C., during the reign of Thutmose I. The hard labor forced on the Hebrews (1:13-14) probably began under Ahmose I. Thus, we can assume another gap between verses 14 and 15, during which the Israelites' suffering continued through Thutmose I's reign.

The king communicated directly with two Hebrew midwives, Shiphrah and Puah. Midwives aided the mother in childbirth, which typically employed the use of birth stools or similar devices. These women probably were recognized as the senior midwives among the Israelites, for certainly there would have been many others.

The king directed these women to see that any newborn Hebrew boys were immediately killed, while newborn girls were allowed to live. This was probably to be done in such a way that the mothers would think their sons had died of natural causes. If carried out, this policy would in time check the growth of the Israelite people and ultimately destroy their identity.

The king's order was not publicly announced but privately communicated. He hoped to quietly accomplish his goal without arousing widespread suspicion or outright rebellion. Why this king, or pharaoh, might expect these women to comply with his wishes is unclear, unless he thought the fear of his power would compel them to obey.

Bold actions (Exod. 1:17-19). If the midwives feared the king, they feared God far more. They did not obey the command, but continued to preserve the lives of newborn Hebrew boys. Their attitude was the same as that of Peter and the apostles when they were ordered not to teach or speak in the name of Jesus. They disobeyed the command, stating, "We ought to obey God rather than men" (Acts 5:29).

Such disobedience to authorities is reserved only for those rare occasions when we are *commanded* to do what is wrong or to not do what is right. Otherwise, civil authorities are to be respected and obeyed, even if they themselves are evil (cf. Rom. 13:1-6).

The Egyptian king soon found out his order was not being followed, and he called in the two midwives and demanded an explanation for why they had "saved the men children alive" (Exod. 1:18). The two women told the pharaoh that the Hebrew women were "lively," or vigorous. They claimed that these women were stronger than the Egyptian women and delivered their babies even before the midwives could arrive to help with the births. This presumably prevented any attempts the midwives might make to carry out the king's order.

There was undoubtedly some truth to the claim of the midwives. The pampered Egyptian women probably demanded help throughout delivery, while the Israelite women, accustomed to hard work, were hardier and often could give birth without a midwife's assistance.

However, Exodus 1:17 indicates deliberate disobedience on the part of the midwives. This means the explanation they gave the king was not entirely honest. There is no indication the king sought to punish the two midwives. He either accepted their explanation or, more likely, decided that any action against them would be counterproductive.

Divine reward (Exod. 1:20-21). The two midwives refused to implement the pharaoh's evil plan, and consequently "God dealt well" with them (vs. 20).

Before explaining what form this blessing of the midwives took, the author Moses added that the Israelite people continued to multiply and become "very mighty" (vs. 20). They were still suffering in bondage, but the one thing their Egyptian taskmasters still wanted was to prevent their growth, but this they could not do.

We might question why God honored the midwives if, in fact, they had not been entirely honest in speaking to the king. The answer is that God did not honor them for deceiving the pharaoh. He honored them because they "feared God" (vs. 21). Every human being is guilty of sin, but this does not prevent God from honoring and blessing His children when they are faithful to Him. We can all take comfort in this.

God had already rewarded the midwives by protecting them from the pharaoh, but Exodus 1:21 explicitly states the primary way in which God blessed them: "he made them houses." This does not refer to physical structures but to households, or families. It may be that midwives typically did not have children of their own in that day, but God blessed these two with families because they had feared and obeyed Him.

One commentator noted that the naming of the two midwives in Exodus 1:15 is meant as an honor, especially "when one realizes that neither Pharaoh nor his magicians nor the elders of Israel nor any other characters save those in Jacob's and Moses' families are named in the first five chapters of Exodus" (Stuart). They are presented as heroes of the Hebrew people because of their obedience to God.

A new edict (Exod. 1:22). The frustrated and enraged pharaoh made one final, desperate attempt to stop the growth of the Israelites. He "charged all his people" to cast every newborn son into the river. By calling on "his people," he was demanding that the Egyptians participate in the killing of Israelite boys. The river, the Nile, was considered a god by the Egyptians, so casting the infants into the river could

have been presented to the people as doing the will of this god.

As with most decisions made in anger and haste, this one was doomed to failure. In fact, the edict probably was not in effect for long. It lasted long enough, however, to alter events in Egypt in a profound way, as we shall see in Exodus 2.

This first chapter of Exodus reminds us that we should never grow too comfortable in this world. We are citizens of heaven (Phil. 3:20), and this world is not our friend. Opposition and suffering are inevitable here. Our role is to be obedient to our heavenly King regardless of the consequences. Only then will we have an eternal impact on this temporary world we currently call home.

—*Jarl K. Waggoner.*

QUESTIONS

1. How did Israel fare in the period immediately following Joseph's death?

2. What did the new king over Egypt fear?

3. What did the king do to address his fear?

4. What resulted from the greater affliction of Israel?

5. Who imposed even harsher treatment on the Israelites?

6. To what types of hard labor were the Israelites subjected?

7. What did the Egyptian king order the Hebrew midwives to do? Why?

8. How did the midwives respond to the king's order? Why?

9. How did God reward the faithful midwives?

10. What final edict did the pharaoh issue in an attempt to prevent the continued increase of the Israelites?

—*Jarl K. Waggoner.*

Preparing to Teach the Lesson

God had brought prosperity to the Israelites in Egypt through Pharaoh's favor toward Joseph (cf. Gen. 47:1-6). But as the years passed, Joseph's authority was forgotten, and the Egyptians and their king began to fear the Hebrews because of their prosperity and proliferation. To protect themselves, the Egyptians enslaved the Hebrews and sought to murder all their male children. But God had other plans.

TODAY'S AIM

Facts: to learn how God faithfully blessed the Hebrews, no matter how much the Egyptians tried to oppress them.

Principle: to learn that no matter how much hatred and evil the world directs toward God's covenant people, God will continue to faithfully bless them.

Application: to realize in your own Christian life that, no matter how bleak your situation, God is working to faithfully bless you in spite of your circumstances.

INTRODUCING THE LESSON

Today we so often see the secular media portraying Christianity as a major threat to the way of life and freedoms that have become the norm for modern society. The secular world both fears and hates Christians, and many would like to take away our religious liberty and silence the free, public preaching of the gospel and the truth of the Scriptures. But as in the days of Exodus, God will show Himself faithful by using that very fear and hatred to deliver His people and bless them greatly.

We must reject the temptation, no matter how strong and reasonable it may seem at times, to return that fear and hatred in kind. It is the Christian's unwavering duty to trust in God's faithfulness to protect and avenge His people as their needs require in His own perfect timing. We must always remember that our battle is not against people, but against the spiritual forces of evil that are behind people's fear and hatred of us (cf. Eph. 6:12). Our sole responsibility is to show God's love toward the lost, preaching and ministering to them in imitation of the Lord Himself.

DEVELOPING THE LESSON

1. Egypt fears God's people (Exod. 1:7-10). After the Hebrews were settled in the Egyptian province of Goshen during the time of Joseph's authority over Egypt, God blessed His people greatly. Not only did they prosper financially, but their population grew to the point that they began to outnumber the Egyptians.

Although there seems to have been no reason for the Egyptians to assume that the Hebrews would ever harbor any hostility toward them, this did not stop them from imagining the worst about their guests. Why this was the case (other than that it was part of God's sovereign plan to reveal His power in the delivering of His people) is a matter for speculation.

Often, when a culture has reached a certain level of languid sophistication and luxury, its impetus to reproduce begins to decline. People begin to grow selfish, viewing the prospects of parental responsibility with increasing disdain. Our own contemporary Western culture seems to have reached this stage. As a result, those who now place a low priority on having and raising children may feel threatened by another class within their society that continues to grow in number, especially if that class represents a foreign culture.

This seemingly unfounded animosity may intensify until the affluent minority begins to take measures to protect themselves from what they perceive as a growing threat to their long-held privileged status. Such was the reaction of the Egyptians to the Hebrews prior to Israel's Exodus.

2. Egypt oppresses God's people (Exod. 1:11-16). The Egyptians quickly formed a strategy for neutralizing the threat from the Hebrews' prolific birth rate and economic prosperity. By making the Hebrews their slaves, they could attempt to control their proliferation and by the same stroke confiscate the Hebrews' riches for themselves.

In addition to enslaving the Hebrews, the Egyptians further oppressed them by appointing ruthlessly cruel masters to oversee them. These tyrants made sure that the lives of the Hebrews were filled with arduous, burdensome labors. These labors included the construction of "treasure cities" (vs. 11), cities designed to store surplus food as well as precious jewels and metals. Adam Clarke, as well as a few other scholars, speculate that the Hebrews' work projects also included the great pyramids (*Commentary on the Bible*, Abingdon).

3. God thwarts Egypt's evil plans (Exod. 1:17-22). Proverbs 19:21 reminds us, "There are many devices in a man's heart; nevertheless the counsel of the Lord, that shall stand." Despite all the measures by the Egyptians to oppress the Hebrews, God was always ahead of them to assure their schemes came to naught.

Our lesson focuses on the midwives to illustrate this: although Pharaoh had instructed them to kill all male Hebrew children at birth, because they feared God, they disobeyed his command, risking death, and preserved the means by which Israel's deliverer would come. Clarke notes that the midwives, "though the law was not yet given, Exod. xx. 13, being Hebrews they must have known that God had from the beginning declared, *Whosoever sheddeth man's blood, by man shall his blood be shed*, Gen. ix. 6."

ILLUSTRATING THE LESSON

The prosperity of God's people was a threat to the Egyptians, but their oppression of God's people only furthered His plan.

EGYPT OPPRESSED THE BLESSED

Bondage and Oppression

GOD

Bless and Multiply

Pharaoh and the Egyptians

God's Covenant People, the Children of Israel

CONCLUDING THE LESSON

Impress upon your students the point that no matter how dark things look, God is at work to bless and prosper them according to His special plans for them.

ANTICIPATING THE NEXT LESSON

Next week we will see that God's purpose was to use the oppression of the Egyptians as an occasion to raise up a deliverer for His people—Moses.

—John M. Lody.

PRACTICAL POINTS

1. Earthly leaders rise and fall; God's power is everlasting and unlimited (Exod. 1:7-9).
2. When God blesses His children with abundance, the enemy often seeks to destroy them (vss. 10-11).
3. Through the strength of God, we can continue to grow during persecution (vss. 12-14).
4. God protects those who fear Him rather than shrink from danger (vss. 15-21).
5. It is unwise for man to pronounce judgment against God's people (vs. 22).

—*Valante M. Grant.*

RESEARCH AND DISCUSSION

1. How can we recognize God-given growth and increase (Exod. 1:7)?
2. How do we know that God is still with us even when people turn against us?
3. Why is it so important for leaders to understand the history of the people they rule?
4. How should believers go about accomplishing tasks that seem impossible?
5. How should we deal with figures of authority who direct us to disobey God (vss. 16-20)?
6. How can we maintain hope in the power of God's deliverance when we are threatened? What bibical promises can we rely on to help us endure persecution?

—*Valante M. Grant.*

ILLUSTRATED HIGH POINTS

Lest they multiply

History is replete with examples of the kind of insidious paranoia that often breeds when a ruling people group hosts another group within its borders. The less-privileged group can be safely tolerated as long as they are not perceived as a threat to the dominant group. If, however, they should grow in size, power, or influence, the privileged group grows uneasy.

This happened in June 1940, when Italy declared war on Britain. Italian families who had lived peacefully in Britain for decades were branded as "the enemy within." Nineteen thousand Italians were interned or deported. One ship transporting such deportees to Canada was torpedoed, killing hundreds.

Jews have historically been victims to this all-too-human behavior. Christians are also subject to it today and will be even more so in the end times.

He made them houses

Last weekend, my husband and I set up our evangelism tent at a local festival. At the end of the day, we noticed that the elderly veterans in the tent next to ours were having a tough time taking down their aging tent stand, so we lent a hand. When they were packed and ready to roll, they stayed to help us with our tent.

Sociologists call this behavior "equality matching." It follows the unspoken rule that every favor indentures the recipient to a debt. When God blessed the houses of the midwives after they had spared the children of the Israelites, was He returning a favor or paying a debt? Not at all. God is in debt to no man!

It is we who owe Him. He created, died for, and forgave us. No matter what we do for Him, the score will never be even.

—*Therese Greenberg.*

Golden Text Illuminated

"The Egyptians made the children of Israel to serve with rigour: and they made their lives bitter with hard bondage" (Exodus 1:13-14).

This quarter's theme is deliverance, which is one of the major themes of God's Word. The term depicts an action that rescues someone for the purpose of setting him free. In this week's lesson, we reflect on the long, hard oppression that God's people, the Israelites, endured. This week's golden text distinctly describes that oppression.

The golden text immediately locates where this oppression took place. The Egyptians, who boasted a long, powerful, and cruel dynasty, exerted their authority and control over the Israelites. God's people were compelled to serve their exacting taskmasters without mercy or relief. In the midst of this severe and unforgiving travail, the prospect of deliverance seemed unimaginable.

The daily experiences of the Israelites were marked by exasperation and grief. God's people experienced constant servitude, characterized by a total absence of peace and well-being. The Israelites did not know what comfortable living meant; instead, their lives were bitter.

The daily bitterness of life and hard bondage involved labor in making bricks and mortar, as well as long hours of work in the fields (Exod. 1:14). Clay was abundant in Egypt, and God's people utilized that clay to make bricks for the construction of massive edifices and entire cities. In making the bricks, the clay was combined with straw.

God's people experienced restless and sleepless lives of tremendous burden. Moreover, they were treated in a barbarous manner that included physical beatings and verbal abuse. The utter cruelty of the Israelites' bondage cannot be overstated.

Unlike later generations of God's people, the Israelites in Egypt had done nothing in particular to deserve the hardships they were enduring. While there were certainly rebels among them, their oppression in Egypt was not a direct judgment for rebellion but simply a part of God's long-standing plan to bring Himself glory (cf. Gen. 15:13-14).

The purpose of all of life is to bring ultimate glory to God. Everything God allows to happen will ultimately bring Him honor and praise—even seasons of hardship and judgment. In light of this, let us consider Exodus 1:13-14 in relation to our lives.

Are you experiencing a season of difficulty that seems to never end? Do the prospects of spiritual deliverance and freedom seem unimaginable? Does God seem to be distant and unconcerned with your present circumstances? Do you bear any personal accountability for your grueling predicament?

I have some good news for you! Asking these questions—and thereby dealing with them with genuine and honest reflection—is the first step to experiencing spiritual deliverance. Through confession and repentance—if needed—and through persevering trust in the Lord and the desire to honor Him, the severity of your bitter life will result in the glorious deliverance God desires for you. When that deliverance becomes a reality, you will delight in His grace, and He will receive the glory, honor, and praise.

—Thomas R. Chmura.

Heart of the Lesson

Have you ever acted or reacted out of fear? Whether intentionally or unintentionally, our minds create the worst possible scenarios to the "what ifs" in life. There are moments when these ponderings help us gather wisdom. Most often, though, these thoughts develop a feeling of fear or dread. In order to protect ourselves from imagined harm, we begin to act and react from our perceived fears. The king of Egypt did this with the Israelites. His fears oppressed an entire people group.

1. The Israelites become numerous (Exod. 1:7). What does the number of Israelites have to do with fear? We have to understand that verse 7 reveals the cause behind the displayed effect written throughout the rest of the chapter. As the Israelites grew in number, they grew in strength. The king of Egypt perhaps did not have an issue with their numbers as much as he feared their strength.

In our own lives we should recognize that whenever we are striving to strengthen ourselves—whether through education, exercise, or skill—there will be those around us who will feel threatened by our advancement.

2. The king devises a plan (Exod. 1:8-14). This king of Egypt did not know Joseph. Why is that important? Relationships can calm our fears and give context to our perceptions. If the king had known Joseph, he would have known that it was Joseph who saved Egypt. Without this context, the king grew fearful.

Therefore, the king devised a plan and put taskmasters in charge to oversee and burden the Israelites, forcing them to build treasure cities.

"And [the Egyptians] made [the Hebrews'] lives bitter with hard bondage, in morter, and in brick, and in all manner of service in the field: all their service, wherein they made them serve, was with rigour" (vs. 14). Despite the oppression, the people of God continued to grow and multiply.

3. Fear brings death (Exod. 1:15-22). The king realized that his plan to oppress the Israelites through hard work was not hindering their growth and strength as a people. Therefore, the king devised a new plan, and he commanded the Hebrew midwives to kill the newborn Hebrew boys.

Unfortunately for Pharaoh, he failed to account for the midwives' loyalty to God. "But the midwives feared God, and did not as the king of Egypt commanded them, but saved the men children alive" (vs. 17). The midwives could have caved to the fear of Pharaoh, but they chose to remain faithful to their God. It is important to remember that the Ten Commandments had not been written yet. The midwives obeyed God based upon what they knew of His character. They chose God over Pharaoh, and God rewarded them for it. Are we willing to obey God even when our lives or livelihood are on the line?

Pharaoh feared the strength of the Hebrews; therefore, he used his power to oppress them, intimidate them, and ultimately, kill them. Pharaoh fell prey to paranoid fears. He assumed that as the Hebrews grew, they would want to take his nation and his position from him. Fear will always cause us to view people and situations through the lens of loss. God will calm our fears as we ask for His perspective.

—*Kristen Reeg.*

World Missions

A three-week-old child is severely burned, his family killed in an attack by Islamist extremists.

A woman runs for her life with her baby on her back as her village burns behind her. She hears shots and finds out later that she was hearing her pastor husband being murdered ("Advancing the Kingdom," *Voice of the Martyrs Magazine,* 2017).

"Remember them that are in bonds, as bound with them; and them which suffer adversity, as being yourselves also in the body" (Heb. 13:3). Scripture directs us to remember children of God who are oppressed. God's people have always suffered in this fallen world, as seen when the Israelites suffered bondage to the Egyptians in Exodus chapter 1. They cried out to God for a long time, and He remembered them.

The people of God still suffer oppression and affliction at the hands of those who do evil. We who enjoy freedom and luxury by comparison should care about their suffering and share our abundance with them.

The Voice of the Martyrs exists for that purpose. For nearly fifty years, VOM has sought to:

- Encourage and empower Christians to fulfill the Great Commission in areas of the world where they are persecuted for sharing the gospel of Jesus Christ.
- Provide practical relief and spiritual support to the families of Christian martyrs.
- Equip persecuted Christians to love and win to Christ those who are opposed to the gospel in their part of the world.
- Undertake projects of encouragement, helping believers rebuild their lives and Christian witness in countries where they have formerly suffered oppression.
- Promote the fellowship of all believers by informing the world of the faith and courage of persecuted Christians, thereby inspiring believers to reach a deeper level of commitment to Christ and become more involved in His Great Commission (VOM Magazine).

Through groups like The Voice of the Martyrs, we can connect with, encourage, and help those of the family of Christ who suffer. We can choose to suffer with them rather than just enjoy lives of ease and luxury, with our eyes turned away from their need. Many of us do not think of ourselves as wealthy; we often think we have nothing to share. But when we hear of believers like Mauricio and Dena, who travel to villages packed in the back of a truck with sacks of grain and chickens and who have had to drop to the floor during a church service because bullets were flying, we realize how blessed we are.

We have freedom to worship our God. We have jobs, food, free time, and money to spend on it. What if we shared more? What if a portion of our lives were set aside to help theirs? If every Christian who could donated an extra ten percent to persecuted believers, imagine how that could change the world! And not just ten percent of money—ten percent of our time and even our prayers. What an impact we could make!

Mauricio says, "We ask the brothers and sisters living in safer places to pray for us.

"I will tell the brothers and sisters that are not living under persecution that it is worth it to serve the Lord. It is worth it to follow Jesus. It is worth it to totally surrender" (VOM magazine).

—*Kimberly Rae.*

The Jewish Aspect

Midwifery is an ancient medical role that has endured through the years. Civilizations both past and present have had professional midwives and schools that have taught midwifery. Such was the case in ancient Egypt and among the ancient Jewish people. Midwives play a special role in the account of Moses' birth in Exodus 1.

Midwives appear early in the Bible. When Rachel gave birth to Benjamin, a midwife was there to assist: "And it came to pass, when she was in hard labour, that the midwife said unto her, Fear not; thou shalt have this son also" (Gen. 35:17). Although Rachel died in childbirth, the son survived and his descendants became one of Israel's twelve tribes.

Midwives were particularly needed in times of potentially difficult births, such as with twins. An example is found in the case of Tamar, whose midwife erroneously identified which baby would be born first: "And it came to pass, when she travailed, that the one put out his hand: and the midwife took and bound upon his hand a scarlet thread, saying, This came out first. And it came to pass, as he drew back his hand, that, behold, his brother came out" (Gen. 38:28-29). When a midwife was not present, friends or relatives assisted in their stead (cf. I Sam. 4:20).

A summary of the activity of a midwife at a child's birth is seen in Ezekiel 16:4. The midwife would cut the umbilical cord, wash the baby in water to cleanse it after birth, rub salt on the skin to dry it and make it firm, and finally swaddle the child for warmth.

The account of the midwives in Exodus 1 provides additional information. As mothers gave birth, they sat "upon the stools" (vs. 16). The Hebrew word translated "stools" only occurs one other time in the Old Testament, where it refers to a potter's wheel (Jer. 18:3). It is derived from a common word for "stone" or "rock" that occurs many times in the Old Testament. In childbirth a mother sat on two stones, with a space between them, to give birth.

An ancient Egyptian painting on the walls of a palace in Luxor shows this occurring in the birth of a royal son, with three midwives attending (*Faussett's Bible Dictionary,* Biblesoft). "Such birthstools are also found depicted in the later forms of the hieroglyphic symbol for 'birth'" (Rubenstein, "The Untold Story of the Hebrew Midwives and the Exodus," www.chabad.org).

A question arises concerning the number of midwives. Two are named: Shiphrah and Puah (Exod. 1:15). With an Israelite population of about two million, how could only two midwives care for the births that must have occurred? A Jewish commentator, Abraham Ibn Ezra (1089-1167), answered that with the most obvious suggestion: these two women were the chief administrators of a group of midwives that probably numbered at least five hundred.

The importance of midwives was also considered in the Jewish Talmud. In the event of a birth on the Sabbath, a midwife was permitted to "profane" it by working, "and all concessions are granted to her as to one engaged in saving human life" (www.jewishency clopedia.com). In addition, the Talmud observes that only women were midwives, no man was ever summoned to assist in a baby's delivery. The practical value of assistance in the ordinary affairs of life was, and still is, a vital part of Jewish culture.

—*R. Larry Overstreet.*

Guiding the Superintendent

One of the major themes of the Bible (if not the major theme) is the idea of rescue and redemption. The Bible itself is the story of our deliverance from the prison of sin and death into the kingdom of God's beloved Son. In addition to this great rescue story, the Bible contains many accounts of how God delivered His people. Our lessons this quarter will examine the first fourteen chapters of the book of Exodus, which give many details about God's first great rescue.

Lesson 1 details some of the terrible mistreatment that the children of Israel experienced under the cruel hand of the world's superpower at that time—Egypt.

DEVOTIONAL OUTLINE

1. Slavery on the Nile (Exod. 1:7-14). About four hundred years before the events of this chapter, God had told Abraham that his descendants would live and suffer in Egypt for four hundred years (Gen. 15:13-14). When famine hit Palestine, the grandson of Abraham (Jacob) took his family down into Egypt. There they were provided for by his son Joseph. The years marched on, and there "arose up a new king over Egypt, which knew not Joseph" (Exod. 1:8).

This new king had a major problem on his hands. The Hebrew population in Egypt was exploding, and he feared that they would soon outnumber his own people and potentially join forces with Egypt's enemies.

Because the king apparently cared more about national security than human rights, he took dramatic steps to deal with the Hebrews. However, it seemed that the more drastic his actions were, the more resilient the Israelites became.

The first step the king took to deal with this problem was to put God's people in forced labor constructing the royal treasure cities. But the more the Egyptians afflicted the Israelites, "the more they multiplied and grew" (vs. 12).

2. Murder on the Nile (Exod. 1:15-22). Forced labor did not work, so the king turned to murder.

The midwives were ordered to kill all male babies. Because of their fear of God (vs. 17), these women deceived the king and protected the defenseless infants (cf. Acts 5:29). When questioned by the king, the midwives told him the Hebrew women were so strong that they were giving birth before the midwives arrived. Finally, out of desperation, the king ordered his people to throw all Hebrew male babies into the Nile (Exod. 1:22).

These events set the stage for God's first great deliverance of the Israelites. It is interesting to note that the text records the names of the midwives but does not tell us who the Pharaoh is. His name is lost in history. This reveals that God is indeed interested in the little people. No one is able to stop the work of God, not even the world's greatest superpower.

CHILDREN'S CORNER

text: **James 2:14-26**
title: **How Faith Works**

Genuine Christian faith is more than talk; it is also action. Genuine Christian faith will challenge a person to focus on others.

To prove this point, the Apostle James looks to the Old Testament for two examples: Abraham, a great man of God, demonstrated his faith by obeying God's command to sacrifice his son; Rahab, a Canaanite woman, also demonstrated her faith by hiding the Israelite spies.

—*Martin R. Dahlquist.*

SCRIPTURE LESSON TEXT

EXOD. 2:1 And there went a man of the house of Levi, and took *to wife* a daughter of Levi.

2 And the woman conceived, and bare a son: and when she saw him that he *was a* goodly *child,* she hid him three months.

3 And when she could not longer hide him, she took for him an ark of bulrushes, and daubed it with slime and with pitch, and put the child therein; and she laid *it* in the flags by the river's brink.

4 And his sister stood afar off, to wit what would be done to him.

5 And the daughter of Pharaoh came down to wash *herself* at the river; and her maidens walked along by the river's side; and when she saw the ark among the flags, she sent her maid to fetch it.

6 And when she had opened *it,* she saw the child: and, behold, the babe wept. And she had compassion on him, and said, This *is one* of the Hebrews' children.

7 Then said his sister to Pharaoh's daughter, Shall I go and call to thee a nurse of the Hebrew women, that she may nurse the child for thee?

8 And Pharaoh's daughter said to her, Go. And the maid went and called the child's mother.

9 And Pharaoh's daughter said unto her, Take this child away, and nurse it for me, and I will give *thee* thy wages. And the woman took the child, and nursed it.

10 And the child grew, and she brought him unto Pharaoh's daughter, and he became her son. And she called his name Moses: and she said, Because I drew him out of the water.

NOTES

18

The Birth of Moses

Lesson Text: Exodus 2:1-10

Related Scriptures: Exodus 6:16-20; Acts 7:20-22; Hebrews 11:23

TIME: 1525 B.C.   PLACE: Egypt

GOLDEN TEXT—"The child grew, and she brought him unto Pharaoh's daughter, and he became her son. And she called his name Moses: and she said, Because I drew him out of the water" (Exodus 2:10).

Introduction

"Providence" is not a word many people today ever hear. Historical documents, however, reveal that it was much more commonly used and understood a couple of centuries ago. The last line of America's Declaration of Independence of 1776 speaks of the signers' "firm reliance on the protection of Divine Providence."

The word appears only once in the King James Bible (Acts 24:2), where it refers to a person's foresight. However, the word represents a theological concept related to God that is found throughout the Bible. Simply put, providence is God's continuing work in controlling all things to bring about the fulfillment of His plan. God's providence entails the use of natural events and processes, as well as people and the decisions they make, to bring about His desires.

Providence is as much God's work as are miracles; both highlight the undeniable revelation of God's power. Moses and the nation of Israel would witness a number of miracles, but the birth and preservation of Moses are testimonies to the providential work of God in preparing the way for Israel's deliverance.

LESSON OUTLINE

I. THE BIRTH OF MOSES— Exod. 2:1-2

II. THE PRESERVATION OF MOSES—Exod. 2:3-10

Exposition: Verse by Verse

THE BIRTH OF MOSES

EXOD. 2:1 And there went a man of the house of Levi, and took to wife a daughter of Levi.

2 And the woman conceived, and bare a son: and when she saw him that he was a goodly child, she hid him three months.

The deliverance of Israel from Egyptian bondage is, of course, central to the book of Exodus. But God had to provide a unique individual to lead a great (but often uncooperative) nation forth from Egypt. That task would take a humble, godly, well-prepared person. In God's providence, He produced just such a man. But, for those individuals he chose to use in this plan, it did not come without challenges along the way.

The work of providing and preparing Israel's deliverer began with his parents. The birth and early life of Moses clearly fell within the period of the edict just described in Exodus 1:22. The pharaoh's law had been issued, calling for the murder of Israel's male infants. In this context, we are told of a man and his wife, both of whom were from the tribe of Levi. Only later do we learn their names: Amram and Jochebed (6:20). Hebrews 11:23 speaks of the godly faith of these two.

In time, the woman conceived and bore a son. This was the child who would be named Moses. A little further study in Exodus reveals that Moses actually had two older siblings, his sister Miriam (cf. Exod. 2:4; 15:20) and his brother Aaron (cf. 4:14; 7:7).

The translation of Exodus 2:2 can be confusing. A boy child was under threat of death if discovered, and it might appear that Moses' mother decided to protect him only because he was a "goodly," or beautiful, child. It is fair to say that every child is beautiful in the eyes of his or her mother and that Jochebed was not unique in desiring to keep her son alive.

Some have suggested there was something unique about the child that gave the parents even greater urgency to protect him. However, the idiom used here has the idea of longing or attraction, being fond of, or wanting to keep; so it could simply be translated, "Longing to have/keep him, she hid him—for three months" (Stuart, *The New American Commentary: Exodus*, Holman).

Hebrews 11:23 again clarifies that both parents were involved in protecting the child. Like the midwives (Exod. 1:17), they feared the heavenly King more than they feared the wrath of Egypt's king. They hid their son for three months so that he would not be discovered and killed.

THE PRESERVATION OF MOSES

3 And when she could not longer hide him, she took for him an ark of bulrushes, and daubed it with slime and with pitch, and put the child therein; and she laid it in the flags by the river's brink.

4 And his sister stood afar off, to wit what would be done to him.

5 And the daughter of Pharaoh came down to wash herself at the river; and her maidens walked along by the river's side; and when she saw the ark among the flags, she sent her maid to fetch it.

6 And when she had opened it, she saw the child: and, behold, the babe wept. And she had compassion on him, and said, This is one of the Hebrews' children.

7 Then said his sister to Pharaoh's daughter, Shall I go and call to thee a nurse of the Hebrew women, that she may nurse the child for thee?

8 And Pharaoh's daughter said to her, Go. And the maid went and called the child's mother.

9 And Pharaoh's daughter said unto her, Take this child away, and nurse it for me, and I will give thee thy wages. And the women took the child, and nursed it.

10 And the child grew, and she brought him unto Pharaoh's daughter, and he became her son. And she called his name Moses: and she said, Because I drew him out of the water.

Through careful planning (Exod. 2:3-4). The parents seemed to realize that at three months of age their son could not continue to be effectively hidden. We do not know exactly what was going on at the time or to what extent the king's edict was followed, but apparently the danger to a male child became unavoidable at this point.

The parents must have given a great deal of thoughtful prayer to their next step and came up with a plan they thought would give their son the best chance to survive. Jochebed placed him in an "ark of bulrushes" (vs. 3). This ark was a small, basket-like vessel that harkens back to the needed asylum provided by the ark of Noah. This ark was made of woven "bulrushes," or "papyrus reeds," which were plentiful along the Nile shoreline.

Moses' mother sealed the ark with "slime" and "pitch" (vs. 3). Both terms refer to bitumen, asphalt, or tar of some type. These would waterproof the basket. The mother placed her son in the ark and put it "in the flags by the river's brink." The "flags" were the papyrus reeds that grew in the water along the river's edge.

Some have surmised that this was simply a hiding place where the child's cries would be covered by the sounds of nature along the river and the mother could come daily and secretly care for him. However, in light of the child's sister being deployed to watch from a distance to see "what would be done to him" (vs. 4), it is very likely the parents had something else in mind.

Their plan to save their son was based on what they knew and had observed, but ultimately they had to leave his future to the merciful providence of God. God was already moving events to secure the protection of Israel's deliverer. Moses' sister, Miriam, simply needed to watch to see what would happen.

In God's providence, the deliverer would be delivered by means of the ark, just as Noah and his family were delivered from God's judgment by means of a very different ark.

Through a compassionate person (Exod. 2:5-6). The ark containing the child was eventually discovered, but thankfully not by those who were looking for Hebrew children to cast into the Nile. Rather, it came to the attention of the "daughter of Pharaoh" and her attendants when she came down to the river to "wash herself."

It is not likely she was bathing but rather ceremonially washing in the Nile. "The waters of the Nile were regarded as sacred, and such washing was more of an ablution with its [supposed] health-giving and fructifying effects" (Barker and Kohlenberger, eds., *The Expositor's Bible Commentary—Abridged Edition*, Zondervan).

Did Jochebed place the ark in this location for the very purpose of having someone—and perhaps the daughter of Pharaoh in particular—find their son along the river's edge? This may well have been the mother's plan, but whether it was or not, God saw to it that the basket floating among the reeds was spotted by just the right person.

Upon spotting the ark, the Egyptian princess had her attendants bring it to her. When she opened it, she found the baby crying and was moved with compassion. Although she immediately recognized the child as a Hebrew, this woman did not share her father's cruel hatred of the Israelites—and especially not of a helpless infant.

Through abundant provision (Exod. 2:7-9). It is probable the pharaoh at this time was Thutmose I (1528–1508 b.c.). If so, this daughter must have been Hatshepsut, who later assumed power in Egypt and reigned as queen. As the daughter of Pharaoh Thutmose I, she was one person who could effectively defy the king's order, or at least secretly get around it.

That this was on her mind seemed

to be clear even to Miriam, who was watching from a distance. Miriam quickly appeared and offered to call a Hebrew woman to nurse the child for her. Miriam did not identify herself as the child's sister, but it is likely Pharaoh's daughter quickly caught on to what was happening, especially when the girl so readily offered a solution to her dilemma.

In her compassion, the princess had already determined to protect the infant in the ark. However, he was not yet weaned, and it was highly unlikely she could find an Egyptian woman willing to take and nurse the child—if she had even thought that far ahead at this point. So she immediately told Miriam to go and bring a nurse from among the Israelites. Miriam, of course, brought her "the child's mother" (vs. 8). Again, Pharaoh's daughter probably realized this was the baby's mother, even if this fact was not stated.

The princess told Jochebed to take the child and nurse him. Unstated here, though undoubtedly discussed by the women, were the details. Presumably, the child would remain with his mother until he was weaned, and then he would be returned to the daughter of Pharaoh. Thus, it could be several years before Jochebed delivered him to the princess.

It would have been at least two to three years, though "perhaps she kept him longer, bringing him frequently to the princess, who must not be allowed to forget him, while at the same time cultivating in his young heart a love and loyalty to the race from which he sprang" (Tenney, ed., *The Zondervan Pictorial Encyclopedia of the Bible*, Zondervan).

Moses must have had at least some continuing contact with his birth parents beyond three years of age, for as an adult he clearly understood his heritage and identified with the Hebrew people, not the Egyptians (cf. Exod. 2:11-12; Heb. 11:24-27).

Not only did Jochebed get to care for her son in the early years of his life, but in God's providence she was even paid for doing so. She "took the child, and nursed it" (Exod. 2:9) on behalf of Pharaoh's daughter, who paid her wages for this service.

With the trauma Moses' parents endured, it is easy to overlook what the pharaoh's daughter did. By taking in the Hebrew child, she was setting herself against the policy of her father. And with multiple attendants present, word of what she had done could have easily gotten out.

In addition, we should not forget that it was likely difficult for her to give up to the Hebrew woman the child she had just claimed as her own. One writer noted, "That she is willing to surrender the child, at least until weaning, says something profound about her respect for the honesty and integrity of these 'Hebrews.' After all, Jochebed can go 'underground' with her baby, and the princess may never see him or her again" (Hamilton, *Exodus: An Exegetical Commentary*, Baker Academic).

Unknown to the princess, the family of Moses had certainly considered all their options and had ruled out the feasibility of going "underground." In fact, taking the child back to nurse him still would have left him in danger unless some appropriate measures were taken. We can assume, then, that the princess provided some sort of protection for the child Moses during this time.

Through gracious adoption (Exod. 2:10). If we think it was difficult for Pharaoh's daughter to give up the baby for a few years, it is hard to imagine how emotionally wrenching it was for Amram and Jochebed to give up their young son to be raised by Egyptians. They had seen God work in wondrous ways to protect him, however, and they could safely entrust him to the Lord to direct his paths even now.

Jochebed brought her son to Pharaoh's daughter, and he became her son. This apparently indicates a formal adoption, giving him all the privileges of being a member of the royal Egyptian family. Interestingly, Hebrews 11:24 tells us Moses "refused to be called the son of Pharaoh's daughter." This, however, points to a decision later in his life to place "concern for his own people" above "a career in Egypt" (Davis, *Moses and the Gods of Egypt,* Baker).

The name "Moses" appears for the first time in Exodus 2:10. There are at least two questions regarding this name that are much debated among scholars. First, is Moses a Hebrew name or an Egyptian name? Second, how does the name fit with the fact that he was drawn out of the water?

Since the Egyptian princess gave him the name, it is most likely of Egyptian origin. However, some scholars argue that the explanation for the name makes more sense if it is Hebrew, since the Hebrew meaning is "drawing out" and the Egyptian meaning is "to bear," or "to give birth to." Gleason Archer, on the other hand, argues that the Egyptian meaning is "son of the water" (Archer, *A Survey of Old Testament Introduction,* Moody).

It is a complicated issue, but it is clear the princess connected the name to the fact that he had been drawn out of the water. By Pharaoh's command, this child was to be cast into the river; by the providence of God, Pharaoh's daughter took him out of the river. The one who would be used to deliver Israel was himself delivered by the working of God.

Interestingly, God is not mentioned in these first ten verses of Exodus. Yet His providential work in these events is undeniable. Moses' parents did what they could to protect him, but once they reached the limit of what they could do, God stepped in and moved people and events to preserve the chosen deliverer of Israel.

The princess was probably the only Egyptian who would dare flout Pharaoh's edict. She was compassionate toward the child Moses and able to protect and provide for him. This was the person God brought to the river that day.

God's presence is not always evident. We might not perceive what He is doing or even understand it if we do. But of this we can be certain: God is present, and He is always at work in this world and in our lives for our good and His glory.

—*Jarl K. Waggoner.*

QUESTIONS

1. In what context was Moses born?
2. What do we know about Moses' family?
3. For how long were Moses' parents able to hide him?
4. What was the parents' plan for saving their son?
5. Were they hoping the baby would be found? Explain.
6. Who found the baby Moses, and how did this person respond?
7. What did Miriam offer to do for the person who found her brother?
8. What role did Pharaoh's daughter give to Jochebed? How long did this continue?
9. What reason did the princess give for naming her adopted son "Moses"?
10. In what ways do we see God working providentially in the events surrounding Moses' birth and infancy?

—*Jarl K. Waggoner.*

Preparing to Teach the Lesson

The pharaoh of Egypt was the most powerful ruler in the known world of Moses' day. But despite bringing all his power to bear to keep God's people under his domination, God merely used his efforts to ensure that Moses would survive (and obtain the necessary skills and education) to become the one who would deliver God's people from Egyptian oppression.

TODAY'S AIM

Facts: to see that God used Pharaoh's cruel plan for the Hebrew children to raise up Moses to deliver His people from Egyptian slavery.

Principle: to realize that all human attempts to oppose God will actually serve only to accomplish His sovereign purposes.

Application: to remember that no matter how strong any opposition to God appears, He will always use it to accomplish His purposes. We can be encouraged to resist the temptation to despair when things appear dark and hopeless, because our God is the one who brings hope out of hopelessness and creates the most brilliant light out of the deepest darkness (cf. John 1:5).

INTRODUCING THE LESSON

We saw in last week's lesson that God sovereignly overruled all the efforts of the Egyptians to oppress the Hebrews and slaughter their children. The Egyptians tried to use the Hebrew midwives to make sure that all Hebrew male infants were murdered at birth, but those midwives had learned to fear the Lord more than they feared Pharaoh; they disobeyed Pharaoh's commands, risking their own lives to protect the infants.

In this week's lesson, we will see that the focus of God's plan for His people was fulfilled in the protection of and provision for His chosen deliverer, Moses. Moses came to grow and mature right under Pharaoh's nose, so to speak.

DEVELOPING THE LESSON

1. A mother's desperation (Exod. 2:1-4). It is important to note that both of Moses' parents were from what eventually became the priestly tribe of Levi. As Adam Clarke notes, "God chose a *religious family* out of which the *lawgiver* and the *high priest* were both to spring" (*Commentary on the Bible,* Abingdon). Also, Moses was not their first child, since his older siblings, Miriam and Aaron, were born before Pharaoh's murderous decree.

Jochebed must have felt extreme desperation for her latest child. She faced the dilemma of either hiding him (and risking the lives of her whole family) or doing nothing and watching her child be killed by the Egyptians.

"Goodly child" (vs. 2) indicates not merely that Moses was normal and healthy, but that he was also a particularly beautiful and attractive child. God likely enhanced his looks in this way not only to motivate his family to risk their own safety to preserve his life, but also to make him desirable to Pharaoh's daughter for adoption.

Once Jochebed realized in desperation that she could no longer hide Moses, she placed his life in the hands of the Lord by placing him in the Nile in a basket made of reeds and pitch. She put her faith in the Holy One of Israel, who would oversee his survival now that she herself could no longer do so. But Miriam, his sister, made sure to watch and see what would become of her little brother.

2. God's sovereign preservation (Exod. 2:5-10). Jochebed's faith proved to be well founded, for the Lord sovereignly guided Moses' little ark right to the one person who could do him the most good—Pharaoh's own daughter. While she bathed in the river attended by her maidservants, she happened to spy the basket among the reeds and sent her attendants to retrieve it for her.

It would seem that as soon as Pharaoh's daughter laid eyes on the crying baby, her heart went out to him in compassion, even though she knew that, as a Hebrew child, he was condemned to die by the royal decree of her father. As Clarke observes, "Scarcely any thing interests the heart more than the sight of a lovely babe in distress. His beauty would induce even his parents to double their exertions to save him, and was probably the sole motive which led the Egyptian princess to take such particular care of him, and to educate him as her own, which in all likelihood she would not have done had he been only an ordinary child."

As Pharaoh's daughter was deliberating about what to do with Moses, Miriam chose that moment to intervene, pushing the princess toward the right decision by offering to find a Hebrew woman to nurse the child for her. In this way, Moses wound up being nursed and raised by his own mother while under the protection of Pharaoh's household. Moses was adopted by Pharaoh's own daughter and grew to manhood within Pharaoh's royal court! Clarke even speculates that Pharaoh might have terminated his edict against the Hebrew male children and cites this incident as the likely cause, conjecturing that the king's daughter would have lobbied against it after realizing what it might have done to Moses.

ILLUSTRATING THE LESSON

The illustration shows how God sovereignly overrules the wicked plans of earthly rulers.

GOD SOVEREIGNLY OVERRULES

Persecution

Moses

God's Hand

Pharaoh

Protection
Adoption

Pharaoh's Daughter

CONCLUDING THE LESSON

Emphasize God's sovereign work in the life of young Moses. Against the greatest earthly power of that age, the Holy One of Israel prevailed by using the very wicked intentions of His enemies to fulfill His promise to deliver His covenant people from Egyptian bondage and oppression.

Today we too can rely on God to prevail for us against His enemies, no matter how menacing and powerful they may appear. Remind your students that no matter how dark and hopeless the cause of God's people may seem, our almighty, sovereign God is surely at work, turning the powers of His enemies against them.

ANTICIPATING THE NEXT LESSON

Next week's lesson reveals how God prepared Moses to be the deliverer of His covenant people by taking him on a detour into exile from Egypt. Moses had to learn true humility by relying on God alone to sustain him.

—*John M. Lody.*

PRACTICAL POINTS

1. God's plan for our lives begins before we are born (Exod. 2:1-2).
2. Godly mothers tend to make wise decisions that protect their children (vs. 3).
3. God will show us how to do what is necessary when we choose to obey Him (vss. 3-4).
4. God provides safety even in the middle of danger.
5. We need not fear because even unbelievers act according to God's sovereign will (vss. 5-9).
6. God can use the resources of your enemy to strengthen you to fight against them (vs. 10).

—Valante M. Grant.

RESEARCH AND DISCUSSION

1. What difference do faithful parents who trust and obey the will of God make for their children?
2. What can we learn from Moses' parents about trusting God with the things most precious to us?
3. God provided Moses with the necessary skills to deliver the Israelites. What tools does God give us to help prepare us to lead people to Christ?
4. What characteristics of God do we see in this passage? Where else in Scripture do we see these characteristics of God on display?
5. What are some ways that God has kept you safe in dangerous situations? Were you able to trust Him in the midst of it?

—Valante M. Grant.

ILLUSTRATED HIGH POINTS

She could not longer hide him

Throughout church history, Christians have been asked to renounce their faith. Under conditions of persecution, many have died, while others simply became what is known as crypto-Christians (secret Christians). Outwardly, they appeared to be one religion, while inwardly they held another belief. Sadly, this has sometimes led to twisted forms of Christianity. However, like baby Moses, Christ cannot remain hidden forever.

Currently, the world is experiencing widespread revival in some of the planet's most oppressive Muslim countries. Many Islamic people are having dreams and visions of Jesus and ultimately turning to Christ. Crypto-Christians are coming out of hiding.

His sister stood afar off

An eighteen-year-old girl named Katie was deeply moved by the needs of the Ugandan people. After a short-term missions trip, God called her back to Uganda. By the time she was twenty-three, she had adopted thirteen girls. Katie probably had no idea how God was going to use her, but she trusted Him, and He ordered her steps (cf. Ps. 37:23; Prov. 3:5-6).

God is all-powerful and can do anything He wants to do without the help of anyone. However, more often than not, He calls people to take part in accomplishing His will. Just like this young girl in Uganda, Moses' sister, Miriam, was being used by God to accomplish His purposes. She unknowingly helped provide Moses with the tools and upbringing He would need in the future to free the Israelites. Even though we often do not understand our role in God's plans, He uses us to accomplish His will (cf. Rom. 12:2).

—Therese Greenberg.

Golden Text Illuminated

"The child grew, and she brought him unto Pharaoh's daughter, and he became her son. And she called his name Moses: and she said, Because I drew him out of the water" (Exodus 2:10).

Israel, God's first people on earth, is His priceless possession. He created this nation to bring glory to Himself. The Prophet Isaiah writes, "But now thus saith the Lord that created thee, O Jacob, and he that formed thee, O Israel, Fear not: for I have redeemed thee, I have called thee by thy name; thou art mine. . . . Even every one that is called by my name: for I have created him for my glory, I have formed him; yea, I have made him" (43:1, 7).

In last week's lesson, we learned that God's people were suffering cruel bondage in the land of Egypt. God's purpose in allowing this was ultimately to bring glory to Himself. His sovereign plan was to shape and use a unique man through whom He would deliver His people.

God's plan to deliver His people involved the birth of a baby boy and his amazing protection, growth, and nurturing in the midst of a murderous culture. Through a sovereignly engineered set of circumstances, the baby's mother gave him up and received him back again to nurse and nurture (Exod. 2:1-9).

After the child was weaned, his mother gave him back to Pharaoh's daughter, who had originally discovered the infant in his protective basket. This arrangement had previously been agreed upon, and the baby's mother fulfilled her part of the agreement. This was the second time the mother had to separate from her son. However difficult it may have been, she displayed her faithful character.

During the time the boy remained in the care of Pharaoh's daughter, she nurtured him as if he were her own son, possibly through an official act of adoption. Pharaoh's daughter then gave him the name Moses, which is a derivative of an Egyptian term that relates to his being drawn out of the water. Moses' name would be a constant reminder of God's sovereign, protective deliverance that would eventually result in the deliverance of His people from their cruel and punitive bondage.

As the only son of Pharaoh's daughter, Moses would experience all the facets of a royal upbringing. He would be educated like any other son of an Egyptian princess. His upbringing would be appropriate for one being groomed for leadership in Egypt. But God had another plan for Moses. Rather than lead the nation of Egypt, he would become the deliverer of God's people from Egyptian slavery.

When I graduated from high school, I attended a local university for two years. During that time, I fulfilled all my general education requirements for a bachelor's degree. I was not a believer in Jesus Christ, and I eventually abandoned my college education, believing it was a wasted time in my life.

About seven years later, I believed in Jesus Christ as my Saviour and started training for the ministry. To my amazement, all my previously earned college course credits transferred. God had redeemed not only my life but also my wasted years. He delivered me from my sin and prepared me for a life that would bring glory to Himself. What an amazing deliverance!

—*Thomas R. Chmura.*

Heart of the Lesson

Most parents have high hopes for their children. Many desire that their children grow up and do spectacular things. But how many look at their children and think, "You're going to change the world!"?

1. The birth of Moses (Exod. 2:1-2). In the first verse of chapter 2, we learn that both of Moses' parents came from the tribe of Levi. At first glance, this may seem insignificant; however, decades later, God set the Levites apart to be priests. Their purpose was to minister to God and minister to His people. In time, Moses would become a priest, a leader, and a deliverer to the Hebrews.

In verse 2, we read that Moses was a "goodly" child. This does not mean that he did not cry or fuss; it is actually referring to Moses' health and beauty. In other words, Moses was an adorable baby.

2. Moses on the bank of the river (Exod. 2:3-4). At the time of Moses' birth, Pharaoh had ordered the Egyptians to throw all the newborn Hebrew boys into the Nile. Moses' mother had been able to conceal him for three months, but now she feared for his life. She made a basket of papyrus, tar, and resin and placed Moses in it among the reeds in the riverbank. Her heart breaking, not knowing what would happen to her beautiful baby boy, she told Miriam to keep a watch on Moses.

3. Pharaoh's daughter adopts Moses (Exod. 2:5-10). The movies and dramatic stories of Moses would have us believe that it was mere chance that Moses was found. Some stories portray Moses as taking a trip down the river, fighting impossible odds, and by chance floating up to Pharaoh's daughter. But this is not what the Bible says. Moses' mother placed Moses in a strategic place among the reeds of the Nile. Most likely, she knew where the king's daughter and her maidens went to bathe.

Pharaoh's daughter saw the basket that held Moses, and she ordered her maids to bring it to her. "And when she had opened it, she saw the child: and, behold, the babe wept. And she had compassion on him, and said, This is one of the Hebrews' children" (vs. 6). The river that took the lives of untold Hebrew boys and shattered the hearts of untold Hebrew mothers became a source of life for Moses.

At the right moment, a godly boldness must have overtaken Miriam to speak to Pharaoh's daughter and ask if she wanted a Hebrew to nurse the baby. Can you imagine the elation of Moses' mother when Miriam returned to her saying that Pharaoh's daughter had had compassion on the baby and was now seeking a Hebrew woman to take care of him?

In the direst of circumstances, God will provide a strategic plan. Moses' mother must have known in the very depths of her heart that Moses was set apart by God. She was determined to conceal his birth and did everything in her power to save his life.

When we feel like our dreams are hidden in a basket, not knowing if they will live or die, know this: God can give you favor with the right people at the right time. He can send someone to watch over your dreams and speak up for you when you are unable to do that for yourself. And then He can enable you to nurse them and watch them grow.

—*Kristin Reeg.*

World Missions

Last week I suggested that we who live in freedom and safety offer ten percent of our lives to our persecuted brothers and sisters in Christ. Have you taken time to seriously consider and pray about this suggestion?

Let us take some time to pursue what such a commitment might look like. Ten percent of our money is the easiest to envision. On a regular basis, we give ten percent of our income to God for a tithe as He commands us, but then we also set aside another ten percent for the work of Christ around the world. We could give monthly to a specific organization, or allow the funds to accumulate and be available for when we hear about a specific need. (To get the monthly newsletter from Voice of the Martyrs, go to persecution.com.)

What about our prayers? To donate ten percent of our prayer time might mean getting the prayer calendar from VOM and praying for a specific place or need each evening at supper. It could be a certain portion of family devotions. It could mean praying regularly for one or two specific families or current global events that cause God's people suffering.

How can we give our time to the persecuted when they are so far away? Some ideas would include writing letters to believers imprisoned for their faith (this opportunity is provided through VOM), or doing a yard sale or community event to raise money for families of martyrs. Another idea would be to calculate part of every day for a year the time it would take to go on a missions trip to visit and help the persecuted church, and then give that time to go on the trip (for example, American adults average over ten hours per day of taking in some kind of media—TV, computer, radio, phone apps, and more

[John Koblin, "How Much Do We Love TV? Let Us Count the Ways," NY Times, June 30, 2016]. Ten percent of that time, one hour per day, adds up to a total of over fifteen days per year.).

The benefits of giving far outweigh the sacrifice. The eternal benefits are best. God can take even our smallest gifts and place them within His plan for deliverance, as He took a tiny Hebrew baby out of a basket in a river and put him in a palace. However, God provides other benefits when we give ourselves to Him that bless our daily lives.

For example, the average child in America has seen eight thousand murders on television before he finishes elementary school. The number of violent acts seen on TV by the end of high school skyrockets to two hundred thousand ("Television and Health," csun.edu). How much better if our children's connection to violence is in fighting it rather than consuming it for entertainment!

Giving up one TV show, one fast-food meal, one latte—these small sacrifices may not seem like much, but they can add up to significant amounts of not only time and money but also inspiration to change our priorities as well as the focus and hearts of our families and churches.

Let us consider taking up this ten-percent challenge. Would God have us set aside ten percent of our finances, or our family vacation, or our "me" time? Would we be willing to sacrifice this small amount for "the recompense of the reward" (Heb. 11:26) in heaven, the blessing of helping our heavenly family, and the benefit we would see in our own lives from it?

As God calls us to do in Gal. 6:10, "Let us do good to all men, especially unto them who are of the household of faith."

—Kimberly Rae.

The Jewish Aspect

God's providential working is observed throughout Exodus 2. People frequently turn their attention to the faith of Moses' parents as they hid and protected him as a baby. They eventually placed him in the Nile in an "ark of bulrushes" (vs. 3). The timely appearance of Pharaoh's daughter and her rescue of Moses is another testimony to God's work.

It was Moses' own mother, remarkably, who ended up nursing him. "And Pharaoh's daughter said unto her, Take this child away, and nurse it for me, and I will give thee thy wages. And the woman took the child, and nursed it" (vs. 9). Throughout this entire sequence of events, God used the customs of the ancient world to fulfill His plans.

Two Hebrew words are used in the Old Testament to refer to a "nurse." In Ruth 4:16, for example, we read that "Naomi took the child [her grandson], and laid it in her bosom, and became nurse unto it." This term for "nurse" refers to someone who cares for dependent children. It is also used of the woman who cared for five-year old Mephibosheth (II Sam. 4:4) and of Mordecai as the loving guardian of Esther (Esther 2:20).

The Hebrew word for "nurse" in Exodus 2, however, has the root idea of "to suck." Living in a time well before the invention of a bottle and nipple and prior to various feeding formulas, a baby totally depended on breast-feeding for survival. For Pharaoh's daughter to request a woman to provide breast milk for the baby rescued from the Nile was no surprise. She could not feed Moses herself.

How important was a wet nurse in the ancient world? She was not someone who merely stopped by on occasion. She moved in with the family. That often continued not just for the time that a child nursed; it could extend well beyond that.

In Old Testament times a child often nursed for up to three years. The nurse became an essential person in the household. When Rebekah agreed to marry Isaac, for example, her "nurse" (Deborah) went with her and Deborah stayed with Rebekah until her own death (Gen. 24:59; 35:8). "In most instances the nurse seems to remain as servant (Isa. 49:23-24; cf. II Kings 11:2; II Chr. 22:11)" and become an integral part of the family (Buttrick, ed., *The Interpreter's Dictionary of the Bible,* Abingdon).

This important custom existed among both the Jews and the Egyptians. The death rate for women in childbirth was high in ancient cultures. Babies were often in need of a wet nurse simply for their own survival. Moses needed a nurse because Pharaoh's daughter was an adoptive mother and could not nurse him. Since wet nurses were in demand, they were paid well in Egypt for their services. This is indicated by the words that Pharaoh's daughter spoke to Moses' mother: "I will give thee thy wages" (Exod. 2:9).

Egyptian children were commonly breast-fed for up to three years. To become a nurse for someone in the royal family was an honor, since such a woman would become part of the family during those years. The nurse also gained prominent community status. Many of these nurses were women who were already "married to an official in the high court" (Williams, "Wet Nurses in Ancient Egyptian Times," www.unexplainable.net). In God's providence, Moses' own mother became part of the royal household and took responsibility for his upbringing. That influence may well have continued for years.

—R. Larry Overstreet.

Guiding the Superintendent

For several centuries the nation of Israel was enslaved at the hands of the Egyptians. Over time, the slavery became more and more oppressive. The early chapters of the book of Exodus detail how God worked His great plan to deliver His people from a tyrannical nation to reveal His glory.

It is interesting that God's plan to save the Israelites and His plan to save the world both begin with a helpless baby. God reveals His power and glory most clearly in human weakness and humility.

DEVOTIONAL OUTLINE

1. Birth of Moses (Exod. 2:1-4). Divine intervention is the only explanation for Moses' story. By all human standards, he should not have survived childhood.

The circumstances of Moses' birth seemed normal, but things soon changed. Pharaoh had ordered that all male infants be thrown into the Nile River (1:22). Baby Moses' loving parents tried to hide him, but after three months it was impossible to continue this plan.

Moses' mother placed him in a basket, which she set on the Nile River at the place where the king's daughter would come to bathe. Moses' older sister then watched from a distance.

2. Cries of Moses (Exod. 2:5-6). In the providence of God, Pharaoh's daughter arrived at the water's edge and found the basket in the water. When she opened it, the infant Moses was crying. Her heart melted.

3. Upbringing of Moses (Exod. 2:7-10). Moses' sister quickly approached the Egyptian princess with the suggestion that she would go and find a Hebrew woman to nurse the baby. God was indeed at work in this situation despite human opposition. The Hebrew mother not only got her baby back but was even paid to raise him! This is an incredible example of God's sovereignty.

When the baby was old enough, he was brought to Pharaoh's daughter, who adopted him and named him Moses, which means "drawn out," because he was drawn from the water (vs. 10).

Slowly but surely, God was working out His plan. Acts 7:21-22 observes that because of his royal adoption, Moses received the skills and education he needed to lead God's people across the desert and to write the first books of the Bible.

CHILDREN'S CORNER

text: **Genesis 4:1-16**
title: **Cain and Abel**

The importance of faith in a believer's relationship with God becomes clear at the beginning of history when one looks at the story of Cain and Abel.

Cain and Abel were the sons of Adam and Eve and the first children born on earth. Cain became a farmer and Abel was a sheepherder.

One day, they decided to bring offerings to God. Cain's offering came from the ground while his brother brought the firstborn of his flock. God accepted the offering of Abel but did not accept Cain's offering. The author of Hebrews explains why: Abel's offering was brought by faith (11:4). This implies that Abel's offering was from his heart while Cain's offering was a result of grudging obedience.

Cain grew very angry. God confronted him, but to no avail. When the opportunity arose, Cain killed his brother. God judged Cain for his failure. He would be "driven . . . from the face of the earth" (Gen. 4:14) and become a wandering fugitive in the world.

—Martin R. Dahlquist.

SCRIPTURE LESSON TEXT

EXOD. 2:11 And it came to pass in those days, when Moses was grown, that he went out unto his brethren, and looked on their burdens: and he spied an Egyptian smiting an Hebrew, one of his brethren.

12 And he looked this way and that way, and when he saw that *there was* no man, he slew the Egyptian, and hid him in the sand.

13 And when he went out the second day, behold, two men of the Hebrews strove together: and he said to him that did the wrong, Wherefore smitest thou thy fellow?

14 And he said, Who made thee a prince and a judge over us? intendest thou to kill me, as thou killedst the Egyptian? And Moses feared, and said, Surely this thing is known.

15 Now when Pharaoh heard this thing, he sought to slay Moses. But Moses fled from the face of Pharaoh, and dwelt in the land of Midian: and he sat down by a well.

16 Now the priest of Midian had seven daughters: and they came and drew *water,* and filled the troughs to water their father's flock.

17 And the shepherds came and drove them away: but Moses stood up and helped them, and watered their flock.

18 And when they came to Reuel their father, he said, How *is it that* ye are come so soon to day?

19 And they said, An Egyptian delivered us out of the hand of the shepherds, and also drew *water* enough for us, and watered the flock.

20 And he said unto his daughters, And where *is* he? why *is* it *that* ye have left the man? call him, that he may eat bread.

21 And Moses was content to dwell with the man: and he gave Moses Zipporah his daughter.

22 And she bare *him* a son, and he called his name Gershom: for he said, I have been a stranger in a strange land.

23 And it came to pass in process of time, that the king of Egypt died: and the children of Israel sighed by reason of the bondage, and they cried, and their cry came up unto God by reason of the bondage.

24 And God heard their groaning, and God remembered his covenant with Abraham, with Isaac, and with Jacob.

25 And God looked upon the children of Israel, and God had respect unto *them.*

NOTES

32

A Comfortable Exile

Lesson Text: Exodus 2:11-25

Related Scriptures: Acts 7:23-29; Hebrews 11:24-27; Genesis 15:13-16

TIME: 1485 B.C.   PLACES: Egypt; Midian

GOLDEN TEXT—"When Pharaoh heard this thing, he sought to slay Moses. But Moses fled from the face of Pharaoh, and dwelt in the land of Midian: and he sat down by a well" (Exodus 2:15).

Introduction

Patience, we are often told, is a virtue. The Bible affirms this by stressing the importance of being patient as we wait for the Lord and His promised blessings (cf. Isa. 40:31; Jas. 5:7).

An old French proverb succinctly states the value of patience while also highlighting the challenge it presents: "Patience is bitter, but its fruit is sweet." Patience has its rewards, but being patient is difficult.

Impatience is common to all of us but perhaps especially to young people. They often want to achieve long-term goals without taking the necessary, and often time-consuming, steps that would adequately equip them to reach those goals.

Biblical figures are no different from us in this respect. Moses is a prime example. We remember him as Israel's godly deliverer, but we often forget that initially he was not willing to wait on God's timing.

LESSON OUTLINE

I. MOSES IN EGYPT—
   Exod. 2:11-15

II. MOSES IN MIDIAN—
   Exod. 2:16-22

III. ISRAEL IN EGYPT—
   Exod. 2:23-25

Exposition: Verse by Verse

MOSES IN EGYPT

EXOD. 2:11 And it came to pass in those days, when Moses was grown, that he went out unto his brethren, and looked on their burdens: and he spied an Egyptian smiting an Hebrew, one of his brethren.

12 And he looked this way and that way, and when he saw that there was no man, he slew the Egyptian, and hid him in the sand.

13 And when he went out the second day, behold, two men of the Hebrews strove together: and he said to him that did the wrong,

Wherefore smitest thou thy fellow?

14 And he said, Who made thee a prince and a judge over us? intendest thou to kill me, as thou killedst the Egyptian? And Moses feared, and said, Surely this thing is known.

15 Now when Pharaoh heard this thing, he sought to slay Moses. But Moses fled from the face of Pharaoh, and dwelt in the land of Midian: and he sat down by a well.

Moses acts rashly (Exod. 2:11-12). The text of Exodus jumps forward a number of years in Moses' life. He was now about forty years old (cf. Acts 7:23). Stephen's survey of Israel's history in Acts 7 fills in a few of the details of those first forty years of Moses' life in the Egyptian court. During that time he was educated "in all the wisdom of the Egyptians" (vs. 22).

Leon Wood noted that Hatshepsut, the daughter of Pharaoh who raised Moses, was "intellectually endowed herself, [and] would not have been satisfied with anything less than the finest education for her son. . . . He would have been provided the finest in tutors, and his own mental capacity would have been able to absorb all that was taught" (Wood, *A Survey of Israel's History,* Zondervan).

His education would have included instruction in the Egyptian and probably Canaanite languages as well as geography, archery, and horseback riding (Davis, *Moses and the Gods of Egypt,* Baker). All this training made him "mighty in words and in deeds" (Acts 7:22). God was guiding his education to prepare him for the task ahead: he would one day confront Pharaoh and lead the Israelites forth from Egypt and through the wilderness to Canaan. He was not yet fully prepared for that quest, however, as we learn in these verses.

Moses was well aware that he was an Israelite, and he was clearly concerned about his people and anxious to relieve their suffering. This is evident from his reaction to seeing an Egyptian beating a Hebrew slave. It may have been that Moses wanted to see for himself what he had heard about the Egyptians' treatment of the Hebrews. When he saw an example firsthand, he acted impulsively and injudiciously.

Moses looked around, and seeing no one else, he killed the Egyptian man and hid his body in the sand. He succeeded in delivering his fellow Hebrew from punishment, but his vengeance went further than the Egyptian had gone in beating the Israelite. Moses' act was no doubt well-intentioned, and by it he was clearly siding with his oppressed people (cf. Heb. 11:25). However, he acted rashly and violently.

Moses' act exposed (Exod. 2:13-14). The next day Moses came across two Israelites fighting with one another. Moses rebuked the one who was in the wrong, asking him why he was striking his Hebrew brother. The man's reply also took the form of a question—actually two questions—and was a rebuke to Moses: "Who made thee a prince and a judge over us?" he asked. He followed this by asking, "Intendest thou to kill me, as thou killedst the Egyptian?"

Moses surely anticipated that his killing of the Egyptian would be known among the Israelites, for the man he saved would spread the word. So it was not the knowledge of his act but the reaction to it that surprised him. This man knew what Moses had done but was not favorably impressed.

Moses probably immediately recognized the man was also giving voice to what others thought: "They did not welcome Moses' newfound conversion from Egyptian to Hebrew identity" (Stuart, *New American Commentary: Exodus,* Holman). They actually resented him.

The New Testament book of Acts sheds important light on Moses' thinking. With his previous day's deliverance of the Hebrew who was being beaten, Moses "supposed his brethren would have understood how that God by his hand would deliver them: but they understood not" (Acts 7:25). It seems even at this point Moses had some understanding of God's plan for him to deliver his people, and he expected them to accept him. But just the opposite was the case. Moses had acted rashly. Rather than patiently waiting for the Lord to direct his steps, Moses had tried to do things his own way.

How we do things is often as important as what we do. Following the philosophy that the end justifies the means has been the downfall of many people, Christians included. Moses thought killing the Egyptian would secure the respect of the Israelites and cause them to hail him as their long-expected deliverer. But his impatience led only to a presumptuous act that had severe consequences.

Moses' immediate reaction was fear: "Surely this thing is known" (Exod. 2:14), he said. If the Israelites resented him, they would not keep Moses' killing of the Egyptian hidden from the Egyptian authorities. He was a wanted man.

Moses flees from Egypt (Exod. 2:15). Moses assessed the situation accurately. The pharaoh soon heard what had happened and "sought to slay Moses." This pharaoh was Thutmose III, who at this time reigned as co-ruler with Queen Hatshepsut, the adopted mother of Moses. A short time later, Thutmose III succeeded Hatshepsut and expressed his hatred for her by "destroying the representation and the name of Hatshepsut wherever these appeared on monuments in Egypt" (Davis). The hatred he had for her undoubtedly was extended to Moses as well.

Moses, therefore, fled from Pharaoh far to the east "and dwelt in the land of Midian: and he sat down by a well" (vs. 15). "Dwelt" translates the same Hebrew word as "sat down." While Moses would settle in that land, at this point he merely sat down there by a well. This marks the transition to the second act in this drama, as the scene moves from Egypt to Midian.

MOSES IN MIDIAN

16 Now the priest of Midian had seven daughters: and they came and drew water, and filled the troughs to water their father's flock.

17 And the shepherds came and drove them away: but Moses stood up and helped them, and watered their flock.

18 And when they came to Reuel their father, he said, How is it that ye are come so soon to day?

19 And they said, An Egyptian delivered us out of the hand of the shepherds, and also drew water enough for us, and watered the flock.

20 And he said unto his daughters, And where is he? why is it that ye have left the man? call him, that he may eat bread.

21 And Moses was content to dwell with the man: and he gave Moses Zipporah his daughter.

22 And she bare him a son, and he called his name Gershom: for he said, I have been a stranger in a strange land.

A noble act (Exod. 2:16-17). The boundaries of Midian are uncertain. The Midianites dwelled primarily in northwestern Arabia, but they were nomadic people who also occupied portions of the Sinai Peninsula. The Midianites were descendants of Abraham through Keturah (cf. Gen. 25:1-2). Because of their common ancestry, Moses would have much in common with them.

Probably exhausted from his travels, Moses "sat down by a well" (Exod. 2:15) in Midian territory. Seven daughters of a priest of Midian came to the well to draw water for their father's flock (vs. 16), but their animals were driven away by shepherds who were probably unwilling to wait their turn and pushed ahead of the women.

Moses, however, quickly arose and came to the aid of the women and even watered their flock. Moses' response is revealing. He was quick to act against injustice, even when the odds were against him. He was physically strong and energetic. And he was "generous and helpful to people he hardly knew" (Stuart). Such qualities would serve him well in his future role as Israel's deliverer. Yet God had things he still needed to teach him while he was in exile in Midian.

A favorable report (Exod. 2:18-19). Reuel, the father of the seven women, would eventually become Moses' father-in-law. Elsewhere he is known by the name Jethro (cf. 3:1; 18:1). At his first mention (2:16), he is identified as "the priest of Midian." It is hard to know exactly what this means, but as a descendant of Abraham, he might well have worshipped the true God, carrying out the priestly function as Melchizedek had (Gen. 14:18).

When his daughters returned from their duties, Reuel was surprised they had come so soon. Apparently, the shepherds had been a constant source of trouble for his daughters. The women reported that an Egyptian had delivered them from the shepherd and then drawn water and watered their flock. They identified the man as an Egyptian, probably because of his attire and Egyptian speech.

A gracious invitation (Exod. 2:20). Reuel was anxious to honor the man by inviting him to dinner. In fact, he seemed to be surprised his daughters had not already done so. Such hospitality was the norm, though there is no hint Moses was seeking or expecting it.

A blessed outcome (Exod. 2:21-22). These verses cover much of Moses' years in Midian in summary fash-ion. Skipping forward from the dinner invitation in verse 20, they tell us that Moses was content to make his home with Reuel's household. This indicates more than a short-term arrangement. In fact, Moses remained with Reuel and worked for him (3:1) and was given Reuel's daughter Zipporah as a wife.

The years that followed saw Moses and his wife become the parents of a son, whom Moses named Gershom. The name itself means "expulsion" but when pronounced, it sounds like the combination of two Hebrew words that mean "a resident alien there" (Cole, *Exodus: An Introduction and Commentary,* Inter-Varsity). His name would be a reminder that Moses had been ban-ished from his former land and made a "stranger in a strange land" (2:22).

Moses would remain in that strange land of Midian for forty years (cf. Acts 7:30). Already forty years old (vs. 23), Moses had many more years of prepa-ration ahead before he would be ready to deliver Israel. He had absorbed the wisdom of Egypt and thought he was ready when he had killed the Egyptian. But this very act testified that there was much he still needed to learn. His years in the wilderness would give him a very different perspective and create a humble, patient servant who was equipped to deliver and lead God's nation.

ISRAEL IN EGYPT

23 And it came to pass in process of time, that the king of Egypt died: and the children of Israel sighed by reason of the bondage, and they cried, and their cry came up unto God by reason of the bondage.

24 And God heard their groaning, and God remembered his covenant with Abraham, with Isaac, and with Jacob.

25 And God looked upon the children of Israel, and God had respect unto them.

The cry of the oppressed (Exod. 2:23). At this point the scene shifts back to Egypt and reminds us of the size of the task for which God was preparing Moses. The king of Egypt, Thutmose III, died about thirty-five years after Moses fled the country. By removing the man who had been seeking to take Moses' life, God was preparing the way for Moses' return to Egypt (cf. 4:19).

A new pharaoh did not change the situation for the Israelites, however. Their oppression continued, and the people were crying out to God for relief.

If the Israelites had remembered God's promise in Genesis 15:13-16, they would have been anxiously anticipating their promised deliverance. Their exclusive focus, however, seemed to be on the severity of their plight.

The response of God (Exod. 2:24-25). God's response to His people's groaning in bondage is described by three terms. First, He "heard" them. Their prayers were not ignored, but came before the God who is faithful to His people and His promises.

Second, God "remembered" the covenant He had made with Abraham, Isaac, and Jacob (vs. 24). "Remembered" here does not suggest that God had previously forgotten this. Rather, it indicates faithful love and intervention (cf. Gen. 8:1). God was determined to act on their behalf because of His covenant faithfulness, which is expressed throughout the Old Testament by the Hebrew word, "checed," usually translated as "mercy" or "lovingkindness" (cf. Psalm 118:1-29; 136:1-26; 63:3).

The covenant mentioned here is the covenant originally made with Abraham (Gen. 12:1-3) and then reaffirmed with Isaac (26:2-5) and later Jacob (28:13-15). From Jacob, the covenant promises were passed on to his twelve sons, from whom came the twelve tribes of Israel.

The Abrahamic covenant promised the Israelites a land of their own (Canaan), descendants who would become a great nation, and divine blessings. The people were certainly numerous, but they were not in the land

Third, God "looked upon" His people and "had respect unto them" (Exod. 2:25). These are expressions of loving recognition and acknowledgement. God loved them and was genuinely concerned about their plight. Indeed, He was already well along in the process of preparing the one who would deliver them from bondage.

Both Moses and the Israelites were impatient, and we can understand why they were. Like us, however, they could not rush God's timing. Only His timing is perfect. He is always faithful to His people and His promises.

—*Jarl K. Waggoner.*

QUESTIONS

1. What did Moses' education in Egypt involve?
2. How did Moses respond when he saw an Egyptian beating a Hebrew?
3. How did Moses expect the Israelites to respond to what he did? Why?
4. Why did he flee from Egypt? Where did he go?
5. Who were the Midianites, and where did they live?
6. What did Moses do on behalf of the seven women? What did his actions reveal about him?
7. Who was the father of the women, and what did he do for Moses?
8. What did Moses name his first son, and why?
9. What was the Israelites' situation back in Egypt?
10. What is meant by God's "remembering" His covenant?

—*Jarl K. Waggoner.*

Preparing to Teach the Lesson

This week's lesson is a good opportunity for you to teach your students about the qualities that God values most in His servants. Emphasize that these qualities tend to be the opposite of the qualities esteemed by the world.

TODAY'S AIM

Facts: to see that, although Moses may have felt ready to deliver God's people, God needed to teach him humility, patience, and dependence on Him alone.

Principle: to realize that our own strength is not what God desires from us; what He wants from us is humility, patience, and dependence on Him alone.

Application: to emphasize to your students that for them to be ready for any good work in service to God, they must first abandon their pride and self-reliance and learn true humility, patience, and full reliance on God.

INTRODUCING THE LESSON

In I Corinthians 1:27-29, Paul writes, "God hath chosen the foolish things of the world to confound the wise; and God hath chosen the weak things of the world to confound the things which are mighty; and base things of the world, and things which are despised, hath God chosen, yea, and things which are not, to bring to nought things that are: that no flesh should glory in his presence." Moses illustrates this principle superbly, but he had to go through a long schooling by the Lord before he could be used.

DEVELOPING THE LESSON

1. From proud prince to fearful fugitive (Exod. 2:11-15). Although Moses was raised as the adopted son of Pharaoh's daughter, we can be sure that Jochebed, his biological mother, and Miriam, his sister, did not allow him to remain ignorant of his Hebrew heritage. He most likely would have also been made aware of God's promise to Abraham and Joseph concerning the deliverance of His people from Egyptian bondage (cf. Gen. 15:13-14; 50:24).

Perhaps his knowledge of these prophecies was the motivation for Moses' rescue of a fellow Hebrew from being beaten by an Egyptian. Intervening in this conflict, Moses killed the Egyptian and hid the body under the sand (Exod. 2:12). But he soon realized the presumption of his actions when the very next day he was rebuked by a fellow Hebrew while attempting to intercede between two Hebrews who were fighting each other.

Moses came to the sudden realization that his status as self-appointed judge over his fellow Hebrews was neither unanimously recognized nor appreciated. He also realized that his killing of the Egyptian was not a secret and that he would soon be arrested and executed for his crime. Moses fled to the east, beyond the reach of Pharaoh's authority. The "Midian" referred to here is located on the eastern side of the Red Sea near Mount Sinai and is still sometimes known as the "land of Jethro" (Clarke, *Commentary on the Bible,* Abingdon).

There Moses took time to rest beside a well; he was most likely completely unaware that God had brought him to precisely the place and position He desired for him.

2. From fearful fugitive to contented shepherd (Exod. 2:16-22). Little did Moses realize that he had journeyed into the land of the Hebrews' distant relatives, the Midianites. Midian was the fourth son of Abraham and his wife Keturah (cf. Gen. 25:2). Later, the

Midianites became the enemies and oppressors of the Israelites (cf. Num. 25:16-18; Judg. 6:2-6), but at this time they provided a needed refuge for the road-weary Moses. Moses earned the trust and gratitude of Reuel, the priest of Midian, when he rescued his daughters from hostile shepherds who sought to deprive them and their father's flocks of access to the well where Moses had stopped to rest (Exod. 2:15-17). Reuel was also known as Jethro (cf. 3:1).

Jethro's grateful hospitality to Moses soon extended to the gift of his daughter Zipporah as a wife. Moses contentedly settled into the service of Jethro as a shepherd of his flocks, although the name that Moses gave to his first son reveals that he was still painfully aware of how far he had fallen socially; Gershom means "foreigner." Moses had gone from ruling as a prince in Egypt to serving as a foreigner in a strange land.

3. God remembers His covenant (Exod. 2:23-25). While Moses was coming to terms with his lowered status in Midian, back in Egypt the plight of the Hebrews had reached the breaking point. They had become the objects of the Egyptians' increasing fear and enmity.

The reigning Pharaoh had died, and life under his successor had become even more oppressive. "Sighed" (vs. 23) indicates a groan or gasp of grief and pain, or an anguished moaning. The mention that it came to God's attention signals the end of His patience with the Egyptians' oppression of His covenant people.

The declaration in verses 24 and 25 that God "heard," "remembered," and "looked" at a specified point in time is obviously anthropomorphic; that is, it depicts God in human terms as a literary convention. But we should remember that, in reality, God always hears His people's cries. He always remembers His covenant. He always recognizes His covenant people. The depiction of the Lord as having *recently* heard and seen His people's suffering strongly emphasizes that He had sovereignly determined that His righteous wrath toward the enemies of His covenant people had now reached its full measure; the time for visiting His righteous judgment on Egypt had finally come.

ILLUSTRATING THE LESSON

The illustration depicts how the Lord had to strip Moses of his pride, impatience, and willfulness so that he could become the humble, patient, dependent deliverer of God's people.

GOD PREPARED MOSES

Proud
Impatient
Self-reliant

Humble
Patient
Dependent on God

CONCLUDING THE LESSON

Remind your class that the qualities that impress the world are the opposite of the qualities God wants to see in His servants: humility, patience, and total dependence on Him alone.

ANTICIPATING THE NEXT LESSON

Next week's lesson presents us with God's official calling of Moses to become the deliverer of His covenant people from their bondage in Egypt.
—*John M. Lody.*

PRACTICAL POINTS

1. When we respond to evil with evil, we must face the consequences (Exod. 2:11-14).
2. God's love can find us even when we feel lost and alone (vs. 15).
3. Even in poor circumstances, we can still find ways to honor God and serve others (vss. 16-17).
4. The love of God is manifested in us in the way we treat each other (vss. 18-20).
5. If we are Christ's, we too are strangers here (vss. 21-22).
6. God is moved with compassion when His children are in trouble (vs. 23).
7. God always keeps His promises (vss. 24-25).

—Valante M. Grant.

RESEARCH AND DISCUSSION

1. Describe a time when running away felt like the right thing to do. Is it possible to run away from the call of God?
2. How can Christians find peace and comfort in this world through Christ even though they are strangers in it?
3. How can you know that God is leading you even when it seems you are lost (Exod. 2:16-21)?
4. What is the significance of family support when we are called to work for God?
5. Describe the process of preparing for the work of the Lord. How do you know when you are in the right place and on the right track (vss. 23-25)?

—Valante M. Grant.

ILLUSTRATED HIGH POINTS

And looked on their burdens

A poor boy was walking through the forest holding a few sticks. He noticed a hungry old man and wanted to feed him, but he had no food. Then he noticed a thirsty deer and longed to give her a drink, but he had no water. Eventually, he came across a camper who was searching for a few sticks to make a fire. "I have sticks," said the boy. The camper proceeded to pay the boy with both food and water. Quickly, the boy returned to the thirsty deer and the hungry old man.

Moses had noticed the plight of his people and wanted to help them. He had the heart to do God's will, but he was not yet equipped. If God sees in us the compassion for the needs of others, He will supply the rest.

Wherefore smitest thou thy fellow?

Moses was shocked to find strife between his Israelite brethren. The following story shows how things should be between brothers:

Two brothers would farm grounds separated by a small hill. Eventually, the older brother married and had six kids. The younger brother never married. One day the younger brother thought, *Since my brother has more mouths to feed, I'll give him a portion of my grain.* That night he deposited some grain in his brother's silo. The older brother had a similar thought: *My brother has no children to care for him in his old age. I will give him a share of my grain.* When night came, he too deposited bags of grain in his brother's silo.

One night, toting their bags, they chanced upon each other at the top of the hill. At once, understanding the love and support between them, they embraced.

—Therese Greenberg.

Golden Text Illuminated

"When Pharaoh heard this thing, he sought to slay Moses. But Moses fled from the face of Pharaoh, and dwelt in the land of Midian: and he sat down by a well" (Exodus 2:15).

In last week's study, we explored the providential circumstances of Moses' birth. In this week's lesson, we will continue to watch in amazement the unfolding of God's sovereign will in Moses' life as He prepared His servant to be the deliverer of God's people from Egyptian bondage.

When Moses reached adulthood, he witnessed an abusive act committed by an Egyptian taskmaster upon a Hebrew slave (Exod. 2:11). The beating must have been extremely severe and unrelenting, for Moses responded by killing and burying the Egyptian when he thought no one was watching (vs. 12). The following day when Moses tried to resolve a dispute between two of his Hebrew brethren, he discovered that his murderous act was not a secret after all and would soon be known to the Egyptians and Pharaoh (vss. 13-14).

This background information brings us to this week's golden text. When Pharaoh heard of Moses' murderous act, he ordered him arrested and put to death. As chief administrator of Egyptian justice, Pharaoh was responsible for apprehending him and bringing him to justice. Even though Moses occupied one of the highest-ranking positions in the land, his crime earned him the death penalty.

The New Testament commentary on this Old Testament narrative suggests that when Moses heard the response of one of the Israelites who was involved in the dispute, he immediately departed the land of Egypt and "was a stranger in the land of Madian [Midian]" (Acts 7:29). Moses' departure from Egypt was sudden, and Pharaoh was unsuc-cessful in his efforts to apprehend him.

When Moses arrived in Midian, he found a dramatic contrast to the chaos he had recently escaped from in Egypt. The term "dwelt" renders a Hebrew word with a range of meaning, from "dwell," "inhabit," "abide," to "sit." This word is repeated toward the end of the golden text, where it is translated "sat down."

The surrounding context makes it clear that Moses made Midian his home base. His sojourn there started when he discovered a well that was used by many in the area. In exile, Moses was a stranger, so the popular well site would provide him with numerous opportunities to become acquainted with his new environment.

Acts 7:23-25 tells us that Moses was approximately forty years old when he murdered the Egyptian. It also tells us that he thought his Hebrew brethren would understand that he was God's chosen deliverer to set them free from their cruel bondage.

But God had another plan for Moses' life. Yes, he would be the deliverer who would lead God's people to freedom, but his life took an unexpected and dramatic turn that resulted in him spending forty years in exile in Midian (cf. Acts 7:29-30).

God sovereignly uses people whom He has thoroughly and properly prepared to accomplish distinctive tasks for His glory. Do you sense that God may be preparing you for a unique task? Are you currently enjoying a season of waiting? If so, you may be on the verge of a call to demanding yet exciting service that brings glory to God!

—*Thomas R. Chmura.*

Heart of the Lesson

Fear forces us to run. Most of the time, we do not run in the direction of our fears; we run away from them. It is not always wrong to run from our fears. Sometimes the time and the distance from people or situations helps us to gain strength and perspective; nevertheless, we must be aware that the day may come when we are asked to face that fear again.

1. Moses attacks the Egyptian (Exod. 2:11-14). Moses may have grown up in the palace, but he knew he was a Hebrew. Imagine being constantly surrounded by others who are different from you. So when Moses decided to take a journey to the Hebrews' job site and saw an Egyptian taskmaster beating a Hebrew, he reacted. Being raised in the palace as a prince, Moses would have been trained in combat. Rage drew upon his training, and he committed murder. He visited the construction site the next day and saw two Hebrews fighting. Moses inquired about the argument and was shocked to learn that the men knew what he had done to the taskmaster. Once Moses realized that someone knew his secret, the situation forced him to run.

2. Moses flees to Midian (Exod. 2:15-22). In training the Israelites' deliverer, God wasted nothing. When Moses fled Egypt, he ended up in Midian. The Midianites were descendants of Abraham and his wife Keturah, whom he married after Sarah's death. Moses sat down at a well, where he met the daughters of the priest of Midian. Moses showed kindness to the daughters, and ultimately, they invited him to dinner. What began as a simple dinner invitation resulted in a new home for Moses.

When Moses was fearful of what would become of his life, God connected him with the priest of Midian and gave him comfort in the midst of his exile. Moses had been educated and trained for war. Now, Moses would learn about worship, sacrifice, and the humble duties of a shepherd. God was giving him context and understanding in various roles in preparation to one day deliver the Hebrews from the oppression in Egypt and lead them to their Promised Land.

3. God hears the cries of the Hebrews (Exod. 2:23-25). After many years, the king of Egypt died. But the oppression of the Hebrews did not cease. They continued to cry out to God for freedom from their bondage. "And God heard their groaning, and God remembered his covenant with Abraham, with Isaac, and with Jacob" (vs. 24).

Sometimes knowing that God is aware of our troubles is enough to give us the strength to persevere. Other times, the trial is too overwhelming. It is not enough to know that God sees. We need him to intervene.

"And God looked upon the children of Israel, and God had respect unto them" (vs. 25). The word "respect" here does not translate to our modern-day idea of respect. It means God had concern for the Hebrews and had compassion on their situation.

Even though Moses sinned and fled, God still took care of him. The Israelites cried out to God, and He heard and took notice. We do not have to be perfect people for God to intervene on our behalf. We just need to remember that God is good. His love never fails, and He will deliver us from all our fears.

—*Kristin Reeg.*

World Missions

God's call is rarely an easy one. If we are called by God to do anything great for His kingdom, we can expect opposition.

For Moses, that opposition first came from his own people. According to Acts 7:23-29, Moses expected them to understand that he was to deliver them. He already had the idea that he was the deliverer, but he was not yet ready. He had more to learn. God used difficult circumstances to better prepare him for the work. He had been exposed to Egyptian culture (vs. 22), but he needed the additional training of a shepherd so that he could lead the hundreds of thousands of God's people through the desert.

When we hear God's call, opposition might come from many places, especially our circumstances. Satan does not want God's kingdom to advance and prosper. He might send illness, delays, difficulties, and hardships in hopes of stopping us from obeying God's call. For example, say we commit to giving that ten percent of our income to the persecuted church. The next week, instead of an increase in finances to make the giving easier, something happens to lower our finances, such as the car breaking down or the basement flooding. We can expect our commitment to the Lord to be tested, but we should not allow that to stop us.

People can be another source of opposition to answering God's call. Well-meaning family and friends may discourage us from taking that missions trip, giving that extra money, or setting aside that extra time. We might be told to not be so fanatical, to keep our faith personal, or that God can do His work without our help. If committing to missions overseas, we might hear that there are plenty of lost people where we are, that our families need us, that it is selfish to go so far away. Again, nothing should stop us from obeying God's call.

One important consideration is to make sure we ourselves are never part of the opposition to God's calling on someone else's life. We should never be the ones to discourage a person's obedience to God, even if it brings hardship. We should be the encouragers of those who are willing to commit to kingdom work.

The delays and trials God allows often strengthen us for the work. Sometimes what feels confusing and even like a shutdown (imagine how Moses felt!) is really God at work. That's what happened with Erma. She felt God's calling to foreign missions, but then God led her to marry an Iowa farmer. Her heart for missions never diminished, and that was God's plan. Erma "dedicated each of her children to the Lord before they were born and continually prayed for God to lead them."

She passed on her passion for missions to her children. Four of them became missionaries. Ten of her grandchildren became missionaries. Eleven great-grandchildren now serve God in Brazil, Africa, Portugal, Spain, China, Indonesia, and Guatemala ("Growing an Eternal Legacy," *ABWE Message Magazine*, 2017, used with permission). Erma's "delay," or what might have seemed like a no from God, was really the beginning of something much greater!

If we want to do something great for God, opposition will surely come. We must not let that stop us from heeding the call and continuing on—steadfast, immovable—knowing that our work for the Lord is never in vain (cf. I Cor. 15:58).

—*Kimberly Rae.*

The Jewish Aspect

Moses was brought up in Egypt's royal palace as the adopted son of Pharaoh's daughter. In that capacity, he "was learned in all the wisdom of the Egyptians" (Acts 7:22). This royal education "included physics, arithmetic, geometry, astronomy, medicine, chemistry, geology, meteorology and music" (Tompkins, *Secrets of the Great Pyramid,* Harper & Row). A critical omission in Moses' Egyptian learning was that of being a shepherd. God, however, remedied that lack (Exod. 2:11-3:1).

In Jewish history, the sheep was the foremost animal in the sacrificial system. The Jewish patriarchs—Abraham, Isaac, and Jacob and his sons—were all shepherds. The abundance of sheep in ancient cultures is clear. When Israel defeated Midian, part of the spoils were 675,000 sheep (Num. 31:32)!

A shepherd must protect his sheep from all dangers since sheep have no effective defense mechanism (cf. I Sam. 17:34-36). Lost sheep must be sought out (Ezek. 34:12). Sheep must be led to food and water (Ps. 23:2). Sheep have no sense of direction. "Sheep are curious but dumb animals, often unable to find their way home even if the sheepfold is within sight. Knowing this fault, the shepherd never takes his eyes off his wandering sheep" (*Nelson's Illustrated Bible Dictionary,* Thomas Nelson).

Throughout ancient Jewish history, the metaphor of leadership often had its focus on the human leader as a shepherd and the people as sheep. When the Prophet Micaiah predicted Ahab's defeat at the hands of the Syrians, he said, "I saw all Israel scattered upon the hills, as sheep that have not a shepherd" (I Kings 22:17). Just as sheep need a shepherd, so God's people needed a shepherd.

Jacob identified that the ultimate leader of Israel was God as "the shepherd" (Gen. 49:24). "The image of God as a shepherd is a common biblical and ancient Near Eastern image. . . . and may refer to the munificent care of the ideal shepherd (Ps. 23), or the punishment of the straying sheep by the harsh shepherd (Ezek. ch. 34)" (*The Jewish Study Bible,* Oxford).

Israel, like sheep, consistently went astray and got lost (Isa. 53:6). One of the descriptions of God dealing with His people uses the shepherd metaphor: "He shall feed his flock like a shepherd: he shall gather the lambs with his arm, and carry them in his bosom, and shall gently lead those that are with young" (Isa. 40:11).

When Moses fled Egypt, he went to Midian. There he defended the daughters of Jethro, priest of Midian, who came to a well to water their sheep. By the end of that story, Moses had married Zipporah and become a shepherd himself! At that point, he no longer thought in terms of geometry, physics, or astronomy. Over the next forty years, he developed the skills of a shepherd. Those were the exact skills he would need when God called him to lead Israel from Egypt.

Moses spent his last forty years shepherding Israel, a people who certainly needed direction, provisions, and protection. As his life came to its close, Moses understood his role as shepherd of Israel, and he prayed that God would choose as his successor a "man over the congregation, which may go out before them, and which may go in before them, and which may lead them out, and which may bring them in; that the congregation of the Lord be not as sheep which have no shepherd" (Num. 27:16-17). God's people need a shepherd.

—*R. Larry Overstreet*

Guiding the Superintendent

Never underestimate the importance of a seemingly purposeless day. God loves to work His plans through ordinary events. Our lesson this week will look at two totally unrelated events in Moses' life that God used to prepare His servant for the great task of leading Israel out of slavery.

While it seemed that God had totally forgotten His people, in reality He was working behind the scenes to bring about His plan.

DEVOTIONAL OUTLINE

1. Moses kills an oppressive Egyptian (Exod. 2:11-14). After years of living and learning in the Egyptian palace, Moses might have looked and sounded like an Egyptian, but his heart was still with his people, the Israelites, in all their oppression.

One day he observed an Egyptian beating a Hebrew. Moses quickly took matters into his own hands and killed the Egyptian. The next day he tried to break up a fight between two Hebrews. Instead of being appreciative that Moses had defended the Hebrew the day before, one of them asked who Moses intended to kill this time. Truly, Moses was not yet ready to lead his people out of oppression.

2. Moses finds a wife (Exod. 2:15-22). Pharaoh soon learned what Moses had done and tried to have him put to death. Moses fled to the desert in the land of Midian.

Moses eventually happened upon a well and witnessed some female shepherds being threatened by some male shepherds. He drove off the threatening shepherds. The female shepherds happened to be sisters. In gratitude, they invited him home to meet their family.

Their father, Jethro, offered Moses a job. And, as they say, "The rest is history."

Moses married one of Jethro's daughters, and soon they had a son whom they named Gershom, which means "foreigner." this reflects the nature of Moses' time in the desert of Midian.

3. God sees it all (Exod. 2:23-25). What appeared to be many years of random events were in fact all part of God's plan for Israel. He remembered His covenant with Abraham centuries before and was ready to directly intervene to make it come to pass.

CHILDREN'S CORNER

text: **Genesis 12:1-5; 15:1-6**
title: **Abram's Faith in God**

"He believed in the Lord, and he counted it to him for righteousness" (Gen. 15:6). These are some of the greatest words in the Bible. The text is referring to the fact that Abram believed God's promise and, because of this, was declared righteous by God. From that point on, Abram would be known as a man of faith.

God appeared to an old, childless man by the name of Abram who lived in Ur. He commanded Abram to leave his country and journey to an unknown land. For doing this, God would bless him with a large family (12:1-5).

Abram obeyed God and started his journey, but Abram and his wife were too old to have children. Abram thought that he might need to adopt his servant to become his heir to God's promise. God very clearly told Abram that this was not the plan. Instead, God would give him an heir of his own—a son. God told him that his descendants would be like the numberless stars.

In spite of all the evidence to the contrary, Abram believed God's promise. Thus, God declared him to be righteous (15:1-6).

—*Martin R. Dahlquist.*

SCRIPTURE LESSON TEXT

EXOD. 3:1 Now Moses kept the flock of Jethro his father in law, the priest of Midian: and he led the flock to the backside of the desert, and came to the mountain of God, *even* to Horeb.

2 And the angel of the LORD appeared unto him in a flame of fire out of the midst of a bush: and he looked, and, behold, the bush burned with fire, and the bush *was* not consumed.

3 And Moses said, I will now turn aside, and see this great sight, why the bush is not burnt.

4 And when the LORD saw that he turned aside to see, God called unto him out of the midst of the bush, and said, Moses, Moses. And he said, Here *am* I.

5 And he said, Draw not nigh hither: put off thy shoes from off thy feet, for the place whereon thou standest *is* holy ground.

6 Moreover he said, I *am* the God of thy father, the God of Abraham, the God of Isaac, and the God of Jacob. And Moses hid his face; for he was afraid to look upon God.

7 And the LORD said, I have surely seen the affliction of my people which *are* in Egypt, and have heard their cry by reason of their taskmasters; for I know their sorrows;

8 And I am come down to deliver them out of the hand of the Egyptians, and to bring them up out of that land unto a good land and a large, unto a land flowing with milk and honey; unto the place of the Canaanites, and the Hittites, and the Amorites, and the Perizzites, and the Hivites, and the Jebusites.

9 Now therefore, behold, the cry of the children of Israel is come unto me: and I have also seen the oppression wherewith the Egyptians oppress them.

10 Come now therefore, and I will send thee unto Pharaoh, that thou mayest bring forth my people the children of Israel out of Egypt.

NOTES

Moses at the Burning Bush

Lesson Text: Exodus 3:1-10

Related Scriptures: Acts 7:30-34; Joshua 5:13-15; Exodus 6:2-8

TIME: 1445 B.C.   PLACE: Midian

GOLDEN TEXT—"Come now therefore, and I will send thee unto Pharaoh, that thou mayest bring forth my people the children of Israel out of Egypt" (Exodus 3:10).

Introduction

Success in any given endeavor depends on many factors. Character, attitude, aptitude, determination, wisdom, and opportunity are just a few things that contribute to success in one's chosen career. But even with the best intentions, one will rarely succeed at anything without adequate preparation.

Some occupations are best learned as an apprentice, growing into the job. Others require many hours in the classroom. A lawyer typically spends four years in college and another three years in law school.

Becoming a medical doctor means four years of college, four more years of medical school, and another three to seven years in a residency program. And most of us are glad to know our doctor did not take any shortcuts in training!

Few could match Moses' level of training. His preparation lasted eighty years! And every one of those years was needed to adequately prepare him to deliver, lead, and establish a nation of people in the face of almost every obstacle imaginable.

LESSON OUTLINE

I. **THE LORD'S SERVANT—Exod. 3:1**

II. **THE LORD'S APPEARANCE—Exod. 3:2-6**

III. **THE LORD'S PLAN—Exod. 3:7-9**

IV. **THE LORD'S CALL—Exod. 3:10**

Exposition: Verse by Verse

THE LORD'S SERVANT

EXOD. 3:1 Now Moses kept the flock of Jethro his father in law, the priest of Midian: and he led the flock to the backside of the desert, and came to the mountain of God, even to Horeb.

Exodus 3 opens with Moses keeping "the flock of Jethro his father in law" (vs. 1). Moses had left Egypt when he was forty years old (cf. Acts 7:23). He had now lived in Midian another forty years (cf. vs. 30). Those years apparently were spent providing for his family by shepherding the flocks of Jethro.

We can hardly imagine a greater contrast between life in the royal court of Egypt, where Moses had been raised, and the life of a shepherd, an occupation despised by the Egyptians (cf. Gen. 46:31-34). Yet together they provided the unique training Moses would need for the task ahead. Shepherding gave him much time in solitude, allowing him to contemplate his life and the mistakes he had made. It also made him familiar with the geography of the wilderness area through which he would soon lead the Israelites.

The "backside of the desert" (Exod. 3:1) is where Moses now led the flock. "Backside" means "behind," indicating a remote no-man's-land or an open range of grazing land. This was the Sinai wilderness, a peninsula formed by the two forks of the Red Sea. It was a rugged, largely uninhabited area of plains and mountains with few springs, yet it had enough vegetation to feed grazing animals. There Moses came to "the mountain of God, even to Horeb."

Horeb is another name for Mount Sinai (cf. Exod. 19:10-11; Deut. 4:10). Moses called it the mountain of God when he wrote the book of Exodus years later and looked back to his meeting with the Lord there. Moses would also lead his people to this mountain to receive God's commands (19—20). The location of Mount Sinai is uncertain, but it is usually identified with Jebel Musa, a seventy-five-hundred-foot mountain in south central Sinai.

THE LORD'S APPEARANCE

2 And the angel of the Lord appeared unto him in a flame of fire out of the midst of a bush: and he looked, and, behold, the bush burned with fire, and the bush was not consumed.

3 And Moses said, I will now turn aside, and see this great sight, why the bush is not burnt.

4 And when the Lord saw that he turned aside to see, God called unto him out of the midst of the bush, and said, Moses, Moses. And he said, Here am I.

5 And he said, Draw not nigh hither: put off thy shoes from off thy feet, for the place whereon thou standest is holy ground.

6 Moreover he said, I am the God of thy father, the God of Abraham, the God of Isaac, and the God of Jacob. And Moses hid his face; for he was afraid to look upon God.

An incredible sight (Exod. 3:2-3). Moses was eighty years old and doing the work of a simple shepherd, but he was about to learn that his greatest work was still ahead. The Bible tells us the "angel of the Lord" appeared to him from the midst of a blazing fire in a bush. The Angel is the Lord Himself (cf. vs. 4), who appears under this title numerous times in the Bible (cf. Gen. 16:7, 13; 22:15-18; Judg. 6:12-14).

Moses did not realize exactly what was happening. From a distance he saw only a bush burning but not being consumed by the fire. The sight grabbed his attention, and he decided to go near to investigate the strange phenomenon.

The burning bush was not just a means of getting Moses' attention, however. It was a theophany, a visible appearance of the Lord in some form. The Lord is often associated with fire (cf. Gen. 15:17; Exod. 13:21; 19:18; 24:17), which probably "symbolized God's powerful, consuming, and preserving presence" (Barker and Kohlenberger, eds., *The Expositor's Bible Commentary—Abridged Edition,* Zondervan).

A divine warning (Exod. 3:4-5). When Moses turned to look closer, the Lord spoke to him from the bush and addressed him by name. Repeating Moses' name "was a way of expressing endearment, that is, affection and friendship" (Stuart, *New American*

Commentary: Exodus, Holman). Moses, therefore, recognized the One who was calling him was One who loved him, and he answered "Here am I."

Although he was in the presence of a friend, Moses was also in the presence of the holy God, and as such was told not to draw near. He must keep some distance between him and the One in the bush, and he must also take off his sandals because he was standing on holy ground (vs. 5). The very ground was holy, or set apart to God, simply because of the Lord's presence (cf. Josh. 5:15).

Taking off one's shoes was a sign of respect and recognition of "personal defilement, and conscious unworthiness to stand in the presence of unspotted holiness" (Jamieson, Fausset, and Brown, A Commentary, Critical, Experimental, and Practical on the Old and New Testaments, Eerdmans).

In Christ we are welcomed into God's presence (cf. Heb. 4:14-16). However, we must never take such an invitation lightly. When we come before Him, we must recognize His holy nature and our own dependence upon His mercy and grace for every blessing we possess. Indeed, such a humble attitude should characterize our daily lives, for we live every moment before Him.

A clear identification (Exod. 3:6). If Moses had not understood by now who was addressing him, the Lord removed all doubt in this verse. He identified Himself as the God of Moses' own father, as well as the God of Abraham, Isaac, and Jacob. The One speaking to Moses was the God who had spoken to and made His covenant with Moses' ancestors (cf. 2:24).

God was not unfamiliar to Moses. He knew his Hebrew heritage and willingly identified with the Hebrew people, even when he could have lived in luxury with the Egyptians (Heb. 11:24-25). In fact, at least forty years earlier, Moses had some awareness of God's

plan for him to deliver Israel, but he had acted rashly and not in accordance with God's timing (cf. Acts 7:23-25). It seems likely Moses thought that plan had been set aside.

Now, however, the God of his fathers was clearly speaking to him. He had not forgotten Moses or his people. Moses suddenly became fully conscious of God's holiness and hid his face in fear because he was afraid to look directly at God (Exod. 3:6).

The all-powerful God is also perfectly holy. To recognize both His holiness and His power is to realize how weak and sinful we are and how easily and justly He could have destroyed us rather than saved us through Christ. This should humble us and instill in us a holy, fearful reverence for God.

THE LORD'S PLAN

7 And the LORD said, I have surely seen the affliction of my people which are in Egypt, and have heard their cry by reason of their taskmasters; for I know their sorrows;

8 And I am come down to deliver them out of the hand of the Egyptians, and to bring them up out of that land unto a good land and a large, unto a land flowing with milk and honey; unto the place of the Canaanites, and the Hittites, and the Amorites, and the Perizzites, and the Hivites, and the Jebusites.

9 Now therefore, behold, the cry of the children of Israel is come unto me: and I have also seen the oppression wherewith the Egyptians oppress them.

Divine compassion (Exod. 3:7). The One who identified Himself as holy and the God of the covenant now revealed His compassion for His suffering people. He told Moses He had seen the suffering of His people. The idea is that He had watched intently the trials they were going through. He had not forgotten them but had heard their cries due to the suffering inflicted on them by their Egyptian taskmasters. He was well aware of their plight and knew the extent of their sorrows.

The expressions in Exodus 3:7 undeniably revealed God's genuine concern for His suffering people (cf. 2:23-25). They also set the stage for the announcement of His impending deliverance of Israel.

Divine determination (Exod. 3:8-9). God told Moses that He had come to free the Israelites from their slavery to the Egyptians. The idea of coming down or descending is often used in relation to theophanies. It pictures God as giving careful attention to a situation and resolving to act powerfully, "not above history, but in and through history" (Davis, *Moses and the Gods of Egypt,* Baker).

God was determined to act decisively to rescue Israel from their Egyptian oppressors. This would mean removing them from the land of Egypt and taking them to a different land. This promise was in accord with the covenant made with Abraham many years before and affirmed with Isaac, Jacob, and Jacob's descendants. The Abrahamic covenant assured Israel that they would inherit a land of their own (cf. Gen. 12:1, 7; 13:15; 35:12).

God had even specified that Abraham's descendants would be strangers in a foreign land where they would be afflicted for four hundred years. God would then judge that afflicting nation and bring His people back to their land (Gen. 15:13-16). God was about to fulfill that promise.

The land to which God would lead His people is described as a good and spacious land (Exod. 3:8). Neither Egypt nor the desert where Moses led the sheep was good for the Israelites. The land He would take them to would be pleasant and beautiful. It is also described as "flowing with milk and honey." This is a frequent idiom that speaks of the richness and prosperity of a land (cf. Exod. 3:17; 13:5; Lev. 20:24; Num. 13:27).

The land promised to Israel extended from the Nile in Egypt to the Euphrates River in Mesopotamia (Gen. 15:18). Clearly this was a large, spacious land. Israel's complete possession of this area awaits Christ's return and the establishment of His kingdom. However, Israel would soon possess a part of that land, particularly that portion known as Canaan, which lies between the Jordan River and the Mediterranean Sea.

At the time the Lord appeared to Moses, this land was the dwelling place of various peoples. "Canaanites" (Exod. 3:8) is the more general term for people of that land. The other groups represent peoples who were scattered about the land. Lists of the land's occupants are found elsewhere (cf. Gen. 15:19-21; Deut. 7:1).

Some of these people perhaps lived in distinct areas of the land, while others were scattered throughout the general area. However, these nations of Canaan were not covenantally related to each other as Israel's twelve tribes were. They may have shared a common cultural or religious history (cf. Cole, *Exodus: An Introduction and Commentary,* InterVarsity).

The various groups that occupied Canaan, generally called Canaanites, were "terribly degenerate. Their perverted religious practices had so polluted them that their iniquity was as great as it could be (cf. Gen. 15:16). They worshiped a large number of deities who were characterized by wicked behavior that in turn dictated the behavior of the Canaanites" (Benware, *Survey of the Old Testament,* Moody). Their practices included religious prostitution and infant sacrifice.

Exodus 3:9 essentially repeats what is stated in verse 7. It was a further reminder to Moses of God's personal concern for His people.

THE LORD'S CALL

10 Come now therefore, and I will send thee unto Pharaoh, that thou mayest bring forth my people the children of Israel out of Egypt.

Moses must have wondered why God was telling him all this, though he surely was happy to hear it. But God's declaration that He was sending Moses to the Egyptian pharaoh to head up the release of the Israelites and their departure from Egypt was not something he was happy to hear. Moses' earlier failure in Egypt made him feel like he could do nothing to help his people.

Undoubtedly, this is why God so fully revealed Himself to Moses before calling him to go back to Egypt and confront Pharaoh. At the burning bush, the Lord had revealed His holiness, His mercy, and His faithfulness to His covenant promises. The miracle of the bush burning without being consumed revealed something of God's power as well. It was crucial for Moses to understand the nature of God so that he would know the deliverance of Israel was not dependent on him but upon the God for whom nothing is impossible (cf. Matt. 19:26).

This was the final step in Moses' preparation. He possessed the knowledge and experience needed to fulfill his role in God's plan. Now he grasped the nature of the God behind that plan. He was a God who was perfectly capable of using an eighty-year-old fugitive shepherd from Egypt to deliver and lead a great nation of people.

God's providence was evident earlier in Exodus in the birth and preservation of Moses. The burning bush was the first miracle recorded in Exodus; there would be many more. God would demonstrate to Moses, to Israel, and to the Egyptians and their so-called gods that He alone is God, the Holy One who is to be worshipped and obeyed.

We can be encouraged by Moses. He made a terrible mistake that sidetracked his life for many years—or so it seemed. But those years were not wasted. God used them to teach His servant, humble him, and prepare Him for a great work.

You may have made some big blunders in life, but if you are willing to humbly follow and obey the Lord, He can use even your failures to teach and prepare you for His service.

He also uses the Word of God to teach us. We should diligently study God's Word and seek to know more and more of God's nature. As was the case with Moses, this will give us greater appreciation for our Lord and greater faith in Him, which will make us better servants of Him.

—*Jarl K. Waggoner.*

QUESTIONS

1. What had Moses been doing during his forty years in Midian?

2. What did his work in the wilderness teach Moses?

3. Where is Mount Horeb, or Mount Sinai, located?

4. Who was the "angel of the Lord" (Exod. 3:2)?

5. How did the Angel of the Lord address Moses? Why?

6. What instruction did God give Moses?

7. How did the Lord identify Himself to Moses?

8. How did God express His concern for the people of Israel?

9. What did God say He was going to do for the people of Israel?

10. Why did God reveal something of His nature to Moses before He called Moses to go to Egypt and lead the people out of that land?

—*Jarl K. Waggoner.*

Preparing to Teach the Lesson

God has been preparing Moses for a grand and glorious mission on behalf of His covenant people. Now He takes the crucial step that will trigger the actual series of events that deliver Israel from bondage and bring the world's most powerful empire to its knees.

TODAY'S AIM

Facts: to see that God manifested Himself to Moses in a special, visible way and called him as His chosen deliverer for His covenant.

Principle: to understand that God knows the needs of His people and that in His own perfect time, He is sure to answer their cries.

Application: to remember that, although God may not manifest Himself to us as He did to Moses, we should take courage and comfort that He knows all about our needs and will provide for us in powerful and amazing ways.

INTRODUCING THE LESSON

This week's lesson needs little introduction, since it has been the subject of numerous dramatizations in the popular media. Anytime Almighty God chooses to make a visible, personal appearance in human history, it is a signal that cataclysmic events are soon to follow.

DEVELOPING THE LESSON

1. A great sight (Exod. 3:1-3). Our lesson this week seems to pick up right where last week's narrative left off—with Moses tending Jethro's flocks. But forty years have elapsed since Moses had settled down as a shepherd in the household of Jethro, so he was now close to eighty years old (cf. 7:7). Note that his preparation as Israel's

deliverer had not only been very hard, it had also taken a very long time!

On the current occasion, Moses had led Jethro's flocks to the "backside of the desert" (3:1). This indicates an open pastureland that was owned by no one but was open to anyone's flocks for grazing purposes. It might be considered God's country, especially since it was near God's holy mountain of Horeb, which is later called Sinai.

The text tells us ahead of time that "the angel of the Lord" (vs. 2) appears to Moses here. This designation often applies to what amounts to a theophany, that is, a visible manifestation of God Himself. Since God the Son is always the image of God's person and glory (cf. Heb. 1:3), the word "angel" should be taken in its literal meaning of "messenger." That word helps keep our thoughts from jumping directly to the idea of a robed being with wings, as popularly conceived. From all indications, it was not just an angel but God the Son appearing to Moses as the ultimate visible expression of God's glory and image.

To Moses, what he saw struck him right away as a unique spectacle. It was definitely a head-turner, a sight so extraordinary that it cannot be ignored. God made sure that He had Moses' undivided attention on this momentous occasion.

2. Holy ground (Exod. 3:4-6). God had sparked Moses' curiosity, but the first thing He did was warn him to keep his distance. Moses was as yet unaware that this phenomenon was no mere natural oddity. He was close to God's own holy presence, which is potentially lethal for sinful humans (cf. Exod. 33:18-23; Deut. 18:16-17;

Judg. 13:22). Moses was instructed to show proper reverence toward God's presence by taking off his sandals, so he did.

To remove all doubt about whose presence he was in, the Lord identified Himself as the historic God of Moses' Hebrew ancestors (Exod. 3:6). At this revelation, Moses immediately realized the great danger he was in, averting his gaze from God's holy manifestation. Adam Clarke observes, "He was afraid to look—he was overawed by God's presence, and dazzled with the splendour of the appearance" (*Commentary on the Bible,* Abingdon).

3. A great commission (Exod. 3:7-10). As Moses humbled himself in the presence of the Creator of the universe and the Almighty God of his ancestors, God got right to the point of His auspicious intrusion into Moses' life. God had seen enough of His people's affliction, and He had heard enough of their sorrowful cries for deliverance. He would now sovereignly intervene to deliver them from the Egyptians and give them their own abundant land. Not only would God miraculously rescue His people from slavery, He would also miraculously take the land from its present inhabitants—naming the six most prominent nations (vs. 8)—and give it to His covenant people for their very own.

God had come down to graciously call Moses to be His special instrument; he would represent the Lord before the world's most powerful ruler to bring all these astounding plans to reality. God would take this formerly impetuous fugitive, now a humbled shepherd exiled to the remote wilderness, and back him with the full might of His divine indignation against the oppressors of His covenant people. Moses would become the personification of God's mighty arm (cf. Exod. 6:6; Deut. 4:34; 5:15; 7:19; 9:29).

ILLUSTRATING THE LESSON

After Moses experienced God's visible manifestation on the holy mountain, his mission was to go and deliver God's people from Egypt.

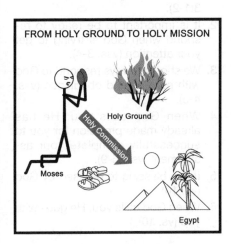

FROM HOLY GROUND TO HOLY MISSION

Holy Ground

Holy Commission

Moses

Egypt

CONCLUDING THE LESSON

We need only think of biblical persons such as Abraham, Jacob, David, and the apostles of Christ to see a divine pattern at work. Our Almighty God delights in calling humble people from obscure situations and raising them to powerful heights that astound and amaze an arrogant, complacent world.

ANTICIPATING THE NEXT LESSON

Now that Moses has been called to deliver God's people, we will see that his path to eventual triumph was not an easy one. He would have to overcome not only his own self-doubt and fear of failure, but also an arsenal of intimidation tactics from the world's most powerful ruler. God would purposely harden Pharaoh's heart against Moses so that the full measure of His wrath and indignation on behalf of His covenant people would be poured out on the worldly pride of Egypt. It is indeed a fearful thing to fall into the hands of the Living God!

—*John M. Lody.*

PRACTICAL POINTS

1. God will reveal Himself to you at exactly the right moment (Exod. 3:1-2).
2. It is important to be ready to respond when God is trying to get your attention (vss. 3-4).
3. We should always respond to God with humility and obedience (vss. 4-5).
4. When God calls you, He has already made provision for you to successfully complete your assignment (vss. 6-9).
5. It is a blessing to be used by God (vs. 10).
6. When God calls you, He goes with you (vs. 10).

—*Valante M. Grant.*

RESEARCH AND DISCUSSION

1. How does the call of God on your life impact your daily routine?
2. How can we know whether God is leading in a situation or not (cf. Rom. 12:2)?
3. Describe God's response to the cry of His people (Exod. 3:7-8).
4. What characteristics have you noticed in the people God chooses to work for Him? Do you see those character traits in yourself?
5. Why do you think God waited until Moses was paying attention to call his name? Has God done this anywhere else in Scripture? Do you ever let your lack of confidence get in the way of something God calls you to do? Why?

—*Valante M. Grant.*

ILLUSTRATED HIGH POINTS

Why the bush is not burnt

Have you ever seen a dollar catch on fire but not burn to a crisp? If you wash a dollar bill in equal parts isopropyl alcohol and water, the water will prevent the bill from being burned while the alcohol around the dollar is consumed. Don't try it at home, but it illustrates how God provides protection for us.

In Exodus 3:2, the Angel of the Lord appears in the burning bush, but the bush is not consumed. Many theologians believe this is a theophany (Old Testament appearance of Christ). Just as the bush was not scorched and the dollar bill is not consumed, so we do not receive our wages for our sin (cf. Rom. 6:23) because Jesus washes us in His righteousness. When we trust in the saving power of our loving caretaker, Jesus, He protects us so we will not be consumed by God's wrath (cf. Deut. 4:24; Lam. 3:22; Heb. 12:29).

God of Abraham, the God of Isaac

Anyone who has looked for a job knows that it can be quite discouraging. You might send out twenty applications before any business even contacts you. However, if you know somebody in the company, you are much more likely to be considered.

By telling Moses that He was the God of Abraham and Isaac, God was revealing His connections; Moses would realize that he was talking to the one true God. (Moses hardly needed to announce his own connection with Abraham and Isaac for the Lord's benefit!) God was being patient with Moses, revealing Himself to the shepherd so he would recognize Him. This was a true sign of the Lord's mercy and grace. But perhaps more important, He had a job for Moses, and He had plenty of authority to ask him to do it.

—*Therese Greenberg.*

Golden Text Illuminated

"Come now therefore, and I will send thee unto Pharaoh, that thou mayest bring forth my people the children of Israel out of Egypt" (Exodus 3:10).

As we conclude this quarter's first unit, the theme of deliverance continues to permeate the golden text. In this week's study, we will consider Moses' dramatic call to be Israel's deliverer from their cruel Egyptian bondage. His timely calling took place in miraculous fashion—at a flaming bush that did not burn up.

Last week's golden text concentrated on Moses' sudden departure to the land of Midian. Moses made Midian his home for a period of forty years. During that time, he befriended Reuel by helping his shepherdess daughters obtain water for their father's flocks (cf. Exod. 2:16-17). As a result, Reuel presented one of his daughters, Zipporah, to Moses, and she became his wife (vss. 18-21). Zipporah conceived and gave birth to a son, whom they named Gershom (vs. 22).

During Moses' prolonged stay in Midian, he watched over his father-in-law's flocks. One day he led them to Horeb, the mountain of God (3:1). At that special place, the Angel of the Lord appeared to Moses in a flaming bush that was not consumed by the fire. At that holy place, God identified Himself to Moses and communicated His desire to deliver His people from their sufferings (vss. 2-10).

In Acts 7:30-34 we read Stephen's account of Moses' call. Stephen notes that when Moses saw the flaming bush, he marveled at the sight and got as close to it as he could (vs. 31).

What happened next must have astounded Moses. When God revealed Himself as the God of his ancestors Abraham, Isaac, and Jacob, Moses reacted with reverential fear and hid his face from sight (Exod. 3:6). God responded with a word of assurance: He was fully aware of the affliction His people were suffering in Egypt these many years (vs. 7). Even better, God was about to rescue them from this oppression and bring them to a secure, fruitful land of their own (vs. 8).

It is in the golden text that God drops His bombshell: He would send *Moses* back to Egypt as the chosen deliverer of His people. Moses, who had fled a pharaoh's wrath, would be the one to personally confront the current pharaoh.

To appreciate the impact of these words, we have to remember that God's call to Moses came abruptly and without warning after a forty-year period of seeming aimlessness. Following the call, God continued to communicate with Moses, preparing him for the spectacular events that would follow. Later (6:2-8), God again spoke with Moses, reaffirming His covenant relationship with His people and assuring him again that He was completely aware of the cruelty of the Israelites' Egyptian bondage; He would bring them safely to their Promised Land.

The Bible amply illustrates the truth that when God calls someone to accomplish His will, He fully equips, provides, qualifies, and enables that person to complete the task (cf. Gen. 22:13-14; 50:19-21; Esther 4:14). In what way do you sense God calling you to share in His work of delivering people from the bondage of sin?

God does not make mistakes. He always acts intentionally and purposefully. Make yourself available to be His servant to His honor and glory.

—*Thomas R. Chmura.*

Heart of the Lesson

Take a moment to reflect on your life. Was there a moment or a decision that you made that changed the course of your life? You may have had one or many of these moments. In Exodus chapter 3, we become observers of one of Moses' such moments.

1. Moses sees the burning bush (Exod. 3:1-3). Moses went from being a prince of Egypt to an obscure shepherd. In those days, shepherds were the least of society. They were not esteemed at all. Moses spent his time protecting the sheep from wolves and other predators, leading the sheep to places of green grass and safe drinking waters, and looking for the sheep that went astray—definitely the perfect training ground for learning humility!

Moses was leading the sheep to the mountain of God when he saw a burning bush. The angel of the Lord had overwhelmed a bush with flames. Bushes on fire were common, but a bush that was engulfed in flames but not consumed by those flames had never been seen before. When Moses saw the bush, it sparked his curiosity. He determined he must investigate.

2. Here am I (Exod. 3:4-6). God called out to Moses from the bush, and Moses responded with "Here am I." If a burning bush started calling out your name, would you respond? Some of us would start running and try to hide among the sheep!

The Bible sometimes tells us how majestic and thunderous the voice of God is (cf. Ps. 29:1-9); nevertheless, He is also love. I imagine He must have spoken tenderly to Moses to draw him closer. God does that with us too. He speaks tenderly to our hearts and whispers until we are drawn into His presence. When God called Moses by name, he was commanded to honor God's presence. As he drew near to God, he was told to remove his sandals as an outward sign of an inner heart submission.

God then identified Himself. "I am the God of thy father, the God of Abraham, the God of Isaac, and the God of Jacob" (Exod. 3:6). Moses would have known that he was from the tribe of Levi. God was letting Moses know that He was the God who is there for all the generations of his people. Moses was having an encounter with the God who had spoken to Abram and made him Abraham. At this revelation, Moses hid his face out of reverential fear.

3. God has seen the sorrows (Exod. 3:7-10). "And the Lord said, I have surely seen the affliction of my people which are in Egypt, and have heard their cry by reason of their taskmasters; for I know their sorrows" (vs. 7). When your soul is filled with tears and torment, it is easy to wonder if God cares. When the pain of waiting seems never-ending, it is easy to doubt if God is interested. Regardless of how you may feel in the moment, God is never apathetic toward your plight.

God told Moses that he had to go back to Pharaoh. We know that Moses was God's chosen one to be the deliverer of His people; however, we forget that Moses had to go through preparation. His preparation took eighty years!

The Israelites were crying out for freedom from their oppressors. Sometimes, the bigger the prayer request, the longer the wait because there are more variables that need to align. The wait does not indicate that God does not care; it is merely further evidence that He is perfecting His plans for you.

—*Kristin Reeg.*

World Missions

Sometimes the hardest opposition to God's call comes from within. When God called Moses, He said:

I have seen.

I have heard.

I know their sorrows.

I am coming to deliver them.

Moses, however, did not focus on these powerful, beautiful truths. Instead, he presented to God all his own inhibitions:

Who am I?

They won't believe me.

I can't speak well.

Send someone else.

When we are called, we might be tempted to give God some of the same "reasons" to not obey. God has responses to all our inhibitions, just as He had for Moses.

I'm not qualified. Last week we read how Moses thought he was to be the deliverer; now we read that he is convinced he is not. Moses had learned humility, which was important. God wanted him to go in the strength of the Lord, not his own strength. Nevertheless, God had qualified Moses in ways he did not even understand. His years in Egypt had purpose, and his time as a shepherd in the desert was important training for all the years of leading God's people like sheep in the wilderness.

If God has called us, He has qualified us—or will. Nothing is wasted with the Lord. Each job, each trial, even our mistakes and failures can be used for good within His work. As in all things, if He calls us, we can trust that His qualifications will be met. The focus should be on trusting Him, not ourselves.

I don't have the personality. When God first led me into missions, I was terrified at the idea of raising support, especially because it meant speaking in churches. I would literally get sick before speaking, but over time things changed. Now speaking to God's people is one of my favorite things to do. That change never would have happened had I not trusted God and moved forward despite myself.

God wants to use extroverts and introverts, those who thrive around others and those who want to be in the background. All types are needed to reach all types!

I don't have the resources (money/health/youth/and so on). Again, the prerequisite is trust in Almighty God, not in ourselves. Oftentimes God chooses those of us who lack something to show that the resources come from Him, not us! Speaking from personal experience, our family was once under-supported by $700 a month. Humanly speaking, it was impossible for us to get what we needed in the very short amount of time we had. But God did it all. Other times He provided food and even diapers when we needed them (and they "happened" to be the right size!). I had friends who came to the field after retirement, letting God fill their senior years with amazing adventures and eternal treasure. When my health failed and being overseas was no longer an option, God allowed me to join an internet ministry so I could still reach people all over the world from my own home.

God is not limited. If we focus on what He says—I AM, I hear, I see, I know the sorrows, and I have a plan to deliver the oppressed—we can go in His strength, trusting that despite our lack and our failings, we will be provided with everything we need to do exactly what He has called us to do.

—*Kimberly Rae.*

The Jewish Aspect

When Moses approached the burning bush, God specifically told him, "Put off thy shoes from off thy feet, for the place whereon thou standest is holy ground" (Exod. 3:5).

Before this time, no one had removed his shoes when worshipping God. God spoke with Abraham, Isaac, and Jacob and did not require this act.

Moses, however, had grown up in Pharaoh's court. He would have known the customs of the Egyptian priests concerning the removal of shoes, who "observed it in their temples" and did so as "a confession of personal defilement and conscious unworthiness to stand in the presence of unspotted holiness" (Jamieson, Fausset, and Brown, *Commentary,* Eerdmans). In that culture, shoes were worn "chiefly as protection from defilement and dust, and hence put off when entering a sanctuary, in order . . . not to bring within the pure place defilement from without" (Edersheim, *Old Testament Bible History,* Eerdmans).

Even though Moses was outdoors and not in a physical "sanctuary," God's presence made the ground holy. Moses was commanded to respect that by his outward reverence. This custom regarding footwear continued to be observed throughout much of Jewish history. In the Mosaic Law, no mention is made of footwear for the priests in their tabernacle/temple service. This may well indicate that they performed their ministries barefoot.

In ancient times, people commonly removed their shoes when entering a home, and they frequently washed their feet. Shoes were put on when preparing to depart and resume activities. This idea of being prepared for activity explains why the Jews kept their shoes on when they observed the Passover: "And thus shall ye eat it; with your loins girded, your shoes on your feet, and your staff in your hand; and ye shall eat it in haste" (Exod. 12:11). Having shoes on was a symbol of Israel's haste in leaving the bondage of Egypt.

The act of removing shoes was practiced in many religions. For example, Greek priests worshipped barefoot shortly after New Testament times (Justin Martyr, *First Apology*).

Contemporary Hindu Brahmins remove their shoes in worship, as do Muslim worshippers. In these cases too, the removal of the shoes is done so that no impurities are brought into the place of worship to contaminate it.

Jews have different practices concerning shoes, especially when it comes to praying. Many believe that a person should wear shoes in prayer, since it is appropriate to wear shoes when in the presence of an honored person: "We must dress in the synagogue as we would dress to go greet a VIP, in dignified and modest clothing" ("Jews and Shoes," www.thoughtco.com).

In many synagogue services, whenever the priestly blessing is said, the *Kohanim* (descendants of priests) must not wear shoes. At this part of the service, they leave the synagogue sanctuary, "remove their shoes outside of the main sanctuary, have their hands washed, re-enter the synagogue, and give the priestly blessing to the congregation" ("Jews and Shoes").

In Jewish practice today, "the symbolism of removing the shoes has faded somewhat (Millgram, "Head Coverings in the Synagogue," www.myjewishlearning.com). But our consciousness of being unworthy to stand in the presence of God without the benefit of His grace should cause us to reverence His holiness.

—*R. Larry Overstreet.*

Guiding the Superintendent

What a difference a day makes! We tend to treat every day as just that—another day. The old desert nomad Moses probably did the same. How could he have anticipated when he woke up that morning that his life would dramatically change forever? For on this special day he would come face to face with God, and he would receive the divine call that would impact the rest of his life on earth—not to mention world history.

The years and centuries of preparation were over. God would finally take specific steps that would culminate in the freedom of the enslaved Israelites.

DEVOTIONAL OUTLINE

1. God appears to Moses (Exod. 3:1-4). What started out as an ordinary day for Moses ended up being the day that would change the direction of his life for the next forty years. While he was tending to his father-in-law's sheep in the desert of Horeb (Sinai), a strange thing happened. There on the desert sands was a bush that was on fire but not being consumed. When Moses went to investigate further, the bush spoke to him!

2. God identifies Himself to Moses (Exod. 3:5-6). God was in the flaming bush! He told Moses to remove his sandals, for he was on holy ground. The Lord then identified Himself as the God of Moses' ancestors—Abraham, Isaac, and Jacob. All Moses could do was hide his face.

3. God calls Moses to lead the Israelites out of slavery (Exod. 3:7-10). God had not been idle. While Moses was herding his father-in-law's sheep, God was observing the plight of Moses' people back in Egypt.

God shared his plans with Moses: "I am come down to deliver them out of the hand of the Egyptians, and to bring them up out of that land unto a good land and a large, unto a land flowing with milk and honey; unto the place of the Canaanites" (vs. 8).

Then God called Moses to be the one who would confront Pharaoh and lead the Israelites out of the land.

God's invisible hand is continually working behind the scenes even if we fail to see it. But when God does act, it becomes very clear. The Lord was indeed aware of the plight of Israel. He was also preparing Moses to lead His people through the desert by putting him in a kind of forty-year desert internship.

CHILDREN'S CORNER

text: **Joshua 2:1-15**
title: **Rahab and the Spies**

In James 2:23-25 we find two Old Testament examples of faith. Abraham is not a surprise, but Rahab is quite unexpected. After all, her nationality, gender, and character do not fit the normal biblical picture of faith. While not part of God's nation, she still provides a stunning portrait of active faith. In a time of great danger, she believed God and acted accordingly.

Before Joshua invaded Palestine, he sent two spies to survey the land. To avoid the local police, the two spies ended up in the home of Rahab. She took extra precautions to hide the men while the authorities searched her house. She sent the authorities looking for the spies in the wrong direction after telling them that the spies had already left.

She told the spies that when she heard about the miracles God had done for Israel, she believed that their Lord was "God in heaven above, and in earth below" (Josh. 2:11). To reward her faith the Israelites spared Rahab and all her family when they attacked the city.

—Martin R. Dahlquist.

SCRIPTURE LESSON TEXT

EXOD. 5:1 And afterward Moses and Aaron went in, and told Pharaoh, Thus saith the L<small>ORD</small> God of Israel, Let my people go, that they may hold a feast unto me in the wilderness.

2 And Pharaoh said, Who *is* the L<small>ORD</small>, that I should obey his voice to let Israel go? I know not the L<small>ORD</small>, neither will I let Israel go.

3 And they said, The God of the Hebrews hath met with us: let us go, we pray thee, three days' journey into the desert, and sacrifice unto the L<small>ORD</small> our God; lest he fall upon us with pestilence, or with the sword.

4 And the king of Egypt said unto them, Wherefore do ye, Moses and Aaron, let the people from their works? get you unto your burdens.

5 And Pharaoh said, Behold, the people of the land now *are* many, and ye make them rest from their burdens.

6 And Pharaoh commanded the same day the taskmasters of the people, and their officers, saying,

7 Ye shall no more give the people straw to make brick, as heretofore: let them go and gather straw for themselves.

8 And the tale of the bricks, which they did make heretofore, ye shall lay upon them; ye shall not diminish *ought* thereof: for they *be* idle; therefore they cry, saying, Let us go *and* sacrifice to our God.

9 Let there more work be laid upon the men, that they may labour therein; and let them not regard vain words.

NOTES

"Let My People Go"

Lesson Text: Exodus 5:1-9

Related Scriptures: Exodus 3:18-20; 5:10-23;
II Kings 18:28-35; Daniel 2:46-47; 4:34-37

TIME: 1445 B.C.   PLACE: Egypt

GOLDEN TEXT—"Moses and Aaron went in, and told Pharaoh, Thus saith the Lord God of Israel, Let my people go, that they may hold a feast unto me in the wilderness" (Exodus 5:1).

Introduction

"Pride goeth before destruction, and an haughty spirit before a fall" (Prov. 16:18). This familiar, though often misquoted, verse is just one of many warnings the Bible gives regarding the destructive power of pride. An elevated view of oneself is completely at odds with the biblical teaching about human sin and depravity. God hates pride (cf. 8:13) and condemns it.

The Bible's warnings against pride are accompanied by real historical examples of the downfall of the proud. (cf. Dan 4:30-33; Acts 12:21-23). God also humbled the arrogant Egyptian pharaoh whom Moses confronted. And, interestingly enough, the person God used

to bring down this exalted king was the once-proud Egyptian prince who now appeared before the king as a humble Hebrew shepherd.

The process would not be easy for either Moses or the Israelites, but the promise would be realized: "God resisteth the proud, but giveth grace unto the humble" (Jas. 4:6).

LESSON OUTLINE

I. MOSES' FIRST REQUEST—
Exod. 5:1-2

II. MOSES' SECOND REQUEST—
Exod. 5:3-9

Exposition: Verse by Verse

MOSES' FIRST REQUEST

EXOD. 5:1 And afterward Moses and Aaron went in, and told Pharaoh, Thus saith the Lord God of Israel, Let my people go, that they may hold a feast unto me in the wilderness.

2 And Pharaoh said, Who is the

Lord, that I should obey his voice to let Israel go? I know not the Lord, neither will I let Israel go.

Moses was not eager to accept God's mission to tell Egypt's pharaoh to allow him to bring his fellow Israelites out of Egypt (Exod. 3:11). In fact,

Moses offered a number of excuses why he could not or should not do so. Moses focused on his inadequacies rather than on the power of the God who was sending him (4:10-16).

Moses' excuses were just that—excuses. However, his attitude was markedly different from what it had been forty years earlier when he had killed a man and then expected the Hebrews to recognize him as their deliverer. Moses had been humbled by that experience and also by his forty years in Midian. There could be no question in his mind or anyone else's that the Israelites' deliverance would come through the mighty work of God alone, not through him.

With his fears answered at the burning bush and God's clear instructions received, Moses set out for Egypt. His brother, Aaron, whom God had promised would serve with Moses as a spokesman (Exod. 4:10-16), was directed by God to meet Moses in the wilderness (vs. 27). Moses informed his brother of all that had happened, and the two of them gathered the elders of Israel together and told them what the Lord had said and done. They believed Moses' report and rejoiced that the Lord was about to deliver them from their oppression.

The people who had rejected the brash young Egyptian-turned-Hebrew forty years earlier now accepted the humble old shepherd who spoke of God's plan for His people. Their faith in Moses and in the Lord would waver in the coming days when more hardship would come. But their acceptance of God's deliverer at this point put them on a course toward freedom.

Moses, along with Aaron, then went to speak to Pharaoh. The pharaoh at this time was Amenhotep II. He ruled Egypt near the zenith of that nation's power, having succeeded Thutmose III, one of Egypt's greatest pharaohs. Just as Moses himself had to be humbled by God, so this powerful and proud ruler also would have to be humbled by God before he would give the Israelites their freedom.

Moses certainly was familiar with the protocol in approaching Egypt's ruler, and perhaps this was useful in getting him and Aaron a hearing before the monarch. The message he brought, however, was straight from the mouth of the Lord. He started his request with the phrase, "Thus saith the Lord" (Exod. 5:1; cf. 4:22-23), which made it clear that Moses was not speaking on his own behalf but was representing the God of Israel.

Moses identified the God whose message he was delivering as the "Lord God of Israel" (Exod. 5:1). "Lord" (Yahweh) is the personal name of God. It speaks of His eternal self-existence. "God" ("Elohim") is in the plural form (i.e. literally "gods") but really is a superlative, meaning "the supreme God." It is a more general name that "emphasizes His strength, power, and superiority over all other so-called gods" (Enns, *The Moody Handbook of Theology*, Moody). This One was the God of Israel. He was not like the gods of the Egyptians, some minor deity among many that the Hebrews created. He was the God who had Himself created all things. He was the true, living God of all the universe, and He had been worshipped by the Israelites from their beginning.

The request—or more properly demand—of the God of Israel was that Pharaoh free the people of Israel so that they might observe a feast to the Lord "in the wilderness" (Exod. 5:1; cf. 3:18). The Lord was telling Pharaoh that he must free the Israelites so they could worship the true God as He required.

Was this a negotiating technique or a test to see if Pharaoh would grant a lesser request before making the greater request for the complete release of the people? Perhaps it was, but it seems more likely that both Moses and Pharaoh understood that the Israelites would not be returning from their feast in the wilderness. Moses was simply using language that would make it easier for Pharaoh to grant the request. "Moses' demand for complete freedom, though couched in polite words, is there from the start" (Cole, *Exodus: An Introduction and Commentary,* InterVarsity).

Pharaoh replied, "Who is the Lord, that I should obey his voice to let Israel go?" (Exod. 5:2). To this he added that he did not know the Lord. He was not so much expressing ignorance concerning Israel's God as he was challenging the Lord's authority over him. He was simply saying, "Why should I obey the God of a people who are in utter subjection to me?"

It is important to remember that Pharaoh himself was considered a god—one of many—in Egyptian religion. To acknowledge the power and authority of the God of Israel was to accept that He was superior to Pharaoh and all of Egypt's gods.

The real conflict was not between Moses and Pharaoh or between Israel and Egypt. At its heart the conflict was between the Lord God and the gods of Egypt, including Pharaoh (cf. Exod. 12:12; Num. 33:4). The Lord was intent not only on freeing His people from oppression but also on humbling Pharaoh and exposing the false religion of Egypt, thus exalting Himself as the one true God. Pharaoh's challenge would be dramatically answered in the days ahead.

MOSES' SECOND REQUEST

3 And they said, The God of the Hebrews hath met with us: let us go, we pray thee, three days' journey into the desert, and sacrifice unto the LORD our God; lest he fall upon us with pestilence, or with the sword.

4 And the king of Egypt said unto them, Wherefore do ye, Moses and Aaron, let the people from their works? get you unto your burdens.

5 And Pharaoh said, Behold, the people of the land now are many, and ye make them rest from their burdens.

6 And Pharaoh commanded the same day the taskmasters of the people, and their officers, saying,

7 Ye shall no more give the people straw to make brick, as heretofore: let them go and gather straw for themselves.

8 And the tale of the bricks, which they did make heretofore, ye shall lay upon them; ye shall not diminish ought thereof: for they be idle; therefore they cry, saying, Let us go and sacrifice to our God.

9 Let there more work be laid upon the men, that they may labour therein; and let them not regard vain words.

The plea repeated (Exod. 5:3). Pharaoh's refusal to listen to the Lord's demand was not unexpected. The Lord had told Moses this would happen and that He would have to "smite Egypt with all [His] wonders" to bring about Israel's release (3:19-20). Still, Moses and Aaron repeated what the Lord had told them to say (cf. 3:18); namely, that he should let them go three days' journey into the desert so that there they might offer sacrifices to the Lord. Presumably the sacrifices would be part of their feast.

They added here that if they did not worship the Lord in the wilderness, He would bring "pestilence" or the "sword" upon them (Exod. 5:3). The one who oppressed the Israelites would, of course, have no concern about their suffering, yet Moses recognized that failure to comply with what God wanted could subject the people to God's punishments.

By mentioning such consequences for failing to obey God, Moses was demonstrating that there was no middle ground for the Israelites. They could not compromise with Pharaoh without offending the Lord. Again, Pharaoh undoubtedly knew the request was not for a three-day holiday but for permanent freedom from slavery.

Pharaoh's accusation (Exod. 5:4-5). Pharaoh's question was actually an accusation. He charged Moses and Aaron with simply trying to get the people out of doing their work. It is possible some of the Israelites, perhaps the leaders, had in fact stopped working briefly and were waiting to hear the outcome of this meeting with Pharaoh. The king commanded, "Get you unto your burdens."

Pharaoh's words in Exodus 5:5 may well have been spoken to himself rather than to Moses and Aaron. Nevertheless, they express the concern of the Egyptian king. The Israelites were indeed "many," and their growing numbers had long been considered a threat by Egypt's rulers.

Earlier attempts to halt the rapid growth of the Hebrew population had failed. Since then, successive pharaohs had continued and even increased the burdens upon them for both economic and security reasons. The Israelites provided cheap labor for the Egyptians, and their tiring work under the watchful eye of taskmasters sapped their strength to attempt an uprising. Giving them any kind of rest from their work would not be considered wise or expedient for Egypt's king.

Pharaoh's command (Exod. 5:6-9). The pharaoh knew the names of Moses and Aaron (vs. 4), probably because they were introduced to him by name. It is quite likely, however, that Amenhotep II had heard of Moses. If so, he had ample reason to believe Moses had more in mind for the Israelites than just avoiding work. The Israelites' hopes for freedom had to be quashed.

Pharaoh's solution was to increase the Israelites' workload. "Pharaoh's argument seems to be that people in bondage dream of freedom only when they have excessive free time or are allowed to idle away valuable time" (Walvoord and Zuck, eds., *The Bible Knowledge Commentary*, Victor).

The order to increase the work of the Israelites was issued that very day to the taskmasters and their officers. The taskmasters were Egyptians; the officers apparently were Hebrew foremen. These officers were later beaten for the people's failure to meet their work quotas (vs. 14).

The order was that in the making of bricks, the Hebrew slaves were to gather straw for themselves. They would no longer be given the needed straw as had been the practice prior to this.

"The ancient Egyptian bricks were made of clay moistened with water and then put into molds. After they were sufficiently dry to be removed from the molds, they were laid in rows on a flat spot exposed to the sun, which gradually hardened them" (Freeman, *Manners and Customs of the Bible*, Logos). Bricks made with straw mixed in with the clay "proved to be stronger than those lacking straw, due to the chemicals released by the straw as it decomposes in the clay" (Tenney, ed., *The Zondervan Pictorial Encyclopedia of the Bible*, Zondervan).

The making of bricks had long been one of the primary tasks assigned to the Israelites, along with working in agriculture (cf. Exod. 1:14). Those who made the bricks, however, apparently had never been tasked with gathering their own straw or stubble for the bricks. From now on they would be required to do so.

Although the gathering of the straw for brick making was now added to the people's labors, the quota, or "tale" (Exod. 5:8), of bricks they were expected to make did not change. The same amount would still be required of them, while the amount of labor required would increase.

Amenhoptep II believed the increased demands would leave them no time to be idly thinking about going to worship and sacrifice to their God. Douglas Stuart suggested the Pharaoh's omission of the Lord's name (Yahweh), which he had used in Exodus 5:2, was an intentional expression of "disdain for Yahweh—who was to him in effect merely 'the god these people worship'" (*New American Commentary: Exodus*, Holman). The God he scorned, however, would soon prove Himself superior to Pharaoh and every other so-called god of Egypt.

In Exodus 5:9, the pharaoh repeated the purpose of his plan. He reasoned that by putting more work upon the shoulders of the Israelite slaves, they would not listen to "vain words." The Hebrew here means deceptive or lying words. This is what Pharaoh thought of Moses' words and what he wanted others to think of them as well. Pharaoh believed that increasing the Israelites' burdens would discredit Moses' message of hope for the captives.

In the short term, Pharaoh's plan succeeded. Moses had returned to Egypt and assured his people the Lord had heard their cries and would deliver them from their oppression. But the heavier burdens Pharaoh placed upon the Israelites immediately turned them against Moses (cf. Exod. 5:20-21).

Pharaoh's scheme ultimately was doomed to failure, however, for he was not merely defying the human leader of Israel; he was defying the God of Israel. In time, the words of Moses, which Pharaoh considered lies, would be proved true in a most convincing way.

We see in this chapter of Exodus a very different Moses than the one who forty years earlier had killed an Egyptian in a fruitless attempt to protect his people. He was still as bold as he had been earlier, but now his boldness was accompanied by a wisdom and humility produced through forty years

of leading sheep in Midian (cf. Num. 12:3). Now he was content knowing he was doing the right thing at the right time within God's plan. His humble faith in the God of Israel would be used to both lead his people and to humble the proud Egyptian king.

We should never think that doing what God has commanded us to do is going to make things easy for us. In fact, just the opposite is likely to result. We need not be discouraged, intimidated, or fearful. Rather, we can be content, knowing that as we honor God by our faithful obedience, He will honor us with "greater riches than the treasures in Egypt" (Heb. 11:26).

—*Jarl K. Waggoner.*

QUESTIONS

1. How did Moses' attitude differ from what it had been forty years earlier?

2. How was Moses received by the elders of Israel?

3. Who was the pharaoh at this time? What do we know about his power?

4. What message did Moses and Aaron deliver?

5. What did Pharaoh mean when he said he did not know the Lord?

6. In what sense did the conflict go beyond Moses and Pharaoh? Whom did it really involve?

7. Of what did Pharaoh accuse Moses and Aaron?

8. What was the Pharaoh's real concern regarding the Israelites?

9. What order did Pharaoh give in relation to the Israelites? Why?

10. Why was his plan ultimately doomed to failure?

—*Jarl K. Waggoner.*

Preparing to Teach the Lesson

When a sinner is born again through repentance and faith in Christ as Lord and Saviour, that person experiences the Holy Spirit's creation of a new life within him. This is accompanied by divine joy, a deliverance from the guilt and power of sin, and a new hope in God's promises for the future.

But often along with the blessings of salvation come new challenges and testing. Satan becomes aware that God has transferred a soul from the kingdom of darkness into the light of the kingdom of God's beloved Son. This often precipitates dire opposition and attacks from the spiritual powers of wickedness. Rather than finding that life becomes easier, the new believer often experiences greater hardships and challenges.

Such was the case with the children of Israel after they had put their faith in God's chosen deliverer, Moses.

TODAY'S AIM

Facts: to note that Moses and Aaron confronted Pharaoh in the Lord's name, but Pharaoh scoffed at both the Lord and their request, making the Israelites work harder than before.

Principle: to realize that, often, when people begin their new journey of faith in the Lord, life becomes harder, not easier, and their faith is tested.

Application: to understand that if your students' lives have become more difficult since becoming believers, this is nothing to be discouraged about. It merely means that their faith is being tested and refined to prove its authenticity and increase its strength.

INTRODUCING THE LESSON

In the preceding chapter, Moses and Aaron had presented their credentials as the Lord's emissaries to the elders of Israel. The elders had responded with faith and humble worship, placing their full confidence in Moses as God's appointed deliverer (Exod. 4:29-30).

DEVELOPING THE LESSON

1. Moses and Aaron confront Pharaoh (Exod. 5:1-5). Hopes must have been high among the people and elders of Israel on the day that Moses and Aaron first approached the throne of Egypt's pharaoh to present God's demand that the king let His people go. Moses and Aaron had already delivered God's message to the Hebrews: the Lord had seen their affliction and heard their cries because of their hardship and suffering at the hands of their Egyptian taskmasters.

Aaron and Moses had also performed miracles to prove the truth of their claim that Moses was God's divinely empowered prophet and deliverer. With God on their side, how could they fail? Thus, Moses and Aaron came before the throne of Pharaoh and faithfully delivered God's command: allow the Hebrews to cease from their labors and journey three days to an appointed place in the wilderness, where they would feast and offer sacrifices in worship of the Lord.

It is important to note here that Moses and Aaron were addressing Pharaoh using the actual proper name of the Lord (in Hebrew: *Yahweh*). This is the first time in the Bible that God's actual name was used to confront an earthly empire. The Lord wanted Pharaoh to know exactly whom he was dealing with, so that when Egypt with all its vaunted gods had been thoroughly defeated, the world would know and fear Him as the only true and living God.

But if the Hebrews were expecting

Pharaoh to submit to the Lord upon this initial encounter, they must have been very disappointed. Pharaoh was completely unimpressed with the Lord and His emissaries. He questioned the Lord's authority and scoffed at the Lord's command, refusing to give it even passing consideration. Adam Clarke notes, "Pharaoh spoke here under the common persuasion that every place and people had a tutelary deity [that is, a tribal or national deity], and he supposed that this Jehovah might be the tutelary deity of the Israelites, to whom he, as an Egyptian, could be under no kind of obligation" (*Commentary on the Bible,* Abingdon).

In response, Pharaoh began to mockingly question why Moses, Aaron, and the rest of the Hebrews were not out shouldering their assigned burdens like good little slaves. He chided them for wasting time and energy with meaningless requests when they should be performing their rightful labors.

2. Pharaoh increases Israel's oppression (Exod. 5:6-9). Building on his imperious warning to Moses and Aaron, Pharaoh observed that since his many Hebrew slaves had time to be idle, they must need more work to do. To accommodate this need, Pharaoh instructed his overseers to no longer provide the Hebrews with straw to make bricks. From now on, the Hebrews would have to not only meet their usual quota of bricks but would also have to gather their own straw to make them. From that point on, the Hebrews had to both harvest straw and produce the same quota of bricks as usual.

Pharaoh explained that his purpose in adding to the Hebrews' workload was to prevent them from having time to waste on foolish ideas such as feasting and sacrificing to their God. Thus, knowingly or not, Pharaoh

had arrogantly taken up the gauntlet cast before him by the Lord God of Israel. He mocked Moses and Aaron, Israel, and especially God Himself. His haughtiness would prove to be a grave underestimation of the One he was dealing with.

ILLUSTRATING THE LESSON

Aaron and Moses confront Pharaoh on behalf of Israel, but Pharaoh scoffs at their cause, increasing Israel's oppression and testing their faith in God.

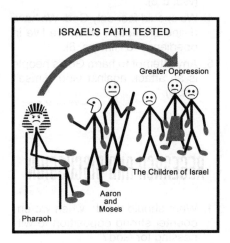

CONCLUDING THE LESSON

It is easy to have faith in God when life is going along smoothly and conflicts between biblical teaching and everyday living are scarce. But when the world, the flesh, and the devil target you for temptation, persecution, or intense suffering, maintaining your faith is possible only by relying on God to give you the patience and endurance to persevere.

ANTICIPATING THE NEXT LESSON

In next week's lesson, the Lord will bring the first plague upon Egypt by directing Moses to turn all the waters of Egypt to blood.

—*John M. Lody.*

PRACTICAL POINTS

1. God's power is greater than any power or authority on earth (Exod. 5:1).
2. When world leaders do not recognize God's authority, He uses humble things and people to teach them humility (vss. 2-5).
3. Oppression and hardship are merely opportunities for God to demonstrate the power of His love (vss. 6-8).
4. We should fear only God. We have divine protection when we live in obedience to Him (vs. 8).
5. Any attempt to harm God's people is an attack against God Himself (vs. 9).

—*Valante M. Grant.*

RESEARCH AND DISCUSSION

1. What should we do when we encounter strong opposition to witnessing for God?
2. What should believers do when they are prohibited from worshipping God?
3. How can believers living in freedom pray for and otherwise support believers living in oppression?
4. Why is it so important to live lives of gratitude to God (Exod. 5:1)?
5. Compare and contrast the limitations of worldly leaders with the omnipotence of God.
6. What is the ultimate result of blatant defiance against a command of God?

—*Valante M. Grant.*

ILLUSTRATED HIGH POINTS

Who is the Lord, that I should obey?

"Who is the Lord, that I should obey his voice?" This is a defiant yet not unexpected boast from the feared ruler of a mighty nation. Historically, monarchs have shown similar contempt for authority.

In 1649, after years of civil war in England, King Charles I was put on trial for tyranny. He challenged the court's authority over him in unyielding statements: "I would know by what power I am called hither. . . .Remember, I am your King. . . .a King cannot be tried by any superior jurisdiction on earth."

It is difficult for those with great power to do anything but scoff at the idea of any higher authority. In the end, the court had King Charles executed.

It is wise to recognize God's authority hastily. Every human, defiant or not, is indeed subject to Him.

They be idle; therefore they cry

A coin collector told his family he was leaving them a fortune. However, when he died, what appeared to be a valuable 1913 Liberty Head nickel (worth three million dollars) was determined to be a fake. Yet after gathering dust for forty years, the coin was reassessed in 2003 and finally recognized for its worth.

The Israelites wanted to worship God, but Pharaoh saw it as an excuse to be idle. In a similar way, devotion to the ways of the Lord by Christians can often be misinterpreted by onlookers. Like Pharaoh, mere observers are quick to misread the motives of worshipping believers.

Christianity may be labeled fake or worthless by many, but one day the true value of our inheritance will be fully revealed.

—*Therese Greenberg.*

Golden Text Illuminated

"Moses and Aaron went in, and told Pharaoh, Thus saith the Lord God of Israel, Let my people go, that they may hold a feast unto me in the wilderness" (Exodus 5:1).

This week's golden text brings us into Unit II, "Preparation for Deliverance." This second unit focuses on the immediate and necessary preparations for the deliverance of God's people from the cruelty of Egyptian bondage. These preparations, mainly in the form of destructive plagues, were necessary because of Pharaoh's rebellious and hardened heart (cf. Exod. 5:2).

The golden text concentrates upon Moses and Aaron's first verbal interaction with Pharaoh. Prior to this interview, God had revealed to Moses several crucial details of his preparation for the meeting (cf. 3:18-20). First, God revealed to Moses what his initial request should be. Assuring Pharaoh that he had met with God, Moses was to request permission for God's people to travel three days into the wilderness in order to offer animal sacrifices to the Lord in worship.

Second, God revealed to Moses with absolute certainty that Pharaoh would not grant his request (vs. 19). The Egyptian king would stubbornly and arrogantly refuse to allow God's people to leave Egypt.

Finally, God disclosed to Moses what His response would be to Pharaoh's stubborn disobedience (vs. 20). The Lord would exert His mighty power and perform "wonders" in the land. This, of course, was a reference to the judgment of plagues He would send upon Egypt. As a result of God's authoritative judgments, Pharaoh would ultimately allow God's people to leave Egypt.

Reassured by this divine information, Moses and Aaron prepared to confront Pharaoh. Remember, because he was raised by a previous pharaoh's daughter, Moses had been thoroughly trained in all the protocols of Egyptian royalty. He knew both when and how to request a meeting with Egypt's king. As representatives of God's people, Moses and Aaron entered Pharaoh's palace and presented their request.

Moses and Aaron's request was exactly what God had told them to make. They began with the announcement that they were speaking not only as representatives of the Israelites but also as representatives of "the Lord God of Israel." This truth placed their request on the level of a divine imperative.

Moses and Aaron then stated the details of their request. They asked Pharaoh to let God's people leave Egypt so they could worship the Lord with a feast in the wilderness. This would involve offering Him animal sacrifices. Their request was bold, but it reflected a respectful consideration for Egyptian sensibilities. Animals were sacred to the Egyptians. Being removed from the Egyptian population would not only allow the Hebrews to freely exercise their worship but also prevent the Egyptians from becoming infuriated by exposure to animal sacrifices.

Moses and Aaron's initial interview with Pharaoh was a significant part of God's plan to deliver His people from Egyptian captivity. God's plan was all-encompassing; that is, He not only prepared Moses as His deliverer, but He also prepared Pharaoh as the recipient of His powerful judgment.

Is God calling you into a unique ministry opportunity? He will thoroughly and adequately prepare you for His service.
—*Thomas R. Chmura.*

Heart of the Lesson

If we were to think of Moses' most quotable quote, it would be, "Let my people go!" As children we used to sing, "Pharaoh, Pharaoh, . . . let my people go." Sometimes when we say something over and over, it loses meaning. Too much familiarity can keep us from fully grasping the significance. For example, our minds may know that God loves us, but our hearts do not believe it. So when we think of Moses saying, "Let my people go," we may miss the full implications and ramifications of those words.

1. Who is the Lord (Exod. 5:1-2)? Moses and Aaron went before the king of Egypt declaring that the Lord God of Israel said, "Let my people go, that they may hold a feast unto me in the wilderness" (vs. 1). Can you imagine the scoffing and look of absolute incredulity on Pharaoh's face as he replies, "Who is the Lord"? In Egypt, Pharaoh was the mediator between the gods and men. He was the high priest. He did not know the God of the Hebrews; therefore, he was not inclined to obey His commands.

In the same manner, we cannot expect those who do not know our God to live as if they did. Let us strive to uphold our moral standards while extending love to those who do not know our God.

2. Let us go (Exod. 5:3-4). Pharaoh was not easily convinced or compelled to let the Israelites go and worship a God whom he did not know. Not surprisingly, his initial response to the request was a resounding "No!"

Moses and Aaron again asked Pharaoh to let the Israelites go and worship their God. This time, they specified the timeframe: a three-day journey into the desert. Pharaoh did not want to lose his workforce, so Moses and Aaron also added a warning by saying, "lest he fall upon us with pestilence, or with the sword" (vs. 3). In other words, the king of Egypt had a choice; he could either let the people go for a short period to worship their God, or he could lose his workforce forever because of what the Hebrew God might do if Pharaoh refused. The choice was Pharaoh's.

3. Pharaoh afflicts the Hebrews further (Exod. 5:5-9). As far as stories go, Pharaoh is the typical bad guy. In this portion of Scripture, he increases the workload of the Hebrews. From our perspective, the king of Egypt's reaction to a valid request appears extreme. At this point, Moses had not said that the Hebrews would never return to their work in Egypt. Pharaoh could even have sent his army with the Israelites into the desert to ensure they returned after their time of worship.

Pharaoh's reaction stemmed from his own pride. In this moment, he felt insulted. He was infuriated that he, the Egyptian mediator between the gods and men, had been served an ultimatum from a God he had never heard of. Pride is a form of insecurity. It insinuates that we do not measure up to expectations of who we think we are.

Responding to this perceived offense, Pharaoh decided to punish the Hebrews. Why? He reasoned that they had too much idle time on their hands if they had time to plan a religious holiday in the desert. Therefore, by making the Hebrews work harder, he was making sure they were too busy to daydream about such trivial things. Moses said, "Let my people go." For Pharaoh, those words meant more than a vacation; they were an insult to his rulership and to his station as a god.

—*Kristin Reeg.*

World Missions

When we go, give, or pray, we can do so in full confidence because God has called us, and our strength and authority come from Him, not ourselves. Moses was able to stand face to face with the most powerful man in the world and make demands because he spoke on God's behalf.

When following God's will, we need fear nothing. Missionaries throughout the ages have found this to be true. Their words can spur us on as they answer our questions:

Why go, do, give?

"God had an only Son and He made Him a missionary" (David Livingstone).

"We are debtors to every man to give him the gospel in the same measure in which we have received it" (P. F. Bresee).

Should it be easy?

"If Jesus Christ be God and died for me, then no sacrifice can be too great for me to make for Him" (C. T. Studd).

"All my desire was the conversion of the heathen . . . I cared not where or how I lived, or what hardships I went through, so that I could but gain souls to Christ. I declare, now I am dying, I would not have spent my life otherwise for the whole world" (David Brainerd).

"What can we do to win these men to Christ?" (Richard Wurmbrand, referring to those persecuting him).

Will it be worth it?

"Never pity missionaries; envy them. They are where the real action is—where life and death, sin and grace, Heaven and Hell converge" (Robert C. Shannon).

"He is no fool who gives up what he cannot keep to gain that which he cannot lose" (Jim Elliot, missionary and martyr).

Do we have to be especially able or super spiritual?

"God isn't looking for people of great faith, but for individuals ready to follow Him" (Hudson Taylor).

"It is possible for the most obscure person in a church, with a heart right toward God, to exercise as much power for the evangelization of the world, as it is for those who stand in the most prominent positions" (John R. Mott).

"God uses men who are weak and feeble enough to lean on him" (Hudson Taylor).

Thomas Hale, missionary to Nepal, once said, "The biggest hindrance to the missionary task is self. Self that refuses to die. Self that refuses to sacrifice. Self that refuses to give. Self that refuses to go."

Like Moses, we may have plenty of reasons why we should not be the ones called upon to do great things for God. We can share those reasons with God and even ask Him to send someone else, but if God answers those reasons as He did with Moses—*I will be with you, I will provide for you, I am the one with the plan, I will carry it out*—we need to recognize His sovereignty and power and trust His choice.

God wants to deliver the lost and oppressed. He wants His persecuted children supported and encouraged. He seeks laborers for His harvest.

Let us not be the ones who hold back. Let us move forward in courage and confidence, knowing that "faithful is he that calleth you, who also will do it" (I Thess. 5:24).

Has He called you?

—*Kimberly Rae.*

The Jewish Aspect

Readers of Exodus 5 approach the chapter with preconceived ideas that can be the exact opposite of the actual situation of the time. Moses told Pharaoh, "Thus saith the Lord God of Israel, Let my people go, that they may hold a feast unto me in the wilderness" (vs. 1). When Pharaoh refused, Moses responded, "The God of the Hebrews hath met with us: let us go, we pray thee, three days' journey into the desert, and sacrifice unto the Lord our God; lest he fall upon us with pestilence, or with the sword" (vs. 3). How did the Jews understand the "feast" and "sacrifice"? What did they think it meant for God to "fall upon" them?

Today's readers may assume that the Israelites had been faithfully offering sacrifices to God during their time in Egypt. We would think they knew the historical events concerning past sacrifices performed on altars by their ancestors: Abraham (Gen. 12:6-7; 13:18; 22:9), Isaac (26:23-25), Jacob (33:18-20; 35:1-7). Surely the Jews in Egypt would be diligently offering their sacrifices on altars dedicated to the Lord.

But this was not the case. In Ezekiel 20 God reviewed the history of Israel in Egypt. He spoke about their rebellion against Him then. When God determined to "bring them forth of the land of Egypt" (20:6), He told them directly to "defile not yourselves with the idols of Egypt" (vs. 7). Even at the time of the Exodus the Israelites rebelled against God, and "neither did they forsake the idols of Egypt" (vs. 8). When the Jews were in Egypt, they actively worshipped the gods of Egypt.

Into that setting Moses entered. He told Pharaoh that "the Lord God of Israel" (Exod. 5:1), the "God of the Hebrews" (vs. 3), wanted the Israelites to offer a sacrifice to Him. The concept of a festival like this was common in ancient cultures. They were observed regularly in Egypt.

It was commonly believed in ancient times that the status and well-being of a nation reflected the power and authority of their "god(s)." Moses introduced Pharaoh to the "Lord" (Jehovah, Yahweh). This was a new God to Pharaoh. He therefore no doubt looked at the Hebrews to evaluate their God, and he "estimated the character and power of this God by the abject and miserable condition of the worshippers and concluded that He held as low a rank among the gods as His people did in the nation" (Jamieson, Fausset, and Brown, *A Commentary,* Eerdmans).

Pharaoh considered the God of the Hebrews as a second-rate deity. He felt he had nothing to worry about concerning such a lesser god. Add to that the fact that the Hebrews themselves had been previously worshipping the gods of Egypt, and he saw no need to grant Moses' request.

Even if Moses was correct that the God of the Hebrews would "fall upon us with pestilence, or with the sword," that did not matter. Ancient cultures commonly believed that if they neglected their gods, those gods could bring violent death to them. In Pharaoh's mind, however, such a lesser god as the one Moses spoke of could not do much damage, especially to a people who had consistently ignored him in the past.

The lessons of Exodus 5 were not just for Pharaoh. They were for the Israelites as well. They needed to be confronted with their spiritual condition, not just with their need for physical deliverance. Such a lesson continues to be needed by all who claim to follow Yahweh.

—R. Larry Overstreet.

Guiding the Superintendent

If Moses had harbored any hope that taking Israel out of Egyptian bondage would be an easy task, that hope was soon dashed. He would quickly learn just how difficult it would be to make Pharaoh release his slave force. The struggle with the king of Egypt begins with Moses' simple appeal to let the Israelites go and worship their God.

DEVOTIONAL OUTLINE

1. Moses' request (Exod. 5:1-3). Moses and his brother Aaron appeared before Pharaoh with a simple request from the Lord God of Israel: "Let my people go, that they may hold a [worship] feast unto me in the wilderness" (vs. 1).

This was not a simple request to go into the desert for a picnic or a party. The word used for "feast" refers to a religious journey and celebration that is still practiced today in Jewish and Arab cultures.

Pharaoh responded by asking the identity of this Lord God. After all, Pharaoh believed that he himself was a god! He did not know this God, so naturally he was not inclined let Israel leave his country. Little did he know, he was asking for a great lesson in theology! Before this lesson is over, Pharaoh will have learned exactly who the Lord God is.

Moses and Aaron told Pharaoh that if he would not let the Israelites go, the Lord God would strike Egypt with pestilence (plague) and sword.

2. Pharaoh's refusal (Exod. 5:4-9). Pharaoh was not intimidated. He reacted with defiance and further oppression. He decided that the slaves had too much time on their hands if they could entertain ideas about going off to worship their God.

Pharaoh instructed his slave drivers to increase the workload. They were no longer to provide straw for making bricks. The slaves would have to find it on their own. However, the daily quota of bricks would not change. This act of cruelty became only the opening salvo in a protracted conflict with Pharaoh.

CHILDREN'S CORNER

text: **Ruth 1:1-8, 15-22**
title: **Ruth and Naomi**

Like Rahab before her, the notable thing about Ruth was not her gender or nationality, but her faith. She gave up all that was familiar to her to step out in faith and travel with her mother-in-law to Israel. Her faith was a faith in action.

There was famine in the land of Israel. A man named Elimelech and his wife, Naomi, along with their two sons, left Israel and settled in the neighboring land of Moab. Then Naomi's husband died. The two sons took local Moabite women for wives. Ten years later, the two sons also died.

When the famine ended back in Israel, Naomi decided to leave Moab and return home. She encouraged her two daughters-in-law to stay in their homeland while she headed back; there was no future for them in her old homeland. Her daughter-in-law Ruth refused to stay in Moab and told Naomi she was coming back to Israel with her.

Ruth acted on her faith. She told her mother-in-law that she would not leave her but would live with her and worship her God. She cast her fate with Israel and their God.

Eventually, God would greatly reward her faith. She would become an ancestor of King David and, ultimately, of Jesus Christ (Ruth 4:16-22; Matt. 1:5-16).

—*Martin R. Dahlquist.*

SCRIPTURE LESSON TEXT

EXOD. 7:14 And the LORD said unto Moses, Pharaoh's heart *is* hardened, he refuseth to let the people go.

15 Get thee unto Pharaoh in the morning; lo, he goeth out unto the water; and thou shalt stand by the river's brink against he come; and the rod which was turned to a serpent shalt thou take in thine hand.

16 And thou shalt say unto him, The LORD God of the Hebrews hath sent me unto thee, saying, Let my people go, that they may serve me in the wilderness: and, behold, hitherto thou wouldest not hear.

17 Thus saith the LORD, In this thou shalt know that I *am* the LORD: behold, I will smite with the rod that *is* in mine hand upon the waters which *are* in the river, and they shall be turned to blood.

18 And the fish that *is* in the river shall die, and the river shall stink; and the Egyptians shall lothe to drink of the water of the river.

19 And the LORD spake unto Moses, Say unto Aaron, Take thy rod, and stretch out thine hand upon the waters of Egypt, upon their streams, upon their rivers, and upon their ponds, and upon all their pools of water, that they may become blood; and *that* there may be blood throughout all the land of Egypt, both in *vessels of* wood, and in *vessels of* stone.

20 And Moses and Aaron did so, as the LORD commanded; and he lifted up the rod, and smote the waters that *were* in the river, in the sight of Pharaoh, and in the sight of his servants; and all the waters that *were* in the river were turned to blood.

21 And the fish that *was* in the river died; and the river stank, and the Egyptians could not drink of the water of the river; and there was blood throughout all the land of Egypt.

22 And the magicians of Egypt did so with their enchantments: and Pharaoh's heart was hardened, neither did he hearken unto them; as the LORD had said.

23 And Pharaoh turned and went into his house, neither did he set his heart to this also.

24 And all the Egyptians digged round about the river for water to drink; for they could not drink of the water of the river.

NOTES

74

A Plague of Blood

Lesson Text: Exodus 7:14-24

Related Scriptures: Exodus 7:1-13; 8:1-32; Revelation 16:3-7

TIME: 1445 B.C.   PLACE: Egypt

GOLDEN TEXT—"Thus saith the Lord, In this thou shalt know that I am the Lord: behold, I will smite with the rod that is in mine hand upon the waters which are in the river, and they shall be turned to blood" (Exodus 7:17).

Introduction

We look at the vast night sky filled with countless stars, and we agree with the Psalmist David: "The heavens declare the glory of God" (Ps. 19:1). We look at a newborn baby and marvel at the miracle of birth and meditate on the obvious design of God in every person.

The evidence for the existence of our eternal, all-powerful Creator is present in the creation that surrounds us. It is fully sufficient and undeniable. Yet human beings have an amazing capacity for denying the undeniable. Millions of people look at the same sky we do and their own newborn children and still reject God's existence.

The explanation for such denial, of course, is not a lack of evidence provided by God. It is fallen human nature, which loves the darkness of sin and therefore refuses to come to the light of Christ (John 3:19-20).

This was the challenge Moses faced. Pharaoh refused to believe in the Lord and obey Him, even in the face of miraculous signs.

LESSON OUTLINE

I. **ANNOUNCEMENT OF THE FIRST PLAGUE—Exod. 7:14-19**

II. **ENACTMENT OF THE FIRST PLAGUE—Exod. 7:20-21**

III. **RESPONSE TO THE FIRST PLAGUE—Exod. 7:22-24**

Exposition: Verse by Verse

ANNOUNCEMENT OF THE FIRST PLAGUE

EXOD. 7:14 And the LORD said unto Moses, Pharaoh's heart is hardened, he refuseth to let the people go.

15 Get thee unto Pharaoh in the morning; lo, he goeth out unto the water; and thou shalt stand by the river's brink against he come; and the rod which was turned to a serpent shalt thou take in thine hand.

16 And thou shalt say unto him, The LORD God of the Hebrews hath sent me unto thee, saying, Let my people go, that they may serve me in the wilderness: and, behold, hitherto thou wouldest not hear.

17 Thus saith the Lord, In this thou shalt know that I am the Lord: behold, I will smite with the rod that is in mine hand upon the waters which are in the river, and they shall be turned to blood.

18 And the fish that is in the river shall die, and the river shall stink; and the Egyptians shall lothe to drink of the water of the river.

19 And the Lord spake unto Moses, Say unto Aaron, Take thy rod, and stretch out thine hand upon the waters of Egypt, upon their streams, upon their rivers, and upon their ponds, and upon all their pools of water, that they may become blood; and that there may be blood throughout all the land of Egypt, both in vessels of wood, and in vessels of stone.

Necessity of the plague (Exod. 7:14-16). Moses' first meeting with Pharaoh had produced only greater burdens for the people of Israel. As a result, Moses' people were angry with him (5:20-21), and Moses complained to the Lord that He had not yet delivered the people from their bondage (vss. 22-23).

Moses did not realize it at the time, but that deliverance would not come quickly. This was because God wanted to do more than deliver His people. He also wanted to deliver a very clear message to Pharaoh, the Egyptians, and the world; namely, that He alone is the Lord.

The Lord proceeded to encourage Moses by reviewing His plan and His covenant promise to Israel (Exod. 6:1-5). He further assured Moses of freedom and blessing for the people (vss. 6-8). Still, the Israelites would not listen to Moses (vs. 9).

The Lord again charged Moses and Aaron to go to Pharaoh and demand Israel's release, even though He warned that the Egyptian monarch would not listen to them (Exod. 6:10-13). When they went before Pharaoh again, Aaron threw down his rod, and it miraculously transformed into a snake. When the king's magicians somehow seemed to duplicate the feat, Aaron's snake swallowed the others. The demonstration of divine power did not seem to make an impression on Pharaoh, and he refused to listen to Moses and Aaron (7:10-13).

The Lord spoke to Moses, saying, "Pharaoh's heart is hardened, he refuseth to let the people go" (vs. 14). While this must have seemed obvious to Moses, it was a reminder that the king's stubbornness was no surprise to God and that it would continue for some time. The statement also pointed to the necessity of the coming plagues.

The ten plagues God would send upon Egypt were designed to punish Egypt and bring about Israel's release. They would also strengthen the faith of the Israelites as they witnessed God's power and the fulfillment of His promise. A final and important purpose of the plagues was to humiliate the gods of Egypt and totally discredit Egyptian religion (cf. Exod. 12:12; Num. 33:4). Each of the plagues directly challenged one or more of Egypt's gods.

The Lord ordered Moses and Aaron to confront Pharaoh again. They were to go to the bank of the river and wait for the king to come there. Aaron was to take with him the rod that had previously turned into a snake. The word for "river" used throughout this passage is of Egyptian origin and refers specifically to the Nile. Apparently the king came there on a regular basis (cf. Exod. 8:20), probably to perform some religious rite.

Upon seeing the pharaoh, Moses was to remind him of the Lord's demand that he release the Hebrews and that he had failed to do so to this point. Pharaoh was probably becoming rather annoyed with Moses and Aaron by now, but the two were about to add something new to the ongoing struggle—a plague that would devastate the land and affect all of Pharaoh's people.

Nature of the plague (Exod. 7:17-19). The words the Lord gave Moses to speak to the Egyptian king reveal both the purpose and the nature of this first plague. First, the plague was designed to make the pharaoh know that the God of Israel is the "Lord." It was meant as an answer to the king's earlier question, "Who is the Lord, that I should obey his voice?" (5:2). He was about to discover something of this God and His power.

Second, the words reveal the form of the coming plague. Aaron's rod would be used to strike the water, and the river would be turned to blood. As a result, the fish in the river would die, the river would stink, and the water would be unfit for drinking.

This plague would be especially noteworthy due to its corruption of the Nile River. It is hard to overstate the Egyptians' dependence on this great river. It was critical to them for transportation, commerce, and agriculture. Without the annual flooding of the river, "Egypt would be as desolate as the deserts on either side. The Egyptians fully recognized this fact, and in thanksgiving for the blessings of the Nile, hymns were written. Not only were gods associated with the Nile, but fertility, blessing, and happiness were also associated with the faithfulness of this river" (Davis, *Moses and the Gods of Egypt,* Baker).

The divine pollution of the Nile would create tremendous hardship for the Egyptians, if only for a short time, and it would be a testimony to the power of the Lord. It would also strike a blow at Egypt's religion. The Nile itself was worshipped as sacred. In addition, Hapi (Apsis) was the god of the Nile, and Isis was the goddess of the river. Osiris was another god closely associated with the Nile. The turning of the river to blood would demonstrate how

powerless these false deities were, for they would be unable to reverse the plague or give relief to the Egyptians. The Nile, the source of life for Egypt, would be turned into a source of death.

Exodus 7:20 takes us forward in the narrative to the moment of confrontation between Moses and Aaron and the pharaoh of Egypt. At the Lord's instruction, Moses told Aaron to stretch out his rod and strike the waters of Egypt. Here our understanding of the nature of this plague is expanded, for not only was the Nile River affected, but so also were the streams, rivers, ponds, and pools of water in the land. The water in all these places became blood. In addition, water stored in wood buckets and stone jars also turned to blood.

It is likely most, if not all, of the water mentioned here ultimately came from the Nile. The "streams" (vs. 19) were probably branches off the main river. The "rivers" were irrigation channels, and "ponds" can refer to marsh areas or pools of standing water. The "pools" consisted of water collected in cisterns or reservoirs. All such water was turned to blood "throughout all the land of Egypt."

ENACTMENT OF THE FIRST PLAGUE

20 And Moses and Aaron did so, as the LORD commanded; and he lifted up the rod, and smote the waters that were in the river, in the sight of Pharaoh, and in the sight of his servants; and all the waters that were in the river were turned to blood.

21 And the fish that was in the river died; and the river stank, and the Egyptians could not drink of the water of the river; and there was blood throughout all the land of Egypt.

Moses and Aaron did exactly as the Lord commanded. Upon meeting the pharaoh, Aaron struck the Nile with his rod, and the river immediately turned to blood. The fact that he did this in front of Pharaoh and his servants left no doubt as to the agent of this miracle. It was clearly not a natural occurrence but a work of the God of Israel.

As foretold by the Lord, the fish in the river died, the Nile became putrid, and the water was unusable. In addition, the water throughout the land turned to blood. The physical impact would have been immediate since water is essential to life. The spiritual impact likewise would have been significant as the Egyptian people fruitlessly implored the gods of the Nile, the gods of the various fish, and the crocodile god for help and relief.

A number of questions are often raised in regard to the plague of blood. Perhaps foremost is whether the waters turned into actual blood. Many commentators suggest the word "blood" is used here simply of the color of the water and point to the prophecy in Joel 2:31 of the moon turning "into blood." There the blood clearly seems to be a reference to the mere appearance of the moon as red.

A simple discoloring of the water by some natural means, however, would not account for the immediate change upon Aaron's rod touching it. Neither would it explain "the extensiveness of death to the fish. Though the chemical makeup of the red substance is unknown, to the Egyptians it looked and tasted like blood" (Walvoord and Zuck, eds., The Bible Knowledge Commentary, Victor) and was properly described as such. It also had the effects we would expect if it were genuine blood.

This question raises another one: Did God use naturally occurring events to bring about the plagues? Some writers have gone to great lengths to explain the plagues in natural terms: A volcanic eruption polluted the Nile and turned it red. Frogs were forced from their natural habitat and died on dry land. The death of the frogs attracted gnats and flies, and on it goes.

While God can and does use His creation—sometimes in amazing ways—to accomplish His purposes, the plagues can be explained only by supernatural intervention. This is certainly true if, as suggested, the blood was by all appearances real blood. The timing, the element of prediction, and the growing intensity of the plagues also point clearly to miraculous works of God, not natural events Moses somehow exploited to the benefit of Israel.

Another question is this: Did the Israelites suffer the results of this plague as well? Nothing is said about their being exempt from it, so perhaps it was God's way of reminding them of the Lord's power and assuring them that He was perfectly capable of effecting their release.

Also, half of the ten plagues are explicitly said to have made a distinction between the Egyptians and Israelites (Exod. 8:22-23; 9:3-4, 25-26; 10:22-23; 12:23, 27), thus protecting the latter from their devastating effects. So it is quite possible there was such a distinction made in all ten plagues. The very fact that there was any distinction, of course, argues that the plagues were undeniably miraculous, not natural.

RESPONSE TO THE FIRST PLAGUE

22 And the magicians of Egypt did so with their enchantments: and Pharaoh's heart was hardened, neither did he hearken unto them; as the Lord had said.

23 And Pharaoh turned and went into his house, neither did he set his heart to this also.

24 And all the Egyptians digged round about the river for water to drink; for they could not drink of the water of the river.

The magicians' response (Exod. 7:22a). Probably at Pharaoh's request, his magicians "were able to counterfeit the miracle of Moses and Aaron to the degree that Pharaoh was satisfied. In light of pharaonic pride it probably would not take very much to satisfy the wicked heart of this man" (Davis).

This was probably a matter of simple trickery, though it is possible they could have performed the act by means of demonic power. As one writer aptly noted, however, "One would have thought to reverse the effect would have been more helpful: but doubtless that lay beyond their powers" (Cole, *Exodus: An Introduction and Commentary,* InterVarsity).

We might wonder where they got the water to perform their trick if all the water had turned to blood. The answer is probably to be found in Exodus 7:24; underground water apparently was the one source unaffected by the plague.

The pharaoh's response (Exod. 7:22b-23). Pharaoh's heart was hardened so that he would not listen to the Lord's demand to release the Israelites. He was resolute, and he turned and went into his house. The expression "neither did he set his heart to this" simply means he did not take to heart the meaning of this plague. He seemed unconcerned. Indeed, as pharaoh he would be spared much of the suffering his people endured because he could probably obtain the necessary resources to find usable water for himself.

The people's response (Exod. 7:24). Finally, we get a glimpse of how the common people of Egypt responded to the plague of blood. All the Egyptians dug near the river desperately looking for water to drink. It seems that underground water was not polluted, but it required considerable effort to obtain it.

Exodus 7:25 seems to indicate the plague of blood lasted seven days. Most people cannot survive much longer than a week without water. The Egyptians were certainly tested by this plague and would have done whatever was necessary to obtain the needed water, including digging new wells.

Pharaoh was adamantly opposed to Moses. His pride would not allow him to acknowledge the Lord and His authority, even when he witnessed a miracle that directly insulted his own gods and brought suffering to his people.

We must acknowledge that we can never overcome another's opposition to God by either physical or intellectual means. We can only do what we are called to do: be patient, faithful witnesses to the truth of God and allow Him to do His work in His way and in His time. And, like Moses, we can trust God to use our feeble efforts in His plan. The river of blood was just a first step in the Lord's plan to direct Pharaoh's heart.

—*Jarl K. Waggoner.*

QUESTIONS

1. What message did God want to deliver to Pharaoh and the Egyptian people?
2. What purposes were the plagues designed to accomplish?
3. At what river were Moses and Aaron to meet Pharaoh?
4. What significance did the river have to the Egyptians?
5. How would the miraculous pollution of the river strike a blow at Egypt's religion?
6. Besides the river, what other water sources were turned to blood?
7. What resulted from this first plague on Egypt?
8. Was the water turned into actual blood? Explain.
9. Can the turning of water into blood be explained naturally?
10. How did Pharaoh respond to the plague?

—*Jarl K. Waggoner.*

Preparing to Teach the Lesson

What is the Lord's chief goal in all His dealings with the universe He created? John Piper puts it succinctly: "The Scriptures teach throughout that all the works of God have as their ultimate goal the display of God's glory" ("The Glory of God as the Goal of History," www.desiringgod.org). The Lord's desire to glorify Himself is pointedly expressed throughout the Old Testament prophecies by the exclamation, "Know that I am the Lord!" (cf. Exod. 6:7; 7:5, 17; 8:22; 14:4; I Kings 20:13, 28; Isa. 49:23; Ezek. 6:7, 10, 13, 14; Joel 3:17).

In the case of our current lessons in Exodus, we have perhaps God's most dramatic display of His glory in His devastating judgments on Egypt and its gods, as well as in His power to deliver His people from their oppressors.

TODAY'S AIM

Facts: to note that because Pharaoh would not let the Hebrews go, God struck all the waters of Egypt, turning them to blood. But Pharaoh's magicians also changed water to blood, so Pharaoh's heart was unmoved.

Principle: to understand that the Lord is in the business of glorifying Himself as the champion and defender of His covenant people. He allowed Pharaoh to further harden his heart against Moses so that His supreme judgment would continue to be displayed against Egypt and its gods.

Application: to realize that no matter how daunting the opposition may appear to us, as God's covenant people in Christ we can be confident in the Lord's power to defend us and bring victory on our behalf.

INTRODUCING THE LESSON

In last week's lesson, we saw that although Moses and Aaron had commanded Pharaoh in the name of the Lord to let His people go, Pharaoh had mocked the Lord not only by refusing to obey Him but also by substantially increasing the workload of his already beleaguered Hebrew slaves. In doing so, Pharaoh had haughtily provoked the Lord to wrath and judgment upon Egypt. As Hebrews 10:31 warns, "It is a fearful thing to fall into the hands of the living God."

DEVELOPING THE LESSON

1. The plague of blood (Exod. 7:14-21). The Lord had given Pharaoh an additional opportunity to repent of his arrogance and hardness of heart after the first audience he had granted to Aaron and Moses (cf. vss. 8-13). But Pharaoh remained unimpressed with the Lord's miracles and as hardened as ever. "In this thou shalt know that I am the Lord" (vs. 17) is an emphatic declaration. Pharaoh had provoked the Lord's vengeful wrath, and now he would begin to reap a very bitter harvest indeed!

Moses and Aaron were told by the Lord to go and confront Pharaoh as he made his customary visit to the Nile. Adam Clarke elucidates that this outing was "probably for the purpose of bathing, or of performing some religious ablution. Some suppose he went out to pay adoration to the river Nile, which was an object of religious worship among the ancient Egyptians" (*Commentary on the Bible,* Abingdon).

It is important to realize that the waters were not merely turned red to look like blood; they were literally turned into actual blood! The native fish and other aquatic animals could not survive in it. Their decaying carcasses further polluted the Nile to the point of making it an object of utter disgust (vs. 21).

The plague extended beyond the waters of the Nile itself to all its tributaries, reservoirs, adjacent ponds, and even to the household urns and vessels that the Egyptians were using to store water (vs. 19)! The Egyptians even resorted to digging into the ground near the Nile, hoping to find water that was filtered enough to be potable (vs. 24).

The significance of this initial plague on Egypt's waters was twofold. First, it was directed against their preeminent god, Osiris, whose blood was said to be the Nile's waters. Polluting Osiris's own bloodstream showed he was no god at all compared to the Lord. The plague was also a judgment on the gods Khnum, the guardian of the Nile's source, and Hapi, the spirit of the Nile.

Second, as Clarke observes, "The plague of the bloody waters may be considered as a display of retributive justice against the Egyptians, for the murderous decree which enacted that all the male children of the Israelites should be drowned in *that* river."

2. Pharaoh's hard heart (Exod. 7:22-24). In confronting Pharaoh this time, the Lord's purpose was no longer to give him further opportunity to submit but to unconditionally visit the first of the many great plagues against Egypt. These would display God's superior power and glory to the world: "But Pharaoh shall not hearken unto you, that I may lay my hand upon Egypt, and bring forth mine armies, and my people the children of Israel, out of the land of Egypt by great judgments. And the Egyptians shall know that I am the Lord, when I stretch forth mine hand upon Egypt, and bring out the children of Israel" (vss. 4-5).

As seen in a previous encounter (vss. 11-13), the magicians of Egypt were able once again to imitate the Lord's miracle. But since virtually all the water in Egypt was already blood, their demonstration must have been on a puny scale. It was sufficient, however, to harden Pharaoh's heart against the Lord.

ILLUSTRATING THE LESSON

Because of Pharaoh's hard-heartedness, the Lord brought a plague of blood upon Egypt's water supply, showing His supremacy over Egypt's preeminent god, Osiris.

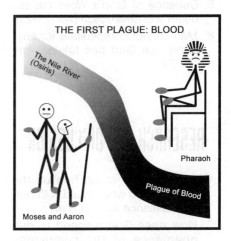

THE FIRST PLAGUE: BLOOD

The Nile River (Osiris)

Pharaoh

Plague of Blood

Moses and Aaron

CONCLUDING THE LESSON

Just as the Lord glorified Himself by defending and delivering the Hebrews, He desires to glorify Himself today in your life. Glorify Him by loving Him and focusing on serving Him as the center of your daily living. "For it is God which worketh in you both to will and to do of his good pleasure" (Phil. 2:13).

ANTICIPATING THE NEXT LESSON

Because of Pharaoh's refusal to let Israel go despite the first six plagues, the Lord directs Moses to bring the seventh plague upon Egypt: thunder and hail.

—John M. Lody.

PRACTICAL POINTS

1. God controls your enemies, and He prepares you to deal with them (Exod. 7:14).
2. When God sends you, He goes with you and directs your path (vss. 15-16).
3. God's actions are never subject to error or defeat (vss. 17-19).
4. When God moves on your behalf, your enemies can only stand and watch (vs. 20).
5. Defiance of God's Word causes death and destruction (vss. 21-23).
6. Man cannot compensate for anything that God has taken away (vs. 24).

—Valante M. Grant.

RESEARCH AND DISCUSSION

1. How can we stand firm on the Word of God when faced with outright defiance against Him?
2. How does God respond to disobedience of His commands (Exod. 7:16-17)?
3. Why must we rely on God's strength to defend us from our enemies?
4. What is the best way to witness to ungodly people?
5. Can we determine by ourselves what path in life we should take? How should believers make decisions?
6. Think about today's world leaders. What similarities or differences do you see between them and Pharaoh?
7. What example can we take from Moses and Aaron when dealing with people who do not fear God?

—Valante M. Grant.

ILLUSTRATED HIGH POINTS

Pharaoh's heart is hardened

God knew that the heart of Pharaoh had hardened.

Petrified wood is material that was once organic but, over time, has transitioned into rock. What was once a living organism, able to multiply and possibly bring forth fruit, became devoid of organic matter. The process begins when the tree branch breaks off and falls away from its living source. Then, swept away, it is buried underground. In the dark, it begins to fill with mineral-laden water, which forms around its very cell structure and slowly solidifies. The original organic matter decays, leaving behind only the mineral, in the exact form of the original plant—a stone replicate.

Let us stay in the light and close to our source, guarding against allowing sinful matter (pride, worldliness, unbelief) to seep into our hearts (cf. Dan. 5:20; Mark 6:52; Luke 21:34).

Get thee unto Pharaoh

An old Scottish woman would throw a stick into the air whenever she came to a crossroad. When it landed, she would go whichever direction it pointed. However, one day she was seen throwing it multiple times. When questioned, she explained that she wanted to go to the right, but the stick kept pointing to the left. This is often how we treat God's will. We ask God to bless our plans, but when we receive a call to action that was not part of our plan, we resist His leading.

Moses made up many reasons why he should have been excused from participating in God's plan. We like to think of our Lord merely as a receiving God. However, we sometimes forget that He also requires action from His people. His followers are sent out again and again, that we might actively do His will.

—Therese Greenberg.

Golden Text Illuminated

"Thus saith the Lord, In this thou shalt know that I am the Lord: behold, I will smite with the rod that is in mine hand upon the waters which are in the river, and they shall be turned to blood" (Exodus 7:17).

God's preparation for the deliverance of His people involved several unique personalities: Moses, Aaron, and Pharaoh. These individuals were the main participants in the historic saga of God's people and their liberation from Egyptian bondage. We have already noted how God prepared Moses to be His earthly deliverer of the Israelites. Although somewhat reluctant and hesitant, Moses ultimately obeyed God's call.

As God continued His preparatory work that would result in the deliverance of His people, the king of Egypt temporarily came to the forefront of the proceedings. This arrogant, unbelieving, and cruel ruler would have to have his spirit broken. He would have to be brought into a state of humble subjection to God Almighty before he would release God's people from their oppressive imprisonment.

God would accomplish His powerful work in Pharaoh's heart through a series of ten supernatural plagues. Starting with the first plague (blood), each succeeding plague would be increasingly severe. The ultimate purpose of the plagues was to liberate God's people from Egyptian slavery. They would accomplish this by authenticating the sovereign authority of Almighty God and bringing Pharaoh to the point of submission to His authority.

Fully committed to being God's faithful servants, Moses and Aaron confronted Pharaoh. In order to authenticate their claim that they represented the Lord, Aaron obeyed God's prior revelation and "cast down his rod before Pharaoh, and before his servants, and it became a serpent" (vs. 10).

Pharaoh's deceptive magicians duplicated Aaron's feat, but Aaron's serpent-staff completely devoured the magicians' serpent-staffs. Nevertheless, Pharaoh's heart began the hardening process that resulted in protracted disobedience (vss. 11-13). Now was the exact time for Moses and Aaron to commence God's judgment of supernatural plagues.

Moses introduced the first judgment, the plague of blood, with words of divine affirmation. Egypt was at the height of its power and glory, and God wanted to overwhelm Egypt's glory with His superior glory. God wanted everyone to know that He, Yahweh, is the one, true, living God of the universe.

God would accomplish this task by using Moses as His spokesperson and Aaron as His laborer to turn the waters of the Nile River into literal blood (cf. vs. 19). Moses made the divine proclamation, and Aaron used his rod to strike the Nile's water.

The turning of water into blood was a significant starting point for God's judgments. The Egyptians not only deified the Nile River, but they were also dependent upon it for sustenance of life. As God prepared His people for deliverance, He struck the first mighty blow at the heart of Egyptian life.

When God decided to strike a mighty blow at the heart of our sin, He again used blood—the sinless blood of His Son, Jesus Christ. As a result, everyone who fully trusts in Jesus as his or her Saviour receives forgiveness and eternal life.

—*Thomas R. Chmura.*

Heart of the Lesson

When our enemies attack us or oppress us, it is natural to wonder if God sees our pain. We know that Pharaoh ordered the death of all newborn Hebrew boys, who were to be thrown into the Nile. What we do not know is how long that edict lasted. It does not seem to have been a onetime event, like Herod's order to kill all boys in Bethlehem up to two years old. God took notice of the lives that were stolen and remembered all the blood that was shed in the Nile because of Pharaoh's decree. Just as Pharaoh's order affected all the Israelites, when God acted, the plagues affected all the Egyptians.

1. The Lord commands Moses (Exod. 7:14-19). The Lord spoke to Moses and told him that Pharaoh was not ready to let the people go. Moses was to go with Aaron to the bank of the Nile while Pharaoh was out by the water. God told them to bring the staff that had transformed into a snake because they were going to use it again. God told Moses and Aaron exactly what to do and exactly what to say. There was no guessing what was required of them. God is the same yesterday, today, and forever. There is no guessing what He requires of His people today—to proclaim the gospel to the world. God gave Moses and Aaron a strategy to combat the king of Egypt. God will speak through His Word and to our hearts and give us a strategy to fulfill His will.

2. Blood everywhere in Egypt (Exod. 7:20-21). Moses and Aaron did exactly as the Lord commanded. They went to Pharaoh and told him to let the Hebrews go and worship their God. Pharaoh refused, so Aaron lifted his staff and struck the water, turning it to blood. Just as the Lord had declared, blood was everywhere in Egypt—including in all their wells and fountains.

Pharaoh watched the Nile turn to blood, but it is important to emphasize that *all* the waters turned to blood—not only the Nile, but also the ponds. The plague of blood lasted for seven days. It is possible that the water transforming to blood was a reminder to Pharaoh of the deaths of the Hebrew babies. God is a just God. Even though His justice may tarry, wait for it. His ways are not our ways; even in His acts of justice we can hear a call for us to turn our hearts toward Him.

3. The copycat Egyptian magicians (Exod. 7:22-24). When Aaron's staff hit the water and blood appeared, Pharaoh became fearful. However, when his magicians were able to duplicate the effects, his heart hardened. Which is greater? Turning the water into blood or turning it back into water? Why did the king of Egypt want his magicians to do the same thing? Why did he not ask them to change the blood back to water? That would have been more beneficial. The Egyptians were forced to dig for water along the Nile, and by the mercy of God, they found fresh water.

When we encounter things that we do not understand, we can be stubborn—just like Pharaoh. We can see genuine moves of God and yet still respond in disbelief. Why? Because when we experience something that cannot be understood by mere human reason, it is easier and safer for us to discount it. Pharaoh witnessed a miracle and hardened his heart. May God increase our faith to believe!

—*Kristin Reeg.*

World Missions

God had promised a great victory. He sent Moses, and the people rejoiced at first. Then Pharaoh refused to let them go and made their oppression even worse.

God sent Moses to do miracles, but the first ones were mimicked by the Egyptians. For a time, God allowed the Egyptians to believe their gods were as powerful as Him. Things got worse for God's chosen people before they got better.

Sometimes turning to Christ can carry a heavy cost. Stories do not always have happy endings in this life.

One wonderful story of following Christ is loosely depicted in the movie *The Inn of the Sixth Happiness*. Missionary Gladys Aylward, serving in an obscure village in China, overcomes again and again. The story culminates in the inspiring depiction of how she led one hundred orphans over the mountains to safety during World War II.

Reality, however, continued beyond the movie. In eternal terms, Gladys was much more of a hero than what the movie showed, at great cost to herself.

Despite amazing victories, such as her transformation of the prison system in the area and almost single-handedly stopping the horrific practice of foot binding, Gladys suffered much.

After the war, once she recovered from a terrible illness, she returned to China. She surely received much advice to stay in Europe. Her response was single-minded: "Life is pitiful, death so familiar, suffering and pain so common, yet I would not be anywhere else. Do not wish me out of this or in any way seek to get me out, for I will not be got out while this trial is on."

Her own opinion of her abilities was low: "I wasn't God's first choice for what I've done for China . . . I don't know who it was . . . It must have been a man . . . a well-educated man. I don't know what happened. Perhaps he died. Perhaps he wasn't willing . . . and God looked down . . . and saw Gladys Aylward . . . And God said— 'Well, she's willing.'" However we might regard the theology behind this humble claim, God used Gladys to bring many Chinese to faith in Christ, including hundreds of university students.

This was a great victory, but then the Communists took over the university. The believing students were subjected to harsh indoctrination.

After three months, two hundred Christian students were called out to the market square. The persecutors began by asking a seventeen-year-old girl what her position was now.

The girl came to the platform and spoke clearly: "Sir, when I went for my three months' indoctrination, I thought Jesus Christ was real. I thought the Bible was true. Now I *know* Jesus Christ is real; I *know* this Book is true!"

Not one of the two hundred rejected their faith. One by one, each was beheaded. It had to have been one of the worst horrors imaginable for Gladys to watch them be murdered. Evil surely seemed to prevail. But despite the pain, Gladys knew each of those students would spend eternity in heaven because the message they believed came from God, not her.

When we follow God into the darkness, things might get worse and begin to look like evil is prevailing. We must remember that we are doing God's will and giving His message if we are to endure, knowing that however things appear on earth, God's stories have a happy ending that is eternal and far greater than anything we can imagine.
—*Kimberly Rae.*

The Jewish Aspect

The Jews rebelled against God and His worship. When God determined to "bring them forth of the land of Egypt" (Ezek. 20:6), He told them directly to "defile not yourselves with the idols of Egypt" (vs. 7). At the time of the Exodus, the Israelites had rebelled against God, and "neither did they forsake the idols of Egypt" (vs. 8). The Hebrews in Egypt were actively worshipping the gods of Egypt. That is critical in understanding the full impact of the initial three plagues.

About 125 gods and goddesses were widely worshipped in Egypt, and about 25 were dominant deities, but there were about 2000 known gods and goddesses worshipped to some degree ("The Ancient Egyptian Gods," www. ancient-egypt-online.com). Some of the gods and goddesses of ancient Egypt were local deities. Others were revered throughout the kingdom.

When God brought the plagues, He said it was "against all the gods of Egypt I will execute judgment: I am the Lord" (Exod. 12:12). Jethro, Moses' father-in-law, recognized that the deliverance from Egypt demonstrated that "the Lord is greater than all gods" (18:11). As Israel approached the Promised Land, Moses reviewed the Exodus, asserting that "upon their gods also the Lord executed judgments" (Num. 33:4).

The Israelites needed to grasp the full importance of how the plagues proved the identity and superiority of the Lord. Because of that, "The first three plagues covered the whole land, and fell upon the Israelites as well as the Egyptians; with the fourth the separation commenced between Egyptians and Israelites, so that only the Egyptians suffered from the last six, the Israelites in Goshen being en-tirely exempted" (Keil and Delitzsch, *Commentary on the Old Testament,* Hendrickson). The people, however, learned slowly. Hundreds of years later, the psalmist wrote, "Our fathers understood not thy wonders in Egypt" (Ps. 106:7).

When God turned the Nile into blood, He demonstrated His authority over several Egyptian gods. Each year in summer the Nile flooded its banks. At that time, the pharaoh presided at a religious ceremony to honor the river and its gods. A painting found at Gebel Silseleh, about forty miles north of Aswan in southern Egypt, shows a pharaoh making an offering to Hapi, a Nile divinity who was considered the life-giving father of all living things.

It was probably at this exact time that God, through Moses, turned the Nile's water into blood. The god of the Nile was Hapi, and its goddess was Isis, queen of the gods. The god Khnum was worshipped as the guardian of the Nile. The Nile's water was considered to be the bloodstream of Osiris, the lord of the dead. Thus the first plague showed God's supremacy over four major gods of Egypt.

The ten plagues may have begun in June with the Nile turning to blood, and they concluded the following April, the time of the Passover. If this is correct, all ten plagues fell upon Egypt in a time span of only ten months. The plague struck the gods that the Hebrews in Egypt had worshipped. The question for them was, Would they remember? Clearly, "Marvellous things did he [God] in the sight of their fathers, in the land of Egypt" (Ps. 78:12), yet after God brought them out of Egypt, "they sinned yet more against him by provoking the most High" (vs. 17).

—R. Larry Overstreet.

Guiding the Superintendent

Egypt was a narrow ribbon of a country that stretched along the Nile River. Beyond this ribbon on either side was a vast wasteland and desert. Egypt could only survive because of the water from the river. Very seldom did the Egyptians venture beyond the confines of the river.

Moses' early attempts to get Pharaoh to release the Israelites to go into the desert to worship God were met with hard-hearted refusal. God decided to get the king's attention by attacking the very source of Egypt's life—the Nile.

DEVOTIONAL OUTLINE

1. Moses' miracle (Exod. 7:14-21). The Egyptians relied on the river's water for everything in life, from irrigation for their fields to fish for their table.

God instructed Moses and his brother Aaron to meet Pharaoh when he came to the Nile. They repeated their request to Pharaoh to let the Israelites go into the desert for worship.

In their first meeting, Pharaoh had questioned who this God of Moses was. This time, God told Moses that the king would know who the Lord God was when Aaron struck the river with his staff. When he did this, the river turned to blood and all the fish died. The smell was unbearable. Everywhere there had been water, there was now blood.

2. The magicians' false miracle (Exod. 7:22-24). With their enchantments, the court magicians were able to duplicate the actions of Moses. Pharaoh responded as God had predicted—with a hard heart. The king turned around and went back to his palace. He really did not take God's warnings seriously. His people were left to fend for themselves as they tried to find water.

Moses and his brother were learning that getting Pharaoh to release his slaves was going to be a prolonged battle.

The Nile River was considered divine—one of many gods of the Egyptian nation. This would be only the first of many gods that Israel's God would attack before He would attack the most important god of Egypt—Pharaoh himself.

CHILDREN'S CORNER

text: **Job 2:1-10**
title: **Job: Hurting but Still Trusting God**

There are about as many reasons humans suffer as there are humans. Perhaps one of most mysterious reasons for suffering is that, often without their knowledge, people are caught up in spiritual warfare between good and evil. Job is probably the best example of one who suffers for no apparent reason.

One day Satan stood before God. God asked Satan, Had he seen that Job feared Him and shunned evil? Satan insisted that Job's motives and character were far from pure. He declared that Job feared God only because God blessed him. He even implied that Job was not righteous, just selfish. Satan earnestly believed that Job had ulterior motives for his upright behavior; if God took away everything good that Job had, he would surely curse God.

Surprisingly, to prove Satan wrong God allowed Satan to attack Job. Satan immediately caused many painful sores to break out all over Job's body. So painful was the attack on his body that the only relief he could find was from scraping his sores with broken pottery. In addition, Job's wife suggested that he curse God. Job still did not turn on God.

Job is a great example of a person who, in spite of great testing, maintains his faith in God.

—*Martin R. Dahlquist.*

SCRIPTURE LESSON TEXT

EXOD. 9:27 And Pharaoh sent, and called for Moses and Aaron, and said unto them, I have sinned this time: the LORD *is* righteous, and I and my people *are* wicked.

28 Intreat the LORD (for *it is* enough) that there be no *more* mighty thunderings and hail; and I will let you go, and ye shall stay no longer.

29 And Moses said unto him, As soon as I am gone out of the city, I will spread abroad my hands unto the LORD; *and* the thunder shall cease, neither shall there be any more hail; that thou mayest know how that the earth *is* the LORD'S.

30 But as for thee and thy servants, I know that ye will not yet fear the LORD God.

31 And the flax and the barley was smitten: for the barley *was* in the ear, and the flax *was* bolled.

32 But the wheat and the rie were not smitten: for they *were* not grown up.

33 And Moses went out of the city from Pharaoh, and spread abroad his hands unto the LORD: and the thunders and hail ceased, and the rain was not poured upon the earth.

34 And when Pharaoh saw that the rain and the hail and the thunders were ceased, he sinned yet more, and hardened his heart, he and his servants.

35 And the heart of Pharaoh was hardened, neither would he let the children of Israel go; as the LORD had spoken by Moses.

NOTES

Pharaoh's Hardening Heart

Lesson Text: Exodus 9:27-35

Related Scriptures: Exodus 9:1-26; Acts 8:18-24

TIME: 1445 B.C.   PLACE: Egypt

GOLDEN TEXT—"When Pharaoh saw that the rain and the hail and the thunders were ceased, he sinned yet more, and hardened his heart, he and his servants" (Exodus 9:34).

Introduction

We all know the disappointment we feel when someone makes us a promise and then fails to follow through on it. If confronted, the person who made the promise always seems to have some excuse for not keeping his or her word. The excuse often is less than convincing, however, and we are left to think that the person never really took the promise seriously.

What might strike us as odd is that many people more readily break their promises to God than their promises to people. Perhaps it is because God is unseen and thus does not seem to present an immediate threat to hold them accountable. Promises made to God in the midst of trying circumstances are often forgotten when the trial subsides.

In this lesson, we find two people making promises. Pharaoh promised to release the people of God, and Moses promised to intercede for Pharaoh to bring relief from the plague. Only one man kept his promise. It is not hard to guess which one it was.

LESSON OUTLINE

I. **THE PROMISE OF PHARAOH—** Exod. 9:27-28

II. **THE PROMISE OF MOSES—** Exod. 9:29-30

III. **THE DEVASTATION OF CROPS—Exod. 9:31-32**

IV. **THE FAITHFULNESS OF MOSES—Exod. 9:33**

V. **THE HARDENING OF PHARAOH—Exod. 9:34-35**

Exposition: Verse by Verse

THE PROMISE OF PHARAOH

EXOD. 9:27 And Pharaoh sent, and called for Moses and Aaron, and said unto them, I have sinned this time: the LORD is righteous, and I and my people are wicked.

28 Intreat the LORD (for it is enough) that there be no more mighty thunderings and hail; and I will let you go, and ye shall stay no longer.

The first plague on Egypt was the turning of the water to blood (Exod. 7:14-24). This was followed by five more plagues: frogs (8:2-15), lice (vss. 16-19), flies (vss. 20-25), death of livestock (9:1-7), and boils (vss. 8-12). Each of these plagues was more intense than the previous one, and each one humiliated the Egyptians and their false gods. The pharaoh of Egypt, however, remained unmoved: "He hearkened not unto them; as the Lord had spoken unto Moses" (vs. 12) and would not let the Israelites go free.

At this point the Lord explained in detail the purpose of all the plagues. They were designed not only to free the people of Israel but also to show Pharaoh and his people that the Lord is supreme. He is all-powerful, and His name is to be "declared throughout all the earth" (9:16). Yet, to this point Egypt's king had exalted himself (vs. 17).

The Lord had already demonstrated His power and the powerlessness of Egypt's gods, including Pharaoh himself, who was considered a very eminent god. The final four plagues would bring even more intense devastation and suffering in order to accomplish God's purposes.

Moses announced that the seventh plague would bring an especially destructive hailstorm upon the land. It would be accompanied by rain, wind, thunder, and fire that "ran along upon the ground" (vs. 23). The fire is understood by many to be lightning, but it is not the normal word for lightning, perhaps indicating this was some never-before-seen phenomenon. Indeed, the storm would not only destroy crops, but even kill people and livestock in the field.

Egypt was greatly dependent on the Nile River, which flows north into the Mediterranean Sea. Most of the population then, as now, resided near the river. The farmlands were watered almost exclusively by water from the river since rainfall was minimal. The nation that normally would have welcomed rain instead dreaded the storm the Lord brought upon the land.

By this time, some of the Egyptians had learned to take Moses at his word, so they put their animals under shelter where they would be protected (vs. 20). Those who continued to ignore the word of God through Moses took no such precautions and suffered even greater losses than they otherwise would have (vs. 21).

The intensity of the storm is described in Exodus 9:24-25. It was like nothing ever seen before in Egypt. Yet it was confined to areas inhabited by the Egyptians. The Israelites, living in the region of Goshen, saw no hail (vs. 26). Clearly this was a supernatural event and a powerful testimony to everyone that the God of Israel was working on behalf of His enslaved people.

After each of the previous plagues, we are told that Pharaoh hardened his heart and would not heed God's demand to let the people go (7:22; 8:15, 19, 32; 9:7, 12). Now, for the first time, there appeared to be a change of Pharaoh's attitude as he called for Moses and Aaron.

Upon their arrival, Pharaoh made three confessions. First, he said, "I have sinned this time" (9:27). "This time" probably suggests only a partial confession. In fact, it can be argued that "I have sinned" could be translated "I have been unfair" (Stuart, *New American Commentary: Exodus*, Holman). It certainly was not a sincere confession of his sin and probably was motivated more by desperation than repentance.

Second, Pharaoh stated, "The Lord is righteous" (vs. 27). Even if he was not sincere, this statement was clearly accurate. In addition, it was an acknowledgment of the Lord, whom the king had rejected earlier as utterly insignificant, if not entirely nonexistent (5:2). Pharaoh was now conceding that the Lord did have some power. He would even ask Moses to pray to the Lord on his behalf (9:28).

Finally, the pharaoh confessed, "I and my people are wicked" (vs. 27). This was a confession of guilt. As we will see, Pharaoh's words were not confirmed by his actions. The fact that he was willing to speak these words, however, points to the effectiveness of the plagues in moving the king toward eventual compliance with the Lord's command. Indeed, Pharaoh asked Moses to pray to the Lord to end the extraordinary thunder and hail. If relieved of this devastation, Pharaoh promised he would let the Israelites go right away.

THE PROMISE OF MOSES

29 And Moses said unto him, As soon as I am gone out of the city, I will spread abroad my hands unto the Lord; and the thunder shall cease, neither shall there be any more hail; that thou mayest know how that the earth is the Lord's.

30 But as for thee and thy servants, I know that ye will not yet fear the Lord God.

Moses assured the pharaoh that as soon as he left the city, he would spread his hands to the Lord in supplication and the thunder and hail would cease. Spreading the hands and reaching heavenward was a posture of prayer (cf. II Chron. 6:13; Ezra 9:5). Moses would pray for the Lord to end the plague, but he would wait to do so until he was out of the city. This seems to convey Moses' complete confidence in God's protection and in the Lord's answering his prayer, for outside the city in the open was where the storm would have been most deadly.

The answer to Moses' prayer was meant to teach Pharaoh that the earth is the Lord's. He needed to take to heart the truth that the entire earth belongs to the Lord. God is sovereign over creation and can bring destruction upon it if He wills. Pharaoh, who fancied himself a god, was at the mercy of God's destructive storm. Yahweh, the only true God, was the one in control.

Moses was under no illusions about Pharaoh. The king's words sounded encouraging, but Moses knew he did not really respect the Lord God (cf. Exod. 9:30). Moses, who had complained after his first meeting with Pharaoh that the Lord had not yet delivered Israel (5:23), had now learned that God's plan to deliver the Hebrews also included the humbling of Pharaoh and Egypt's false gods. He knew that this was a monumental work that would take time. God needed to be fully glorified by the spectacle of Egypt's punishment.

THE DEVASTATION OF CROPS

31 And the flax and the barley was smitten: for the barley was in the ear, and the flax was bolled.

32 But the wheat and the rie were not smitten: for they were not grown up.

Exodus 9:31-32 acts as a parenthesis in the narrative, giving a summary of the devastation that had taken place as a result of the hailstorm. The text notes that the flax and barley, which were nearing the time of harvest, were destroyed by the storm. Flax was important in the making of linen clothing, which was highly valued by the Egyptians. Barley was used for bread, beer, and animal food.

The loss of these crops was a great blow to the Egyptians. However, two other crops, wheat and "rie" (vs. 32), survived the hailstorm. "Rie" refers to spelt, a low-grade species of wheat. These crops, which were more needful for humans, were harvested about a month later than flax and barley. Though the "shoots were up and growing, and surely were smashed down by the hail, they were able to recover" (Stuart).

Why did God see fit to include such details here? There are probably at least three reasons.

First, the ancient world was primarily agricultural, and readers would naturally be interested in what kind of damage was done by the plague. In fact, knowing this would reveal to them the power of the Lord in a way that might not be so evident to those unfamiliar with agriculture.

Second, there is an indication of God's mercy in this description. The Lord's judgment did not destroy the crops on which the Egyptians were most dependent. If Pharaoh had followed through on his promise to release the Israelites (vs. 28), the essential crops would have been spared. His failure to do this, however, led to the loss of the wheat in the locust plague that followed (10:1-19).

Third, the specific mention of the crops that were destroyed emphasized again the impotence of Egypt's gods. Nut was the goddess of the sky in Egyptian religion, and Shu was god of the atmosphere. Set was the god of storms. Yet these gods offered no help. "Those who had labored long and hard in the hot sun witnessed in a few moments the total destruction of their crops. Their desperate cries to their deities had not brought relief" (Davis, *Moses and the Gods of Egypt*, Baker). The message was clear: "The earth is the Lord's" (9:29). Yahweh, not the false gods of Egypt, was the only source of relief and hope.

THE FAITHFULNESS OF MOSES

33 And Moses went out of the city from Pharaoh, and spread abroad his hands unto the LORD: and the thunders and hail ceased, and the rain was not poured upon the earth.

True to his word, Moses left the city and immediately spread out his hands before the Lord in prayer. The Lord heard his prayer, and the storm, with its rain, thunder, and hail, ceased. Moses' faithfulness to his word stands in stark contrast to the actions of Pharaoh that followed.

THE HARDENING OF PHARAOH

34 And when Pharaoh saw that the rain and the hail and the thunders were ceased, he sinned yet more, and hardened his heart, he and his servants.

35 And the heart of Pharaoh was hardened, neither would he let the children of Israel go; as the LORD had spoken by Moses.

As soon as Pharaoh saw that the rain and hail and thunder had stopped, "he sinned yet more" (Exod. 9:34). The idea is that he sinned again; that is, he once again willfully did what was wrong. His particular sin is spelled out in the rest of this verse and the next: he hardened his heart and refused to obey God's command to release the people of Israel.

While Moses quickly kept his word to Pharaoh by praying for the plague to end, the Egyptian king just as quickly abandoned his promise to let the Israelites go. He was joined in this determination by other members of his royal court.

These servants were not only attendants but also advisers to the pharaoh. They supported him by approving his actions and becoming as hardened as he was. Given the pharaoh's position and power, they were undoubtedly reluctant to raise an opposing opinion. Only upon the announcement of the next plague did any of them suggest the king let the Israelites go (10:7).

Through this plague and the previous ones, the Lord had revealed Himself to Pharaoh as the supreme, all-powerful God. He had demonstrated His righteousness (cf. 9:27), faithfulness, and persistence. And He had shown that the earth belongs to Him (vs. 29). Pharaoh had been humbled and forced to mouth compliance with the Lord's demand (vs. 28). Pharaoh's heart was not really moved but hardened against Moses, Israel, and Israel's God.

The hardening of the heart speaks of stiffness, stubbornness, or obstinacy. The expression is used throughout Scripture to describe "the idea of stubborn human resistance to God" (Tenney, ed., *The Zondervan Pictorial Encyclopedia of the Bible,* Zondervan).

In the case of Pharaoh, the Bible speaks repeatedly of his hardening his heart, but it also speaks of his heart being hardened by God (cf. 4:21; 7:3, 13; 9:12; 10:1, 20, 27; 14:4, 8). How are we to understand this? Some suggest God's hardening of Pharaoh's heart was a response to the king's hardening of his own heart. Others believe God unconditionally hardened Pharaoh's heart, yet still held him accountable for his actions. This seems to be a case where we must affirm that both God and Pharaoh were responsible for the hardening.

God clearly hardened Pharaoh's heart so that the Lord's wonders might be multiplied in Egypt (7:3). In fact, God said that He raised up Pharaoh for the very purpose of revealing His power so that His name might be declared throughout the earth (9:16). The Lord used the downfall of this powerful ruler to demonstrate His own sovereignty (cf. Rom. 9:17-18).

At the same time, Pharaoh, like all who willingly resist the Lord, was rightly held to account for his actions (cf. Ezek. 18:20). We may find it hard to reconcile these two ideas, but then, as finite humans, we can never fully grasp the ways of the infinite God.

Leaving behind the difficult theological question regarding the hardening of Pharaoh's heart, there is a very practical issue to address here. Why would a man like Pharaoh resist the Lord in the face of such overwhelming evidence that He is indeed all-powerful, righteous, and sovereign over the earth? The king's stubborn pride in his own power, ability, and supposed deity dissuaded him to keep his promise and give in to the demands of Israel's God.

Pride exalts us and thus naturally leads us to resist God. The more we value ourselves, the less we value God. Let us not stubbornly and selfishly pursue our own desires, but instead let us put the plan and desire of God above all things. It is through abandoning a self-centered life that we find true life and contentment (cf. Matt. 6:33; 16:24-25; Phil. 2:5-9).

—*Jarl K. Waggoner.*

QUESTIONS

1. What was God's purpose for the plagues?
2. What phenomena were involved in the seventh plague?
3. How did the Israelites fare during the seventh plague?
4. How had Pharaoh reacted to the previous plagues?
5. What did the king confess to Moses and Aaron?
6. Of what did Moses assure the Egyptian king?
7. Did Moses believe Pharaoh would release the Israelites as he said he would?
8. What is the religious significance of the details regarding the destruction of crops?
9. How did Pharaoh respond to the ending of the plague?
10. How did God use the Egyptian king to accomplish His purposes?

—*Jarl K. Waggoner.*

Preparing to Teach the Lesson

Besides offering a richly rewarding study of how the Lord manifested His almighty power over the greatest empire on earth, bringing them to their knees and delivering His covenant people from slavery, these chapters in Exodus also provide a fascinating and instructive look at how an unbeliever reacts when confronted with the claims of the Lord upon his life.

TODAY'S AIM

Facts: to see that Pharaoh seems to repent and become willing to free the Hebrews, but as soon as the plague of thunder and hail is lifted, he hardens himself again and refuses to free them.

Principle: to understand that people who seem genuinely contrite about their sins can often become recalcitrant again when their fear of judgment subsides.

Application: to understand that when dealing with people's attitude toward their sins, we should seek the Holy Spirit's discernment about the honesty of their contrition.

INTRODUCING THE LESSON

Pharaoh's varied reactions to the Lord's command run the gamut from skepticism to outright mockery to feigned or calculated repentance and finally to threats of physical violence. An analysis of his responses can be very helpful in anticipating and understanding the reactions of people to the claims of the gospel in our own day.

DEVELOPING THE LESSON

1. Pharaoh and Moses (Exod. 9:27-32). How encouraging Pharaoh's confession sounds! He admits that he and his fellow Egyptians have sinned,

that the Lord is righteous, and that he and his countrymen are wicked. But here is the first clue that Pharaoh's repentance is less than genuine: he implies that the freedom of the Hebrews is contingent upon the ceasing of the plague of hail and thunder that was currently devastating Egypt's landscape.

"Mighty thunderings" (vs. 28) literally translates as "voices of God," which is idiomatic for thunder that is superlatively loud. This expression is amplified by the words of Psalm 29:3-8: "The God of glory thundereth. . . . The voice of the Lord is powerful; the voice of the Lord is full of majesty. The voice of the Lord breaketh the cedars. . . . The voice of the Lord shaketh the wilderness." It is difficult to know which the Egyptians feared more—the destruction of their crops or the constant thundering of the voice of Israel's God in their ears.

The plague of hail and thunder, like the rest of the plagues upon Egypt, was intended as a specific judgment on Egypt's gods. In this case, the deities under judgment by the Lord were Nut, the goddess of the sky, and Set, the Egyptian storm god. The Lord displayed His supremacy over both idols in definitive fashion.

As we read Exodus 9, verses 31 and 32 give us an insight into Pharaoh's real motives. The barley (beer) and flax (linen) crops had been destroyed. When the hail struck the land, these two crops had been nearly ready for harvesting. But the wheat and rye crops were still viable, since the ears of grain for these two crops had not yet appeared and therefore had not been ruined for use as food. These two remaining crops actually formed the greater part of Egypt's annual food supply. Thus, if Pharaoh could persuade Moses to call off the hail now, most of the food crop would be saved. Pharaoh could then backtrack on his agreement to release the Hebrews once their supply was out of immediate danger.

Pharaoh thought he was so clever! He believed that Moses could be duped by his contrite act. If Moses stopped the hail, the Egyptians would have no incentive to free the Hebrews from slavery. But Pharaoh was really too smart for his own good, since Moses revealed (vs. 30) that the Lord was fully aware of Pharaoh's deceit; He knew that Pharaoh had no intention of letting the Israelites go.

In fact, as revealed in Exodus 10:1, it was the Lord who was continuing to harden Pharaoh's heart for the purpose of unleashing His full wrath and judgment on Egypt. The Lord was making Egypt an example before the world of what happens to any nation, even the most powerful one on earth, that dares to defy Him.

2. Plague relief and renewed hardening (Exod. 9:33-35). It surely indicates an irrational frame of mind to fully realize, on the one hand, that the Lord is sovereign over all that happens to you and your country and yet, on the other hand, to persist in scheming and conspiring to resist submitting to Him. But such was Pharaoh's frame of mind as he continued to experience the devastation that resulted from defying the Lord, yet persisted in that defiance to his own ruin.

In verse 33, Moses follows through on his promise (made in verse 29) to end the plague of hail, fully aware that Pharaoh would persist in his refusal to let the Israelites go. It is chilling to behold the inexorable progression and escalation of the Lord's plan to completely devastate Egypt. God used Pharaoh's own stubborn arrogance to

bring the nation to its inevitable and utter destruction.

In verse 34, it is as if Pharaoh had not even heard Moses foretell his renewed rebellion in verse 30. Pharaoh's behavior has at this point become positively maniacal in its irrational, self-destructive obsession. Disregarding the fact that he is merely furthering the Lord's plans to destroy him and his kingdom, he nevertheless deliberately goes on defying the Lord's command.

ILLUSTRATING THE LESSON

The illustration shows that seemingly sincere repentance may prove false once the fear of punishment is abated.

FALSE REPENTANCE

Thunder and Hail

Fear of punishment removed

Pharaoh hardened his heart again!

Feigned repentance under fear of punishment

CONCLUDING THE LESSON

True repentance is not based on fear but on enduring trust, love, and gratitude toward Jesus Christ. Pharaoh is a poignant negative example of how fear alone is insufficient to produce real, lasting repentance.

ANTICIPATING THE NEXT LESSON

Next week's lesson is about Moses' final encounter with Pharaoh after the Lord sends the plague of complete darkness upon the land of Egypt.

—*John M. Lody.*

PRACTICAL POINTS

1. It is foolish to make a commitment to God that you do not intend to keep (Exod. 9:27-28).
2. If we try to bargain with God, He may grant our request, but He will hold us accountable (vs. 29).
3. God cannot be deceived by insincere repentance (vs. 30).
4. God has all power over every force of nature (vss. 31-33).
5. The devil deceives those who seek only temporary relief instead of true repentance (vss. 34-35).

—*Valante M. Grant.*

RESEARCH AND DISCUSSION

1. What is the result of trying to use God merely to solve your problems (Exod. 9:28)?
2. Why is it so important to always approach God with a sincere heart?
3. How should believers respond to those who seem to repent but whose lives do not line up with the truth (vss. 29-30)?
4. How does God support His people in adverse situations? Describe a time when God stepped in to hold you up.
5. How should you approach a spiritual battle when God has already promised that you will win?
6. What are some practical ways in which you can be sure to praise God even in the good times? Why is it so hard to do this?

—*Valante M. Grant.*

ILLUSTRATED HIGH POINTS

I have sinned this time

The aging tiger, having lost his speed and energy, decided to trick the forest animals into his lair. He began telling them that, at his advanced age, he had turned his life around and become a vegetarian. It was against his principles to hunt small animals anymore.

When the whole forest heard of this, joyful little critters came to his den to wish him well and welcome him into the community. The fox, however, observed that animal tracks led into the opening, but none came back out.

Having cruelly oppressed the Israelites for years, Pharaoh could only manage to say that he had sinned "this time." No wonder John the Baptist encourages us to bring not only words, but "fruits meet for repentance" (cf. Matt. 3:8). We are weighed not by words but by actions (cf. I Sam. 2:3).

The wheat and the rie were not smitten

There was once a former radio executive who had lost his voice. He and his family had lived in the lap of luxury, but now they were in poverty. The man abandoned his family and went on a drinking binge. But one night he opened the drawer in his hotel and found a Bible. He came to know Christ that very night.

Some people need to hit rock bottom before they will confess their sin and turn to God. At seen in our lesson, Pharaoh promised to comply with God's will, but he ultimately chose sin (Exod. 9:34). God nevertheless was merciful by leaving the wheat and rye, delaying His full judgment. The purpose of God's patience is to lead us to repentance (Rom. 2:4-5). He is a gracious, merciful, and just God.

—*Therese Greenberg.*

Golden Text Illuminated

"When Pharaoh saw that the rain and the hail and the thunders were ceased, he sinned yet more, and hardened his heart, he and his servants" (Exodus 9:34).

There is a traditional quotation that states, "If you live in a graveyard too long, you stop crying when someone dies." Please bear with me as I try to illustrate the heart of this saying.

During my tenure as an ordained minister of the gospel, I had several opportunities to conduct funeral services. Most of the funeral home directors I worked with were sensitive, compassionate people. On rare occasions, though, I worked with funeral directors who had allowed their hearts to become hardened to the reality of death. These directors had allowed their daily interaction with death to create an emotional numbness of heart.

Before I accepted Jesus Christ as my personal Saviour by faith, I worked for my parents in their family business. They owned a small delicatessen in Cleveland, Ohio, and I spent my fair share of time slicing lunchmeat orders for our customers. We sold high-quality hard salami that had a penetrating scent. But after several years, I noticed that I could not detect the salami's unique scent. My sense of smell had become dulled, or in a way, hardened.

It is one thing to become insensitive to the reality of death or the unique scent of hard salami, but it is an entirely different and spiritually damaging thing to become hardened in heart to the presence of the one true, living God of the universe. This is exactly the process that God allowed Pharaoh to experience in preparation for the deliverance of God's people from Egyptian slavery.

Matthew Henry, the seventeenth-century English Bible commentator and Presbyterian minister, stated, "No man will say, 'There is no God' [until] he is so hardened in sin that it has become his interest that there should be none to call him to account" (www.illustrationexchange.com). Considered deity in Egypt, Pharaoh was not accountable to anyone. As a result, he felt no compulsion to allow God's people to leave his presence.

God, however, in preparing His people for their spiritual deliverance, was also preparing Pharaoh's eventual subjection as a demonstration of His sovereign authority. God accomplished this objective through a series of increasingly severe and devastating plagues. This week's golden text highlights Pharaoh's hardened response following the seventh plague, the plague of hail.

The plague of hail had a remarkable effect on Pharaoh, prompting him to outwardly confess the divine authority of the Lord God (Exod. 9:27). He humbly asked Moses and Aaron to intercede with the Lord that the hail would cease. In return, he promised to let God's people leave Egypt (vs. 28).

Pharaoh's repentance was temporary. Following the plague's cessation, his true heart condition was revealed. Pharaoh "sinned yet more," and his sinful hardness extended to his servants. As a result, Pharaoh once again refused to let God's people leave Egypt.

Psalm 51:17 states, "The sacrifices of God are a broken spirit: a broken and a contrite heart, O God, thou wilt not despise." Guard your heart, dear reader. Do not allow it to become hardened by sin. Through daily obedience, keep it responsive and soft.

—*Thomas R. Chmura.*

Heart of the Lesson

How often have you tried to "make a deal" with God? For example, if God would get you out of whatever unpleasant circumstance you find yourself in, you promise to serve Him for the rest of your life, give all your money to the poor, or stop a certain sinful behavior. News flash: trying to make a deal with God is not a new thing! In today's lesson we will see that Pharaoh once tried to make a deal with God.

1. Pharaoh makes a deal (Exod. 9:27-28). The Lord told Moses to stretch out his hand to heaven and hail would fall. Moses raised his staff to heaven, and hail came beating down, along with fire, all over Egypt—except in the land of Goshen, where the Hebrews lived. Pharaoh summoned Moses and Aaron and told them that he would let the people go if the God of the Hebrews would stop the hail.

For a moment we might have thought that Pharaoh was really repentant. He even admits his sin! However, desperate times often call for desperate measures. In such moments, people will say whatever they think will return them to a place of comfort and safety. So it was with Pharaoh.

2. Moses agrees (Exod. 9:29-30). After listening to the king of Egypt's bargain, Moses agreed. He told the king that once he got out of the city, he would pray to God to stop the storm. Moses was not fooled, however. He saw right through Pharaoh's act. He knew that the king had not truly had a change of heart. Therefore, in order to ensure his safety, Moses said he would raise his hands in prayer after he got out of the city. This would serve as proof to Pharaoh that the earth was the Lord's.

What does it take to get your attention? Even the hardest of hearts cannot deny certain acts of God. When Moses prayed, the fiery hail came down. When Moses prayed again, the hail and fire stopped.

3. Pharaoh reneges on the deal (Exod. 9:31-35). The storm of hail and fire struck everything in Egypt. The Egyptians' crops of barley and flax were destroyed, but the wheat and the rye were still viable, for they were just beginning to come in.

"And Moses went out of the city from Pharaoh, and spread abroad his hands unto the Lord: and the thunders and hail ceased, and the rain was not poured upon the earth" (vs. 33). When Pharaoh saw that the hail, the fire, and the rain had stopped, he was able to breathe again, realizing that the disaster had ended. He no longer felt the need to honor his commitment to let the Hebrews go to worship their God. He had received what he wanted—a reprieve. The king of Egypt may have thought that he had outsmarted the God of the Hebrews and that he could safely avoid making any decision about allowing the Hebrews to go.

Unfortunately, this is true of many of us too. How often have we stood in the place of Pharaoh in the midst of a horrible situation crying out for mercy? We make empty promises, knowing that God is merciful. And because God loves us, He at times looks past our empty vows. Sometimes simply because we acknowledged Him and called out to Him for help, He hears us. He reaches down from heaven and lends us a hand, not because of anything we have done to deserve His intervention, but because He is good. God is not seeking to make a deal with us in times of trouble. He wants to humble us so that we realize how much we truly need Him.

—*Kristin Reeg.*

World Missions

There are now, and have always been, those with hardened hearts against God and His children. These people tend to be miserable and bitter. A Christian's life might be made miserable by them, but through it all the Christian always has the advantage of grace, God's presence, and hope for eternity.

Aliyah knows this to be true. At her strict Islamic school, she asked questions until her teacher got angry. "I had a lot of fear, and I was just hopeless," she said. She received threats even before she came to Christ.

"I thought, 'What if I die, if these people kill me today? Where am I going to go, as I don't have any assurance in Islam?'"

One night, Aliyah had a dream about Jesus. He told her, "I am the only way and the truth. You don't have to fear anything, because I am the one who will never leave you." Aliyah placed her faith in Jesus, and since then she has been followed, chased by men with knives, and threatened regularly.

"I think whoever believes Jesus and serves Him will suffer," Aliyah says. "I also believe suffering is a gift from God, according to the book of Philippians. We are also not just granted to believe, but to suffer."

Aliyah lives this belief. She shares openly about Jesus, even though the threats keep coming. The Voice of the Martyrs is helping her.

"Just pray for me that God can use me," she asks. "And pray that many come to Christ and know Him. That is more important for me."

Aliyah is an example of how we can hope and continue to serve when hearts around us are hard. Mahad is an example that God can turn even a hardened heart.

Mahad became an imam (Islamic teacher) at age nine, and his most popular topic for his sermons was Christians. "I hated Christians," he said. "I expressed the wish that Allah would send all Christians to hell."

When Mahad was ten, he met an American missionary. He lashed out at him, but the missionary gave him a Bible and said he should read it. "Slowly but surely," Mahad remembers, "I found out that I was lost and needed a saviour. As a Muslim you have to earn your salvation. . . . With Jesus it is grace, only grace."

Mahad's family disowned him and threatened to kill him. Over the years, he was arrested many times for sharing his faith. He moved, joined some missionaries, and began reaching out to young men through basketball. Within a year, sixteen came to Christ. He was arrested, jailed, and then kicked out of the area.

Persecution followed Mahad. Like Paul, he was beaten "several times . . . three times they left me to die." He continued to preach in underground churches.

After a video sharing his faith became known on Muslim media worldwide, Mahad became a wanted man, with hundreds of thousands of dollars offered to whoever would kill him. He lost his job.

The Voice of the Martyrs is helping Mahad as he continues his ministry. He has to move every month now. Life is difficult, but a hard life with God is far better than a hardened heart against God.

"Through all these troubles, I have increasingly experienced the presence of God," Mahad says. "For me to live is Christ and to die is gain" (*Voice of the Martyrs Magazine,* May 2017).

—*Kimberly Rae.*

The Jewish Aspect

The plague of hail was so severe that Pharaoh confessed he had sinned, and he begged Moses to "intreat the Lord" to stop the hail (Exod. 9:28). Moses replied, "I will spread abroad my hands unto the Lord; and the thunder shall cease, neither shall there be any more hail" (vs. 29).

The word translated "spread abroad" is frequently connected with people's prayers in Scripture. When Solomon prayed at the temple's dedication, he "spread forth his hands toward heaven" (I Kings 8:22; cf. 8:54; II Chron. 6:12-13). In his prayer, Solomon also exhorted a listener whenever he repented to "spread forth his hands toward this house" in a prayer of confession (I Kings 8:38; cf. II Chron. 6:29).

In another instance, when Ezra discovered the sinful intermarriages between Jews and Gentiles, he wrote, "I fell upon my knees, and spread out my hands unto the Lord my God" (Ezra 9:5).

This word for "spread abroad" is also used in connection with idolatry. If the people of Israel ever "stretched out [their] hands to a strange god" in idolatrous prayer, God would know "the secrets of the heart" (Ps. 44:20-21). Rebellious and sinful Jews continued to pray and offer sacrifices to God. In response, the Lord said, "And when ye spread forth your hands, I will hide mine eyes from you: yea, when ye make many prayers, I will not hear: your hands are full of blood" (Isa. 1:15).

Similar Hebrew words occur to describe the Jews lifting up or spreading out their hands before God in prayer. These occur with the idea of pleading for mercy (Ps. 28:2), when confessing sin (Lam. 3:41), when in desperate grief (Ps. 88:9), when lamenting difficulty (141:2), or when needing comfort (Lam. 1:17). The Jews also lifted their hands to show their agreement with God's Word, that they would worship Him (Neh. 8:6), and to express a prayerful desire to obey God's commands (Ps. 119:48).

The hand is that part of the body that commonly does work. Because of this, the hand represented the whole individual as he approached God. The person who can confidently enter God's presence is one "that hath clean hands" (Ps. 24:4).

The Hebrew word for "hand" puts the focus on the open palm. As the Jew prayed, he often raised both of his open palms before the Lord; by this he symbolized that he came with nothing of his own into God's presence. The open and outstretched hand symbolized particular desires for the Jews. It showed their earnest request for the Lord's help and assistance. It also demonstrated that they wanted to lay hold of God. The practice continued in Judaism: "Lifting our hands in this fashion has a long history in Jewish tradition" ("Why the Open Hands at Ashrei?" www.chabad.org).

The open, empty, and powerless outstretched hand of the Jew comes before God in prayer. In stark contrast God says, "I will stretch out my hand, and smite Egypt with all my wonders" (Exod. 3:20). Concerning their Exodus from Egypt, Moses reminded the Jews that "by strength of hand the Lord brought you out from this place" (13:3).

The outstretched "hand" of God frequently refers to the great power and might that He demonstrates (cf. Job 27:11; Ps. 31:15; Isa. 59:1). God uses His powerful hand to bestow favor (Ezra 7:6) and strength (vs. 28) upon His servants. Christians, like the Jews of old, come empty-handed before God, beseeching that His hand act on our behalf.

—*R. Larry Overstreet.*

Guiding the Superintendent

According to the Center for Disease Control (CDC) over six hundred thousand people die every year in America from heart attacks; this comprises one-fourth of all annual deaths. Yet there is still one other heart failure that is worse, because it leads not to physical death but to eternal death. The malady is known as hardening of the heart. People who suffer from hardened hearts refuse to make God a part of their everyday lives.

In our lesson this week, we will learn that the king of Egypt suffered from such a problem.

DEVOTIONAL OUTLINE

1. Pharaoh's phony attitude (Exod. 9:27-32). Plague after plague upon Egypt and her pantheon of gods seemed to be having some effect on the king. Pharaoh showed signs of realizing that the plagues were supernatural and could not be explained away. He signaled a willingness to grant Moses' request to let the Hebrew slaves go into the desert to worship their God. It seemed too easy. And it was.

Earlier, Moses had warned Pharaoh that the next plague would be severe; God would send massive hail that would destroy men, animals, and crops throughout Egypt. The land of Goshen, where the Israelites lived, would be spared (vss. 9:18-19, 25-26).

At first it appeared that the rain, thunder, and hail had worked its purpose. It looked like Pharaoh had had enough. He summoned Moses and Aaron and confessed that he had sinned and that the Lord was right. He asked Moses to pray that the plague would be lifted (vss. 27-28).

Moses promised to pray for the removal of the plague but told Pharaoh: "But as for thee and thy servants, I know that ye will not yet fear the Lord God" (vs. 30). The storm destroyed the earlier crops (flax and barley), but the later crops (wheat and rye) had not yet developed.

2. Pharaoh's real attitude (Exod. 9:33-35). Moses prayed just as he had promised. The hailstorm was lifted. No sooner had the storms stopped than Pharaoh and his officials revealed their true colors. They sinned and hardened their hearts. The king again refused to release his slaves.

It became obvious that it would take something much more severe to change Pharaoh's behavior.

CHILDREN'S CORNER

text: **Ezra 8:21-31**
title: **Ezra: Trusting God Through Danger**

Ezra had faith in God. It was more than nice words of faith. It was a faith that directed his life.

Years before Ezra came on the scene, God had punished the Jews for their continual sin by sending them into Babylonian captivity. Ezra was tasked with leading a remnant of the Jewish nation back to Jerusalem.

The road back was long and dangerous. Ezra was concerned about their safe arrival in Jerusalem and about the safety of the material gifts given to them for the temple.

He proclaimed a period of fasting and prayer. He would not rely on the soldiers of the king but would trust God to protect them and get them all safely back to Jerusalem. "The hand of our God was upon us, and he delivered us from the hand of the enemy, and of such as lay in wait by the way" (Ezra 8:31). By faith they made it back to Jerusalem.

—*Martin R. Dahlquist.*

Scripture Lesson Text

EXOD. 10:21 And the Lord said unto Moses, Stretch out thine hand toward heaven, that there may be darkness over the land of Egypt, even darkness *which* may be felt.

22 And Moses stretched forth his hand toward heaven; and there was a thick darkness in all the land of Egypt three days:

23 They saw not one another, neither rose any from his place for three days: but all the children of Israel had light in their dwellings.

24 And Pharaoh called unto Moses, and said, Go ye, serve the Lord; only let your flocks and your herds be stayed: let your little ones also go with you.

25 And Moses said, Thou must give us also sacrifices and burnt offerings, that we may sacrifice unto the Lord our God.

26 Our cattle also shall go with us; there shall not an hoof be left behind; for thereof must we take to serve the Lord our God; and we know not with what we must serve the Lord, until we come thither.

27 But the Lord hardened Pharaoh's heart, and he would not let them go.

28 And Pharaoh said unto him, Get thee from me, take heed to thyself, see my face no more; for in *that* day thou seest my face thou shalt die.

29 And Moses said, Thou hast spoken well, I will see thy face again no more.

NOTES

Final Confrontation with Pharaoh

Lesson Text: Exodus 10:21-29

Related Scriptures: Exodus 10:1-20; Romans 9:17-24; Ephesians 4:17-24

TIME: 1445 B.C.   PLACE: Egypt

GOLDEN TEXT—"Moses said, Thou hast spoken well, I will see thy face again no more" (Exodus 10:29).

Introduction

I vividly remember talking to a blind college friend years ago when he mentioned that he had just touched a cow for the first time. He expressed his surprise at learning how large the animal was, explaining that he had always thought a cow was about the size of a dog.

My own eyes were opened that day, so to speak, as I understood better the challenges of life without sight. A simple thing I had known from childhood and taken for granted had been hidden from my friend for twenty years simply because no one had thought to describe to him in detail the size of a cow.

Given such limitations, it is amazing how well sightless people navigate life and all its obstacles. Their success in doing so is a testimony to their determination to develop skills that will enhance their quality of life.

It is certainly easy to imagine that it would be a frightening experience to be suddenly blinded. The disorientation and acute awareness of our inability would, at least initially, totally immobilize us. This essentially describes that ninth plague the Lord brought upon the preeminent nation of Egypt.

LESSON OUTLINE

I. THE PLAGUE OF DARKNESS—Exod. 10:21-23

II. THE RESULTING ENCOUNTER—Exod. 10:24-29

Exposition: Verse by Verse

THE PLAGUE OF DARKNESS

EXOD. 10:21 And the LORD said unto Moses, Stretch out thine hand toward heaven, that there may be darkness over the land of Egypt, even darkness which may be felt.

22 And Moses stretched forth his hand toward heaven; and there was a thick darkness in all the land of Egypt three days:

23 They saw not one another, neither rose any from his place for three days: but all the children of Israel had light in their dwellings.

Announcement of the plague (Exod. 10:21).
Following the plague of hail and Pharaoh's refusal to release all the Israelites, the Lord sent an eighth plague upon Egypt. Massive swarms of locusts descended upon the land and utterly devastated it, stripping away all vegetation and destroying what crops remained for the people. Only when Moses interceded did the Lord lift the plague (vss. 1-19). Still, Pharaoh's attitude did not change. Indeed, the Lord Himself "hardened Pharaoh's heart, so that he would not let the children of Israel go" (vs. 20).

At this point, the Lord spoke to Moses, announcing the coming of a ninth plague. This plague was not announced in advance to the Egyptian king and his servants, however. Instead, Moses was simply to stretch out his hand toward heaven and the plague would begin. Darkness would fall over the land of Egypt, a darkness that the Egyptians could actually feel.

Since this darkness could be felt, many have assumed it was a blinding sandstorm that made it nearly impossible to see anything. The details in the next two verses would seem to rule out this possibility, as well as the theory that it was a solar eclipse. A storm would not distinguish between the Egyptians and Israelites, and a solar eclipse would not produce such profound darkness or last for three days.

Some have surmised that the darkness was accompanied by a heavy mist that could be felt. However, "felt" (Exod. 10:21) is probably best understood as being used figuratively to describe a darkness so oppressive and foreboding that it was like a substance that could be felt.

Consequences of the plague (Exod. 10:22-23).
Moses did as the Lord instructed, and a "deep darkness" came upon all the land instantaneously and lasted for three days. The darkness was so great that people could not see one another. They were confined to their homes, unable to travel or do anything other than wait in fear.

This was not the darkness they would commonly experience at night but a supernatural darkness and apparently total darkness. If you have ever been deep in a cave or cavern and had your lights go out, you know what total darkness is. You literally cannot see your hand in front of your face. This seems to be what the Egyptians were experiencing. They were essentially blinded, and they were totally immobilized.

The account notes, however, that the Israelites did not experience this darkness. They "had light in their dwellings" (Exod. 10:23). The Hebrew word for "dwellings" here does not normally refer to houses but to dwelling places or areas of dwelling more generally (cf. Gen. 10:30; Num. 15:2; 31:10).

It appears, therefore, the meaning here is that the areas of the country where the Israelites lived were unaffected by the darkness. We know the Israelites lived separately from the Egyptians in the area known as Goshen (cf. Gen. 46:28-34; Exod. 8:22; 9:26) in the eastern part of the Nile Delta. It appears the darkness did not engulf this portion of the land.

In this plague, as in some of the previous ones, the Israelites were exempted from the effects (cf. Exod. 8:23; 9:3-7, 25-26). This made it abundantly clear, at least in retrospect, that it was the God of the Israelites who was at work, protecting His people even as He brought judgment upon the Egyptians and their gods.

As the plagues on Egypt progressed,

they became more and more intense, so that each event was worse than the previous one. This is seen in the increasingly desperate responses and pleas of Pharaoh. We might not think a plague such as darkness would be so terrifying. However, the darkness was indeed profound, and the Egyptians did not know how long it would last. It also seems that whatever light sources they had, such as lamps, did not function in the darkness.

Perhaps even more fearful was that the plague struck at the heart of the Egyptians' religious beliefs. The Egyptians worshipped many gods and goddesses. However, the sun god Re was particularly prominent. He was commonly counted as the creator in Egypt (Frankfort, *Ancient Egyptian Religion: An Interpretation,* Dover).

"Egypt's high god was the Sun God. Lord Sun was now being shut down by Lord Yahweh. If Egypt would not let Israel go to worship their God, then Egypt's god would be darkness" (Ross, *Studies in Exodus,* christianleadershipcenter.org). This god, along with others associated with the sun, was utterly humiliated as the people saw he was powerless to thwart the work of Israel's God. The continuing darkness must have brought a sense of dread over impending judgement.

THE RESULTING ENCOUNTER

24 And Pharaoh called unto Moses, and said, Go ye, serve the Lord; only let your flocks and your herds be stayed: let your little ones also go with you.

25 And Moses said, Thou must give us also sacrifices and burnt offerings, that we may sacrifice unto the Lord our God.

26 Our cattle also shall go with us; there shall not an hoof be left behind; for thereof must we take to serve the Lord our God; and we know not with what we must serve the Lord, until we come thither.

27 But the Lord hardened Pharaoh's heart, and he would not let them go.

28 And Pharaoh said unto him, Get thee from me, take heed to thyself, see my face no more; for in that day thou seest my face thou shalt die.

29 And Moses said, Thou hast spoken well, I will see thy face again no more.

Concession and rejection (Exod. 10:24-26). It is interesting that while Moses and Aaron did not announce this plague in advance to Pharaoh, the king knew the source of it. The supernatural character of the darkness left no doubt it was the work of the Lord, so Pharaoh called on Moses. His summons must have come after the three days of darkness had ended. The demonstration was enough to convince the Egyptian ruler that he needed to make some concessions before something worse befell his country.

Pharaoh told Moses that he and his people, including their children, could leave Egypt to serve their God. However, there was a condition: they must leave their flocks and herds behind.

The Egyptians had suffered tremendous losses among their own animals (cf. Exod. 9:3-6, 18-21), so perhaps Pharaoh was simply seeking to recoup those losses by demanding the Israelites leave their flocks and herds behind when they left.

It seems more probable, however, that he wanted to keep the animals as a guarantee that the Israelites would in fact return after a short time of worship in the desert. After all, these animals were the Israelites' primary asset (cf. Gen. 46:31-34).

Pharaoh was trying to offer a concession to Moses that would pacify the Lord while preserving his own dignity in the face of growing unrest among the Egyptian people. The offer was probably meant as the starting point in a negotiation with Moses.

In human terms, Moses was able to negotiate from a position of strength. In reality, Moses was not interested in negotiating anything. The king's offer might have seemed generous from his own point of view, but it was totally unacceptable to Moses. He was speaking for the Lord Himself, and the Lord demanded animals for sacrifice.

"Sacrifices" (Exod. 10:25) refers to animals killed before the Lord in recognition of the principle of substitution—the sacrificial animal dying in the place of the one offering the sacrifice. "Burnt offerings" were animals completely burned as gifts to God. Though the law had not yet been given to Israel, these concepts of sacrifice were known to Moses' ancestors (cf. Gen. 8:20; 22:2-8, 13; 31:54) and would be encoded in Israel's law. Therefore, Moses demanded they be allowed to take the animals.

Furthermore, in Exodus 10:26, Moses indicated that "some aspects of the Israelite sacrificial system were still to be revealed. Moses and the Israelites could not presume that what they so far understood about how, when, and why to provide sacrifices and burnt offerings to God would not be altered once all the nation had met with him formally in worship" (Stuart, *New American Commentary: Exodus,* Holman).

Moses knew they would have to use at least some of the animals in their worship of the Lord, but he did not know how many. Therefore, he firmly stated, "There shall not an hoof be left behind" (vs. 26). For Moses to accept anything less than this would certainly seem to contradict God's promise that He would bring the people forth "with great substance" (Gen. 15:14) as well as Moses' earlier insistence that the flocks and herds must go with them (Exod. 10:9).

Command and acceptance (Exod. 10:27-29). Once again we are told that "the Lord hardened Pharaoh's heart" so that "he would not let them go." This reminds us that while Pharaoh was responsible for his actions, God was also fully engaged in accomplishing His purpose. Indeed, God had raised up this Pharaoh in order to demonstrate His power and make His name known (9:16).

"This means that every time Pharaoh changed his mind and broke his promise, rather than demonstrating his own personal authority, as he thought, he was actually helping to fulfill God's purpose." It is "a remarkable illustration of human responsibility and divine sovereignty working together to accomplish God's will" (Wood, *A Survey of Israel's History,* Zondervan).

Moses certainly was not surprised by Pharaoh's refusal to let the Israelites go. In fact, despite the king's apparent concession and willingness to discuss Israel's departure—a posture he had taken previously (cf. Exod. 8:8, 25; 9:28; 10:11)—Moses knew he would not release the Israelites at this time. The Lord had made clear from the beginning that it would take the death of Pharaoh's own firstborn to force him to obey God's command (4:23).

Moses' inflexible demands made the Egyptian king furious. In his pride, the exalted pharaoh could not allow himself to comply with the demands of a mere shepherd, one whose very profession was despised by the Egyptians (Gen. 46:34). Neither could the one hailed as a god himself by the Egyptian people permit the God of his slaves to bring him to his knees.

In his anger and defiance of God's command, Pharaoh not only refused to release the Israelites, but he also commanded Moses to depart from him. He warned Moses to take care never to see his face again, for if Moses ever saw the king again he would be killed.

Anger can rob a person of reason, and this seems to have been the case with Pharaoh. Moses had made it very clear that he was merely the messenger of the Lord, conveying the Lord's demand that the king release the captive people of Israel. The plagues upon Egypt had revealed the power of Israel's God, and killing His messenger could not stop such a God from forcing the release of His people from Pharaoh's grasp.

"Pharaoh was trying to get rid of the problem of Yahweh's demands by preventing Yahweh's chosen messenger from bringing those demands to his attention" (Stuart). If Pharaoh had been thinking at all at this point, he doubtless would have concluded that killing Moses would only infuriate the God Moses represented and therefore bring more destruction upon Egypt.

Moses' response was to state, "I will see thy face again no more" (Exod. 10:29). Though Moses left Pharaoh's presence and no longer confronted him directly, he announced the coming of one last plague to the people of Egypt: the death of the firstborn (11:4-8).

Moses' statement that Pharaoh would not see his face again at first glance seems to contradict Exodus 12:31. It is possible that Pharaoh's words "See my face no more" (10:28) simply meant that he did not want Moses voluntarily appearing before him again—and Moses did not. This would preclude an instance of Pharaoh summoning him to appear. It is also quite possible to understand the Hebrew expression in 12:31 as referring to the sending of a messenger to Moses and Aaron rather than Pharaoh personally meeting with them.

This ninth plague on Egypt demonstrated that the God who created the light (Gen. 1:3) also controls the light. It showed again that the God who raised up Pharaoh could also use him, even in his belligerence, to accomplish His own purposes. It also assured the Israelites that the God who heard their cries of suffering could also deliver them from bondage.

What an encouragement it must have been for the enslaved Israelites to realize that this almighty God was on their side, and nothing could thwart His plan for His people. How encouraging it is to know that this same compassionate, all-powerful God is also on our side today.

—Jarl K. Waggoner.

QUESTIONS

1. What was meant by the darkness being something that could be "felt" (Exod. 10:21)?
2. How did the darkness affect the Egyptians? How did it affect the Israelites?
3. What made this plague so terrifying to Egypt?
4. What did Pharaoh offer to do?
5. Why did he say the Israelites must leave their herds and flocks behind?
6. Why did Moses insist the people's animals must go with them?
7. Why did the Lord harden the heart of Pharaoh?
8. Was Moses surprised by the king's refusal to let the people go? Why?
9. Why would Pharaoh not give in to Moses' demand?
10. What threat did Pharaoh issue to Moses?

—Jarl K. Waggoner.

Preparing to Teach the Lesson

Have you ever witnessed to an unbeliever whose persistence in unbelief seemed to defy all your best efforts to bring the light of the gospel to shine upon his understanding? Astonishingly, this can happen even when every circumstance of his life bears witness to a desperate need for salvation!

TODAY'S AIM

Facts: to see that Moses cursed Egypt with a ninth plague—supernatural darkness—but that Pharaoh became ever more hardened against the Lord.

Principle: to understand that the hardness of a sinful heart is not moved to true repentance by even the most extreme threats and punishments.

Application: to realize that the only way a lost soul is brought to repentance is by the powerful calling of the Holy Spirit, who quickens those who are spiritually dead in their sins.

INTRODUCING THE LESSON

To review: since our lesson from Exodus chapter 7, Pharaoh and the people of Egypt have been through a lot! Starting with the Lord's judgment of blood upon the Nile and its gods Hapi and Osiris, the Egyptians have endured a plague of frogs (Hapi was also a frog goddess), a plague of lice (against the earth god, Seb), a plague of flies (against the fly god, Uatchit), a plague of livestock pestilence (against the cattle gods, Ptah, Mnevis, Hathor, and Amon), a plague of boils (against the health gods, Sekhmet, Serapis, and Imhotep), a plague of hail and thunder (see lesson 7), and a plague of locusts (against Serapis, the Egyptian protector from locusts). And the worst plagues were yet to come!

DEVELOPING THE LESSON

1. A thick darkness (Exod. 10:21-23). On this occasion the Lord once again used Moses as His agent of judgment—for the ninth time. This ninth plague would be different; it would be a palpable darkness that would envelop the land, allowing no Egyptian to even move around in his own home. The Egyptians became prisoners of the Lord's darkness within their homes for three entire days.

Take special note that this darkness was not merely the absence of light from the sun or the moon; this darkness utterly filled the interiors of Egyptian homes. Lamps or any other means of artificial illumination were useless to dispel it. The Egyptians were unable to even see one another—within their homes or outside them.

Yet the Scripture pointedly tells us that all the Hebrew households enjoyed light for those same days, allowing no doubt that this plague was divinely directed against Egypt for the benefit of Israel. Note that this light was "in their dwellings" (vs. 23). This may indicate that the darkness also held sway for the Hebrews when they were outside their homes, but the Hebrew term used in this verse is often employed more broadly and may simply refer to the area where they lived.

The Egyptian deities being judged by this plague were the exalted sun god, Ra, and the moon god, Thoth. Both deities were shown to be helpless to provide light either by day or by night against the power of the Lord God of Israel. Adam Clarke sees this plague as emblematic of the spiritual darkness that afflicted the souls of the idolatrous Egyptians. It was their spiritual darkness that was the underlying cause of this and all the other plagues that were visited on them from the Lord. The plague of darkness served as "an awful emblem of the darkened state of the Egyptians and their king" (*Commentary on the Bible,* Abingdon).

2. "I will see thy face again no more" (Exod. 10:24-29). At the fateful last meeting between Pharaoh and Moses, this dejected ruler made a seemingly generous concession to Moses' demands. Pharaoh was now fully amenable to letting the Hebrews go into the wilderness to serve the Lord. He even told them to take their children along with them, implying that he was agreeable to the outcome that they intended to never return to Egypt. His only stipulation was that they leave behind all their livestock.

Moses rightfully balked immediately at Pharaoh's condition. How could they sacrifice to the Lord without bringing their livestock? They must have their livestock, for they could not know how many sacrifices they would need to worship the Lord properly until they arrived at their divinely prescribed destination. Clarke insinuates an additional, ulterior motive on Pharaoh's part that reached beyond mere inexactness or even greed: "Had *six hundred thousand* men, besides women and children, gone three days' journey into the *wilderness* without their cattle, they must have inevitably perished. . . . It is evident from this that Pharaoh intended the total destruction of the whole Israelitish host."

Moses' response carries the force of a boldly implied ultimatum. He is no longer merely a humble supplicant before the throne of Egypt; with his latest demand, Pharaoh has placed himself squarely among those who would seek to destroy the Lord's covenant people. Unaccustomed to being addressed in such a bold, unbending manner, Pharaoh's comeback is nothing less than a barefaced death threat. Moses must flee his presence and be on guard from now on; if he ever shows up in Pharaoh's presence again, he will be summarily executed! Moses' reply was calm and resolute. As far as he was concerned, this was their last meeting. However, Pharaoh would soon have to swallow even this threat when he was forced to call in Moses and Aaron one last time after the death of his firstborn (12:31-32).

ILLUSTRATING THE LESSON

God brought a paralyzing supernatural darkness upon the Egyptians, while their Hebrew neighbors had light; yet Pharaoh persisted in his defiance against the Lord.

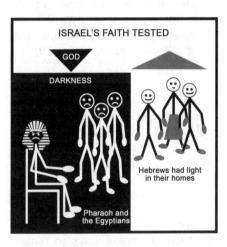

ISRAEL'S FAITH TESTED

GOD

DARKNESS

Hebrews had light in their homes

Pharaoh and the Egyptians

CONCLUDING THE LESSON

The next time you are puzzled or amazed by an unbeliever's spiritual blindness, remember the physical darkness cast over the Egyptians, which was emblematic of their spiritual state.

ANTICIPATING THE NEXT LESSON

Next week, in preparation for the final plague upon Egypt, which again passed over the Hebrews, the Lord gives instructions for instituting the Passover feast.

—John M. Lody.

PRACTICAL POINTS

1. Those who reject the Word of God live in darkness (Exod. 10:21-23).
2. We cannot allow the enemy to keep us from following the plan of God (vss. 24-25).
3. It is important to serve the Lord regardless of the circumstances (vss. 26-27).
4. We must stay faithful to God's teaching without compromise (vs. 28).
5. When backed into a corner, people will resort to extreme, but ultimately empty, threats (vs. 28).
6. When we know God's truth, we can speak with confidence (vs. 29).

—Valante M. Grant.

RESEARCH AND DISCUSSION

1. Describe the responsibility and burden of prayerfully witnessing to someone for a long time. How do you endure such a prolonged spiritual battle?
2. What are some ways to remain diligent when engaged in an extended battle with the enemy?
3. Why do you think God allows some battles to continue for a long time when He has the power to overthrow the enemy in an instant?
4. What is the significance of worship in spiritual warfare (Exod. 10:25)?
5. Unbelievers do not understand how powerful God really is. How can we pray for unsaved people we know regarding this?

—Valante M. Grant.

ILLUSTRATED HIGH POINTS

Even darkness which may be felt

"Dark Night of the Soul" is a poem written by sixteenth-century mystic John of the Cross. It depicts a dark period in a person's life, when questions about faith are rife. Such darkness can be all-encompassing. Such was the darkness cast upon Egypt.

Doctors say depression and anxiety are not always just dark moods; they also can present physical symptoms, including joint pain, back pain, and even extreme thirst. They too are "dark nights" that can be felt.

Even Jesus, feeling forsaken by the Father, cried out, "I thirst" (John 19:28). Yet in His darkest hour, He accessed deep faith and declared, "Father, into thy hands I commend my spirit" (Luke 23:46). Pharaoh, on the other hand, allowed his dark time only to harden his heart.

Light in their dwellings

What would it be like to be blind from birth? You would never be able to see colors, sunlight, or the faces of your loved ones. You would only be able to observe what you could hear, touch, taste, and smell. Unless someone described things to you in great detail, you would have a very hazy picture of the world. God made the Egyptians dwell in darkness, while the Israelites resided in the light. The Egyptians' darkness left them blind, just as the unsaved in the world are blind to the truth.

Believers are the only ones who can describe the truths of the gospel to unbelievers. We can see the world as it really is because we are no longer bound by sin. In a world that seems to be overcome with darkness, Christians can reflect a great light. This light can be seen in their everyday lives.

—Therese Greenberg.

Golden Text Illuminated

"Moses said, Thou hast spoken well, I will see thy face again no more" (Exodus 10:29).

The process of preparing God's people for their deliverance from cruel Egyptian slavery was approaching its climax. God had used His prepared deliverer, Moses, and his brother, Aaron, to confront Pharaoh on several occasions and demand that he let God's people leave Egypt. This week's golden text recounts Moses and Aaron's final face-to-face visit with the Egyptian ruler.

Before we explain the golden text and relate it to this week's lesson theme, I believe it would be helpful to thoughtfully consider God's role in Pharaoh's hardened heart. To accomplish this, we will consider one of this lesson's related Scripture texts: Romans 9:17-24.

God's participation in hardening Pharaoh's heart is first brought to light in Exodus 4:21: "I will harden his heart, that he shall not let the people go" (cf. 7:3; 14:4). The Hebrew term for "harden" in this context means "to make rigid" or "obstinate"; in a sense, Pharaoh's heart was strengthened by God—made strong enough to consistently produce disobedient and evil actions.

From a human perspective, it may seem unjust for God to harden Pharaoh's heart and then punish him for decisions and deeds that were a result of that hardness. Romans 9:17-18 gives us the biblical perspective by stating, "For the scripture saith unto Pharaoh, Even for this same purpose have I raised thee up, that I might shew my power in thee, and that my name might be declared throughout all the earth. Therefore hath he mercy on whom he will have mercy, and whom he will he hardeneth."

The ultimate response to the claim that God's hardening action is unjust is God's absolute sovereign authority over His creation. Simply stated, God is God, and we are not. Or as the Apostle Paul so splendidly stated, "Nay but, O man, who art thou that repliest against God? Shall the thing formed say to him that formed it, Why hast thou made me thus?" (vs. 20).

Alongside God's sovereign authority is the biblical truth that man is sinful by nature (cf. Rom. 3:23), and the fair penalty for man's sin is death (cf. 6:23). Realizing this, God's people must humbly welcome the breathtaking truth of God's sovereign authority and rejoice that His sovereign plan for His children is to glorify Himself through their faithful lives.

This week's golden text summarizes Moses and Aaron's final confrontation with Pharaoh. The plague of thick darkness prompted Pharaoh to partially agree to Moses' demand to let God's people leave Egypt (cf. Exod. 10:24). Following Moses' demand for complete liberation, God hardened Pharaoh's heart, and he abruptly canceled his offer. Pharaoh then dismissed Moses with rude anger (cf. vss. 27-28). In response to the king's fierce dismissal, Moses departed in holy indignation (cf. 11:8).

God was almost finished with His sovereign preparations for the deliverance of His people. To fully accomplish His task, only one more severe, unprecedented plague—the sudden death of every firstborn son in Egypt—remained, along with one more significant Israelite event: the Passover.

As we move toward the end of this quarter's second unit, would you humbly consider how God is preparing you to be set free to glorify Him through your life?

—*Thomas R. Chmura.*

Heart of the Lesson

How many times have you or I said, "Yes, Lord! I will go anywhere! I will do anything! Whatever You need, here I am!"? But then He shows us where He wants us to go. He tells us what He wants us to do. Suddenly, our excitement wanes and our willingness mysteriously disappears. "Lord, I would do anything for You, but please, not that!" We see something similar with Pharaoh. We can feel the tug of war between relenting and tightening his grip. But we already know the rest of the story; it does not end well for Pharaoh.

1. The darkness you can feel (Exod. 10:21-23). Have you ever been in a pitch-black room—a room without windows or any source of light? Consider that the starting point for the kind of darkness that God sent to Egypt. "And the Lord said unto Moses, Stretch out thine hand toward heaven, that there may be darkness over the land of Egypt, even darkness which may be felt" (vs. 21).

There is darkness, and then there is an oppressive, eerie darkness that causes your heart rate to accelerate. Egypt was without light. People could not see each other. The nation did nothing for three days. That is not just darkness; it is an oppressive, impenetrable presence that envelopes everything and defies all illumination.

2. Go worship the Lord (Exod. 10:24-26). Pharaoh was tired of the calamities that had come upon his nation. Exasperated, the king of Egypt finally surrendered and gave the Hebrews permission to go worship their God. But wait! There were strings attached. "And Pharaoh called unto Moses, and said, Go ye, serve the Lord; only let your flocks and your herds be stayed: let your little ones also go with you" (vs. 24). In other words, "Moses, go on your three-day hike. Worship the Lord. Take the women and children with you; however, leave your animals here."

At first glance, the request seems harmless. You think that Moses should have taken the deal. But Pharaoh wanted the Hebrews' livestock for Egypt. Most of the animals in Egypt had died or were diseased. If the Hebrews went away and left the livestock, then the animals would be much easier for the Egyptians to steal. Again, Moses was not a fool. He told Pharaoh the animals were part of the deal. The Hebrews needed them for sacrifices, and the people would not know which ones were necessary for religious rituals until they arrived at the place designated for their worship.

3. Never to be seen again (Exod. 10:27-29). Pharaoh refused to let Moses take the animals with them to worship God. His heart was hardened yet again. Imagine the anger and the frustration that must have been building in the heart of Pharaoh. His empire was crumbling before his eyes. He must have felt as though he was losing both his control over his nation and the respect of his people.

Though Pharaoh was a king, he was still just a man. He was caught between a rock and a hard place. He knew that letting the Hebrews go would stop the plagues, but it would also make him look weak. Because of his pride, he could not afford to be seen as weak. In a moment of rage, Pharaoh told Moses that he never wanted to see him again. Moses and Pharaoh were at an impasse. It was not a flippant statement. Let us learn from Pharaoh's mistakes and surrender to God. He is Lord of all; we definitely are not!

—*Kristin Reeg.*

World Missions

During the plague of darkness that fell on Egypt, the gloom was so thick it could be felt. Even though those all around them could not see, God's people lived in light. What a picture of how our lives are meant to be in this dark world!

The difference was clear between those who followed the God of Israel and those who did not.

It should still be so today. It should be clear to those who walk in darkness that we live in light. Our lives should be a living witness. We are called to be ambassadors of Jesus Christ (II Cor. 5:20), and our lives should reflect a different lifestyle from that of the world.

Evangelism is often thought of as a spoken message, but the message of our lives can speak even louder—for good or for evil.

Our Saviour is dishonored when we do not follow Him in our daily lives. Not only does it grieve God and damage our relationship with Him, but it also harms or destroys any influence we could have with the lost.

A lost man sees his Christian neighbor at a store buying something inappropriate. He had been thinking about going to church, but now he will not consider it.

A lost woman is drawn to a group of ladies wearing Christian T-shirts, only to discover when she nears them that they are gossiping and making fun of someone in vicious terms. She turns away in tears. She had heard that God's children were people of compassion and love, but now she no longer believes it.

These might seem like minor examples, but small things can have a devastating impact. And such actions bring up some crucial questions: How real are Christ and His kingdom to us? Do they occupy more and more of our thoughts each day, or are we paying lip service to Christianity and just trying to add a little God to our lives? If God did not spare His own Son to rescue us from destruction, what makes us think He will ultimately be satisfied with hypocrisy from us?

All believers, whether called into full-time ministry or not, are commanded to present themselves as living sacrifices, "holy, acceptable unto God" (Rom. 12:1). We are not to love the world or the things of the world (I John 2:15), just as the Israelites were not to be drawn to Egypt's idols or unholy practices. We are to be set apart, different. It should be clear that we belong to God, not only in the message we give when we are consciously trying to reach the lost but also in our everyday conversations, our actions and reactions, even our thoughts, because our thoughts show us who we truly are (Prov. 23:7). Do we have a high regard for the commandments of God? Do we obey readily and cheerfully? Do we have peace in circumstances where such peace is beyond understanding (Phil. 4:7)?

Once a nonbeliever moved to America and met a Christian family who treated him kindly, but he wanted to know if their faith went beyond show. How did they act when they did not know anyone was watching? The man went to their home and literally spied on them through their window, watching to see if their faith in Christ was more than just talk.

If that man brought his binoculars to spy into our homes or if he followed us at work or running errands or during leisure time, would he see the light of Christ in our lives?

How we live matters. Our unspoken testimony could matter for eternity to someone who is lost. Let us live in the Light that saves men's souls, and pray that it will radiate through us.

—Kimberly Rae.

The Jewish Aspect

The ninth plague that struck Egypt was darkness. This plague showed that God surpassed the so-called might and power of the Egyptian gods Ra and Horus, both of whom were associated with the sun and its light. This plague never affected the Israelites: "All the children of Israel had light in their dwellings" (Exod. 10:23). God alone controls both light and darkness.

The Jews have observed that "God, before 'stretching out the heavens like a curtain,' 'wraps Himself in light as in a mantle'" ("Light," www.jewishencyclo-pedia.com). And God not only creates light but also fashions darkness (cf. Isa. 45:7).

Scripture refers to light in various contexts. It stresses that God "made great lights," including the sun, moon, and stars (Ps. 136:7-9), and lightning as well (77:18).

Light also has spiritual significance. It "dwelleth with God (Dan. 2:22), and "his brightness was as the light" (Hab. 3:4). Isaiah exhorted the Jews, "Let us walk in the light of the Lord" (Isa. 2:5), and God's Word serves as "a lamp unto my feet, and a light unto my path" (Ps. 119:105).

The biblical record often emphasizes light as God deals with His people. God led Israel by a pillar of fire, for example, "to give them light" (Exod. 13:21). That same pillar was also "a cloud and darkness" to the pursuing Egyptians (14:20). Once again, God directly intervened with the light and dark distinction between Israel and Egypt.

Jewish writings from the first century A.D. taught that before God created the universe He made the angel Adoil, and God said, "I beheld him, and lo! He had a belly of great light. . . . And he came undone, and a great light came out" (2 Enoch 25:1, 3, www.pseudepi-grapha.com). God then made a throne for Himself, and placed light above it.

The Babylonian Talmud (A.D. 200-500) connected light specifically with Moses. "At the time when Moses was born, the whole house was filled with light—it is written here, And when she saw him that he was good, and elsewhere it is written: And God saw the light that it was good" ("Sota 12a," come-and-hear.com/sotah/sotah_12. html).

By the fourth century, Jewish midrash had concluded that at the time of Creation God had wrapped Himself in light "as in a robe and irradiated with the luster of his majesty the whole world from one end to the other" ("Genesis Rabbah 3," sacred-texts. com/jud/mhl/mh105.htm).

Many Jews have believed that light is distinct in creation. An article in the Jerusalem Post, December 11, 2011, verifies that this belief is still common in Judaism. Its writer said that "fundamentally, light does not belong to this world. Rather, it is an emanation of a different essence, from the other side of reality" (Steinsaltz, "The motif of light in Jewish tradition," www.jpost.com).

Jewish midrash proposed: "'God said let there be light' refers to the book of Genesis, which enlightens us as to how creation was carried out. The words 'And there was light' bear reference to the book of Exodus, which contains the history of the transition of Israel from darkness to light" ("Genesis Rabbah 3").

The greatest Jewish "light" was their promised Messiah. God's salvation light would come for Israel (Isa. 51:4-5) and for the Gentiles (Isa. 60:1-3). This promise was fulfilled in Jesus Christ, the Light of the World (John 1:1-9).

—R. Larry Overstreet.

Guiding the Superintendent

Plague after plague had desolated the land of Egypt. Every plague was greater than the one before it. Each was a direct attack on one of the major gods of Egypt. There were only two main gods left—Ra, the sun god, and Pharaoh himself.

In Egyptian hieroglyphs, Ra is pictured as a left-facing falcon with a large yellow disk above his head. Ra was considered to be the source of all created life in the land. It was only fitting that the ninth plague attacked Ra.

DEVOTIONAL OUTLINE

1. Plague of darkness (Exod. 10:21-23). Like the third plague, lice (8:16-19), and the sixth plague, boils (9:8-12), the ninth plague came with no announcement.

Suddenly the skies over Egypt turned totally dark. It was so dark that the darkness could be "felt" (vs. 21). It was almost as if the Egyptians had been blinded and now had to find their way in the blackness.

Unlike a typical dark night, the plague lasted for three days. So dark was the blackness that people were fearful of leaving their homes. Like the other plagues, this darkness was only on the Egyptians. Israel was exempt.

2. Pharaoh's partial concession (Exod. 10:24-26). Moses and Aaron were summoned into Pharaoh's presence. The ruler tried to negotiate with the Jewish leaders. He said they could go and take their women and children and worship but must leave their animals.

This was a nonstarter. Aside from the fact that this was not God's will, Israel would have needed the animals for food and worship. As before, Moses responded with the original request.

3. Pharaoh's rage (Exod. 10:27-29). While plagues had, for all practical purposes, destroyed everything, Pharaoh's heart was hardened. He tried to intimidate Moses with a threat: "In that day thou seest my face thou shalt die" (vs. 28). Moses assured the king that he would never see him again. There was only one more false god in Egypt that would feel the wrath of Israel's God.

CHILDREN'S CORNER
text: **Matthew 14:22-33**
title: **Peter's Faith in Jesus**

It had been a long and trying day of ministry and miracles for Jesus and the disciples around the Sea of Galilee. As evening approached, Jesus worked a great miracle of feeding five thousand men.

Jesus then put his tired disciples into a boat and instructed them to go across the lake while He went to the mountain for a time of prayer.

It was very early in the morning. The disciples were still in the boat, and a great storm broke out on the lake. All of a sudden, what appeared to be a ghost came walking on the water toward the boat. He spoke and revealed to the disciples that he was Jesus.

Peter responded in faith and asked for greater reassurance of who this figure really was. He asked to come to Jesus, and Jesus invited him to walk on the water! As long as Peter kept his eyes on Jesus, he stayed above the surface. However, his faith was shaken by his fear. Soon he became overwhelmed by the storm and began to sink into the waves.

Jesus reached out, grabbed Peter, and admonished him for his lack of faith. The disciples responded to this demonstration of His deity with worship and confession that Jesus was truly God's Son.
—*Martin R. Dahlquist.*

SCRIPTURE LESSON TEXT

EXOD. 12:1 And the LORD spake unto Moses and Aaron in the land of Egypt, saying,

2 This month *shall be* **unto you the beginning of months: it** *shall be* **the first month of the year to you.**

3 Speak ye unto all the congregation of Israel, saying, In the tenth *day* of this month they shall take to them every man a lamb, according to the house of *their* fathers, a lamb for an house:

4 And if the household be too little for the lamb, let him and his neighbour next unto his house take *it* **according to the number of the souls; every man according to his eating shall make your count for the lamb.**

5 Your lamb shall be without blemish, a male of the first year: ye shall take *it* out from the sheep, or from the goats:

6 And ye shall keep it up until the fourteenth day of the same month: and the whole assembly of the congregation of Israel shall kill it in the evening.

7 And they shall take of the blood, and strike *it* on the two side posts and on the upper door post of the houses, wherein they shall eat it.

8 And they shall eat the flesh in that night, roast with fire, and unleavened bread; *and* **with bitter** *herbs* **they shall eat it.**

9 Eat not of it raw, nor sodden at all with water, but roast *with* fire; his head with his legs, and with the purtenance thereof.

10 And ye shall let nothing of it remain until the morning; and that which remaineth of it until the morning ye shall burn with fire.

11 And thus shall ye eat it; *with* your loins girded, your shoes on your feet, and your staff in your hand; and ye shall eat it in haste: it *is* the LORD's passover.

12 For I will pass through the land of Egypt this night, and will smite all the firstborn in the land of Egypt, both man and beast; and against all the gods of Egypt I will execute judgment: I *am* **the LORD.**

13 And the blood shall be to you for a token upon the houses where ye *are:* and when I see the blood, I will pass over you, and the plague shall not be upon you to destroy *you,* when I smite the land of Egypt.

14 And this day shall be unto you for a memorial; and ye shall keep it a feast to the LORD throughout your generations; ye shall keep it a feast by an ordinance for ever.

NOTES

116

The Passover

Lesson Text: Exodus 12:1-14

Related Scriptures: Exodus 11:1-10; Luke 22:7-20;
John 1:29-36; I Corinthians 5:6-8

TIME: 1445 B.C.   PLACE: Egypt

GOLDEN TEXT—"This day shall be unto you for a memorial; and ye shall keep it a feast to the Lord throughout your generations; ye shall keep it a feast by an ordinance for ever" (Exodus 12:14).

Introduction

The observance of Memorial Day was a yearly ritual in my family. While officially a day set aside to remember those who have died in service of our country, Memorial Day was more than that for most people where I grew up. We called it Decoration Day. Family members would gather and go to the local cemeteries with flowers to decorate the graves of departed family members. It was a way of honoring our ancestors, whether they had died in the armed forces or not.

In the case of the nation of Israel, Passover is a reminder of God's miraculous deliverance of His people from bondage. It also pointed ahead to deliverance from sin through Jesus Christ.

LESSON OUTLINE

I. THE TIME OF THE
   PASSOVER—Exod. 12:1-2

II. THE SELECTION OF THE
   PASSOVER LAMB—
   Exod. 12:3-5

III. THE SACRIFICE OF THE
   PASSOVER LAMB—
   Exod. 12:6-11

IV. THE DETAILS OF THE
   PASSOVER EVENT—
   Exod. 12:12-13

V. THE INSTITUTION OF THE
   PASSOVER FEAST—Exod. 12:14

Exposition: Verse by Verse

THE TIME OF THE PASSOVER

EXOD. 12:1 And the Lord spake unto Moses and Aaron in the land of Egypt, saying,

2 This month shall be unto you the beginning of months: it shall be the first month of the year to you.

The Lord had already announced the imminent arrival of the tenth and final plague on Egypt (Exod. 11:4-5)—the death of the firstborn. Moses and Aaron had departed from Pharaoh in anger, while the Egyptian king continued to stubbornly resist God's demand to free the Israelites (vss. 8-10).

At this point, the Lord spoke to Moses and Aaron again. He highlighted the uniqueness and effectiveness of the coming plague by reordering Israel's calendar. The current month in which the final plague and the deliverance of Israel would occur would henceforth be the first month of the year.

This was the month known as Abib (Exod. 13:4), or Nisan (cf. Neh. 2:1). It corresponds to our March–April. This new calendar instituted by the Lord was observed as Israel's religious, or sacred, calendar. A civil calendar was also observed, with the first month beginning in the fall, seven months later.

THE SELECTION OF THE PASSOVER LAMB

3 Speak ye unto all the congregation of Israel, saying, In the tenth day of this month they shall take to them every man a lamb, according to the house of their fathers, a lamb for an house:

4 And if the household be too little for the lamb, let him and his neighbour next unto his house take it according to the number of the souls; every man according to his eating shall make your count for the lamb.

5 Your lamb shall be without blemish, a male of the first year: ye shall take it out from the sheep, or from the goats.

By each household (Exod. 12:3-4). The Lord told Moses and Aaron to instruct the people of Israel with regard to the selection of an animal for a sacrifice. This sacrifice, of course, is related to the last plague, as their instructions make clear.

A lamb was to be chosen and set aside on the tenth day of the month.

"Lamb" (vs. 3) can refer to either a sheep or a goat in Hebrew. The animal would be kept till the fourteenth day of the month. The feast that would come from this lamb was to be observed in individual households. Thus, each household would select a lamb. Small households that could not consume an entire lamb were to join with other families.

By the quality of the animal (Exod. 12:5). Great care was to be taken in the selection of the lamb. First, it had to be "without blemish." This expression means complete, whole, or perfect. It refers to an animal that has no physical defects. This requirement for sacrifices was later incorporated into Israel's law (cf. Lev. 22:19-22; Deut. 17:1).

Second, the lamb must be a male. The third requirement was that it must be of the "first year" (Exod. 12:5). This simply means that it must be one year old. A lamb of this age was just reaching maturity. Again, the animal could be taken from the sheep or the goats.

The animal to be sacrificed had to meet these qualifications in order to make it an appropriate symbol of the Lord Jesus Christ, as we shall see.

THE SACRIFICE OF THE PASSOVER LAMB

6 And ye shall keep it up until the fourteenth day of the same month: and the whole assembly of the congregation of Israel shall kill it in the evening.

7 And they shall take of the blood, and strike it on the two side posts and on the upper door post of the houses, wherein they shall eat it.

8 And they shall eat the flesh in that night, roast with fire, and unleavened bread; and with bitter herbs they shall eat it.

9 Eat not of it raw, nor sodden at all with water, but roast with fire; his head with his legs, and with the purtenance thereof.

10 And ye shall let nothing of it remain until the morning; and that which remaineth of it until the morning ye shall burn with fire.

11 And thus shall ye eat it; with your loins girded, your shoes on your feet, and your staff in your hand; and ye shall eat it in haste: it is the Lord's passover.

The slaughter of the animal (Exod. 12:6). According to the Lord's instructions, the sacrificial lamb was to be kept until the fourteenth day of the month. That it was to be chosen four days before the feast protected against "last-minute arrangements and the possibility of haphazard celebration or lack of availability" (Stuart, *New American Commentary: Exodus*, Holman).

Then, on the fourteenth day of the month, every family group was to slaughter the lamb (vs. 6). "In the evening" literally means "between the evenings." Judaism traditionally understood this to mean between the time when the sun's heat begins to decrease and the sunset, or about 3:00 P.M. (Davis, *Moses and the Gods of Egypt*, Baker). This would coincide with the time of Jesus' death during the Jewish Passover (cf. Matt. 27:45-50).

The blood of the animal (Exod. 12:7). Once the lamb was killed, some of its blood was to be put on the side posts and the "upper door post"; that is, the lintel, or the horizontal beam across the top of the door. The blood was to be placed on each house wherein the lamb was eaten.

Interestingly, the Israelites were not asked to do anything during the first nine plagues. Now they were given detailed instructions concerning the lamb, its blood, and how it was to be prepared and eaten. The previous nine plagues had demonstrated God's power. Having witnessed those miraculous sights, the Israelites were now fully prepared to obey the Lord—and did so.

The act of killing the lamb and putting its blood on the door, which "represented the entry and the protection of the house," had obvious symbolic value, though clearly it was not grasped in its fullness at this time. The act "immediately pointed out the great price of redemption and symbolically it pointed toward the death of Jesus Christ" (Davis). The blood of the lamb would protect the Israelites from the judgment of God, just as the blood of Jesus, the Lamb of God, protects the Christian from divine judgment upon sin.

The eating of the animal (Exod. 12:8-11). Moses and Aaron also relayed the Lord's instructions concerning the preparation of the meal. The lamb was to be roasted over an open fire and eaten that same night, along with unleavened bread and bitter herbs.

Bread could be made much quicker without leaven, or yeast, since there was no waiting for the dough to rise. Unleavened bread symbolized the Israelites' hasty departure from Egypt. In Deuteronomy 16:3, the unleavened bread is also called the "bread of affliction," indicating it also served as a reminder of their years of suffering in Egypt. Bitter herbs were easy to find and simple to prepare. No specific meaning is given to them, but "later Jews saw them as symbolizing the bitterness of Israel's bondage" (Cole, *Exodus: An Introduction and Commentary*, InterVarsity).

The preparation of the lamb is detailed in Exodus 12:8-10. Eating any part of it raw was forbidden. Neither was it to be "sodden," or boiled, in water (vs. 9). The prohibition against eating raw meat was not only a protection against health concerns but also separated the Israelites from "many of the surrounding pagan peoples [who] often ate raw flesh at their sacrificial meals" (Davis).

The lamb was to be roasted whole, with its "purtenance" (vs. 9), or inner parts, over a fire. This would help eliminate any remaining blood (cf. Gen. 9:4). It also was the quickest way to prepare the meat. The meat was to be eaten entirely. If any happened to remain, it was to be burned, not saved for later. This shows that this was "more a meal of religious observance than a meal to provide sustenance over time" (Stuart).

Finally, the meal was to be eaten with "loins girded" (Exod. 12:11), sandals on the feet, and staff in hand. To gird the loins was to tuck the bottom of the cloak into the belt, freeing the legs for travel and work. This action, along with wearing shoes and holding a staff—things normally never done inside a house—meant the Israelites were to eat the meal while fully prepared to travel. The meal itself would be quickly prepared and was to be eaten hurriedly.

The reason given for these instructions was that this was "the Lord's passover" (vs. 11). Up to this point the Israelites had been told only that they should prepare a special meal and put the blood of the lamb on their doors. How this related to what God was going to do was not stated, but it was clear the instructions held some symbolism, and there was some hint that the people should be prepared to leave Egypt at a moment's notice.

This is the first mention of the word "Passover" (*pesach*). The origin of the word is unclear, but the meaning of the event is clearly stated in Exodus 12:12-13, and it would obviously be the Lord's doing. One commentator offers a good summary at this point: "Here there were no priests, no altar, no tabernacle; families were communing in the presence of God and around the sacrificial lamb that was the substitute for each member of that family. The lamb was to be a year-old male because it was taking the place of Israel's firstborn males who were young and fresh with the vigor of life. The bitter herbs were to recall the bitter years of servitude (1:14), and the unleavened bread was

to reflect this event's haste on that first night. This was the Lord's Passover, and this was how Israel was to eat it" (Barker and Kohlenberger, eds., *Zondervan NIV Bible Commentary,* Zondervan).

THE DETAILS OF THE PASSOVER EVENT

12 For I will pass through the land of Egypt this night, and will smite all the firstborn in the land of Egypt, both man and beast; and against all the gods of Egypt I will execute judgment: I am the LORD.

13 And the blood shall be to you for a token upon the houses where ye are: and when I see the blood, I will pass over you, and the plague shall not be upon you to destroy you, when I smite the land of Egypt.

The final plague was coming the very night the meal was eaten, and there would be a clear distinction in this plague between the Egyptians and the Israelites (cf. Exod. 11:7). The Passover would involve the Lord's passing through the land in judgment. In doing so, He would kill all the "firstborn in the land of Egypt, both man and beast" (12:12).

"Firstborn" is a masculine form and refers here to firstborn males. The Egyptians, who had sought to kill Israel's firstborn males (1:15-16), would now suffer the loss of their own firstborns.

This plague would also be the final strike against the gods of Egypt. Their gods had not protected them against all the previous nine plagues, and neither would they prove helpful in this last one. Min, the god of reproduction, and numerous deities who were believed to attend the birth of children would be put to shame. The judgment would also fall upon Pharaoh's firstborn son, who like his father was believed to be divine. The supernatural death of Egypt's firstborn sons would powerfully demonstrate that the God of Israel alone is the Lord, Yahweh.

This last plague would indeed provide the final push to free God's people from bondage. But it would also send an undeniable message to Egypt and the entire world that man-made religion in all its forms and with all its various gods is empty, powerless, and useless. Idolatry is mere imagination that offers no hope, peace, or lasting joy.

The supremacy of God would be manifested by His protection of Israel throughout the plague. The blood upon their houses would distinguish the Israelites' homes from the homes of the Egyptians. The Lord said, "When I see the blood, I will pass over you, and the plague shall not be upon you to destroy you" (12:13). The blood would provide protection.

However, the blood was really a sign, not for God, but for Israel. God knew full well who His people were. The blood was a sign to the people themselves. It was a public testimony of their faith in God that He would protect them and deliver them.

THE INSTITUTION OF THE PASSOVER FEAST

14 And this day shall be unto you for a memorial; and ye shall keep it a feast to the Lord throughout your generations; ye shall keep it a feast by an ordinance for ever.

The Lord declared that Passover was to be observed as a memorial feast throughout Israel's history. As an annual memorial (Exod. 12:14), it would remind the people of God's gracious and merciful deliverance of their nation. "Why such an emphasis on commemoration? Because what is not carefully remembered by a community is very naturally and easily forgotten—and virtually completely forgotten as soon as the oldest members of that community who experienced the original event die" (Stuart). It was crucial that Israel remember this event, for it

demonstrated who their God was: the almighty, merciful, compassionate, gracious God—the only true God.

It was also important that they remember the Passover because it prepared the way through its symbolism for the One the New Testament describes as the "Lamb of God, which taketh away the sin of the world" (John 1:29). The perfect Lamb of God was slaughtered for us. His death and His blood bring deliverance from the bondage of sin.

All this was foreshadowed in the Passover, reminding us that the death of Christ was always in God's plan. In compassion, He looked upon us in all our sin and from eternity past set in motion the plan to provide eternal, spiritual deliverance from sin through the blood of the Lamb.

—*Jarl K. Waggoner.*

QUESTIONS

1. How did the Lord highlight the uniqueness of the final plague?
2. What qualifications must the sacrificial animal meet?
3. When was the animal to be killed? Why is the timing significant?
4. What did killing the lamb and putting its blood on the door symbolize?
5. How was the lamb to be prepared for eating? Why was this important?
6. Why were the people to eat the meal hastily?
7. What distinction would be made in the final plague?
8. How did the death of the firstborn strike a blow against Egypt's gods?
9. For whom was the blood on the doors a sign?
10. Why was it important for Israel to observe Passover annually?

—*Jarl K. Waggoner.*

Preparing to Teach the Lesson

In the first chapter of John's Gospel, John the Baptist is standing with two of his disciples as Jesus comes toward them. As Jesus approaches, John testifies, "Behold the Lamb of God, which taketh away the sin of the world" (vs. 29).

John's testimony would have been easily understood by his disciples as a reference to the lamb of Passover. The blood of the lamb marked the doors of every Hebrew home to protect them from the final plague against Egypt—the death of the first-born.

TODAY'S AIM

Facts: to learn about the history and details of the Passover Feast.

Principle: to understand the significance of the Passover Feast for both the old and the new covenants.

Application: to celebrate and worship God in thanksgiving for Jesus Christ, the ultimate fulfillment of the Passover.

INTRODUCING THE LESSON

Passover is the first and most important celebration of the Jewish calendar. It marks the seminal event that changed the Hebrews into the nation of Israel; they were transformed from an extended family of slave laborers in a foreign land into the chosen nation of Yahweh, the only true and living God and the Creator of the whole universe!

DEVELOPING THE LESSON

1. Preparation for the Passover (Exod. 12:1-5). To show that their deliverance from Egypt was assured, the Lord commanded the Hebrews to institute a celebration of their deliverance that would be repeated each year by all succeeding generations. In fact, their calendar year would from now on begin with that current month called Nisan.

On the tenth day of Nisan, every Israelite household would choose a year-old male sheep or goat to be the main focus of this commemorative feast. The animal had to be perfectly formed, without any physical defect of any kind, and it also had to be perfectly healthy. If a whole lamb was deemed too much food for a smaller household, two households were to share the feast together using the same single lamb—the point being that every Israelite man's household had to participate in this crucially significant celebration.

The chosen lamb would be kept by the family until the fourteenth day of that same month. On the evening of the fourteenth of Nisan (which would be the beginning of the fifteenth day of the month, according to the Hebrew reckoning of days beginning at nightfall), every chosen lamb would be slaughtered for the Passover feast. The blood of the lamb would then be painted upon the two posts and the lintel of the door to each family's home, where a feast would be celebrated.

2. Celebration of the Passover (Exod. 12:6-14). Once the doors to their homes were marked with the blood of the Passover lamb, the whole slaughtered lamb, including the head, legs, organs, and entrails, had to be roasted on a fire; it could not be boiled or baked or prepared in any time-intensive manner, for the emphasis was on the haste of their deliverance. No edible trace of the lamb could remain. Anything not eaten by morning had to be thoroughly consumed by fire. Likewise, the lamb would be eaten with unleavened bread (*matzah*) and bitter herbs. The Mishnah lists herbs such as romaine lettuce, endives or escarole, and horseradish. These herbs were to be eaten uncooked.

The Hebrews had to eat this feast fully clothed for travel. This especially included a belt, shoes, and a walking staff. Note that each detail of the Passover was actually an expression of faith in the surety of the Lord's deliverance. They were to behave in every detail as if their freedom from Egypt was a done deal that would occur at a moment's notice. Just as the Hebrews acted in faith that God would deliver them, the commemorative feast was also a sign of faith that God would send the Messiah.

In verses 12 and 13, the Lord explains the crucial importance of the Passover for them. The lamb's blood on their doors would be a sign to the Lord's Angel of Death (identified as the Lord Himself) as He passed through Egypt to bring death to every firstborn of both humans and animals. The Lord also explicitly describes this visitation as a judgment on all the gods of Egypt (also a reference to its rulers, including Pharaoh and his nobles).

Verse 14 is the Lord's declaration that the Passover should be a memorial feast for all succeeding generations of Israelites forever. Clarke notes four details of this first Passover that were not carried over into subsequent celebrations: "1. The eating of the lamb in their houses dispersed through Goshen. 2. The taking the lamb on the tenth day. 3. The striking of its blood on the door posts and lintels of their houses. And, 4. Their eating it in haste" (*Commentary on the Bible,* Abingdon).

As we look back on the Passover from the vantage of the new covenant, we know that it was a foreshadowing of the atoning death of our Lord Jesus Christ. This is why He is referred to throughout the New Testament as the "Lamb" (cf. John 1:29, 36; Acts 8:32; I Pet. 1:19; Rev. 5:6, 8, 12-13; 6:1, 16).

ILLUSTRATING THE LESSON

The significance of the Passover was that it pointed Israel to the ultimate Passover Lamb of God, Jesus Christ!

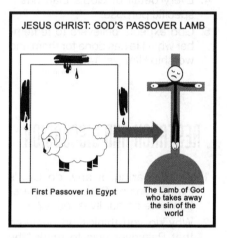

JESUS CHRIST: GOD'S PASSOVER LAMB

First Passover in Egypt

The Lamb of God who takes away the sin of the world

CONCLUDING THE LESSON

For the Hebrews of Egypt, the lamb's blood turned away the wrath of God from their homes as He passed through Egypt. For those of us who are cleansed by faith from all sin, the atoning blood of the Lamb of God saves us from the wrath of God that is coming upon the whole earth (cf. John 3:36; Rev. 16:1).

ANTICIPATING THE NEXT LESSON

Next week's lesson presents us with the terrible visitation of the Lord's final and decisive plague upon Egypt as well as the start of the glorious exodus of the hosts of Israelites from Egypt.

—*John M. Lody.*

PRACTICAL POINTS

1. God gives specific directions for how His people should live. It is important to follow every step of His instructions (Exod. 12:1-11).
2. God protects His people and executes judgment against His enemies (vs. 12).
3. Believers are protected from God's wrath only by the blood of Christ (vs. 13).
4. Every detail of God's plan has a specific purpose.
5. God expects believers to remember what He has done for them and worship Him (vs. 14).

—Valante M. Grant.

RESEARCH AND DISCUSSION

1. What bearing, if any, do God's instructions on Passover preparation have on our lives today?
2. Why do you think God declared that Passover was to mark "the beginning of months" and "the first month of the year" (Exod. 12:2)?
3. Why was it crucial that the Passover lamb be "without blemish" (vs. 5)?
4. Why was such an important celebration as Passover to be eaten in haste (vs. 11)?
5. How does the Passover memorial relate to New Testament believers (vs. 14)?
6. God always wants us to remember the message of the gospel. What "memorials" do we have to help us do this on a daily basis?

—Valante M. Grant.

ILLUSTRATED HIGH POINTS

Unto you the beginning of months

Being a car guy, Eric could be found working on his Mustang for hours. He decided to fulfill his dream for his cherished metal baby and install a dual exhaust. For this he would need a new bumper, which he ordered online.

That weekend, he opened the box, only to discover the wrong bumper had been sent. It was clear that he would still have to deal with the parts company for some time.

Though the Passover marked a new phase for the Israelites, they needed to continue to follow God in this newly found freedom because He was the only one who had the parts for them to truly live a life free from spiritual bondage.

Your staff in your hand

Lester, the inventor, came through the bus station dragging his two heavy suitcases. When a stranger asked him the time, Lester's face lit up. Proudly, he pointed to his latest invention—his watch. This watch could announce the time in every zone. It had GPS and could easily be switched from timepiece to an FM radio, a satellite receiver, or a distance measurement device. It was even capable of storing up to three hundred books.

"I must have this watch!" the stranger exclaimed. "What if I give you $1,000?"

"Sir, it is not yet ready."

"I will give you $15,000."

Lester agreed, and as the stranger walked away, pointed to the cases and exclaimed, "Don't forget the batteries!"

Just as the Israelites had to be ready to leave Egypt in haste, when we decide to follow God, we must be ready to leave behind the things of this world, no matter how important or impressive they may seem.

—Therese Greenberg.

Golden Text Illuminated

"This day shall be unto you for a memorial; and ye shall keep it a feast to the Lord throughout your generations; ye shall keep it a feast by an ordinance for ever" (Exodus 12:14).

"At the one-hundred-year anniversary of the arrival of missionaries to the Congo, a large celebration was planned. In commemoration of the lasting impact of the work of the original missionaries, speakers were invited to address the gathering. Special music, a festive meal, and other activities were planned as a memorial to this important occasion.

"As the story goes, an aged native came forward and introduced himself to the crowd as the last person alive who was privy to a terrible secret. The old man confessed that one hundred years earlier, when the missionaries first came, the natives didn't know whether to believe the message they carried. So, in order to test their sincerity, they devised a plan.

"Slowly, secretly, systematically, they began to poison the missionaries. Then they watched intently as mothers said good-bye to children, as husbands said good-bye to wives, as friends and colleagues said good-bye to one another. The old man explained that it was only as they saw how these missionaries died, that the truth of their message was confirmed. As a result, many of the people believed and embraced the Gospel message" (www.illustrationexchange.com).

As we complete this quarter's second unit and its theme of preparation for deliverance, we focus on an Israelite observance called the Passover. This week's golden text declares that God established this significant occasion as a memorial for His people, for it would forever remind them of their freedom from slavery to their cruel Egyptian taskmasters. With the estab-lishment of Israel's Passover, God's preparations for deliverance would be complete.

Like the situation described in our opening illustration, Israel's memorial Passover would involve the reality of death—specifically the death of every firstborn Egyptian son. In stark contrast, however, the pervasive reach of death in Egypt would not result in a widespread turn to the Lord by unbelieving Egyptians. What it would do was allow God's people to escape His judgment of death, and it would eventually portray the salvation dynamic of Jesus' death on the cross.

The night of the first Passover was the night of the tenth plague. On this night, God's people were to take an unblemished lamb and sacrifice it (cf. Exod. 12:3-6). They were to then place the lamb's blood on the frames of their household doors (vs. 7). In addition to this, the Israelites were to eat a memorial meal, fully prepared to leave the land of Egypt in haste (vss. 8-11).

Even to this day, Jewish people all over the world obediently celebrate the Passover. Does the Jewish Passover have any spiritual significance to Christians? The answer is definitely yes! For believers in Jesus Christ, Jesus is their Passover (cf. I Cor. 5:7; Rev. 5:12).

The blood of the sacrificial Passover lamb spared the Israelites from the plague of death. Likewise, the blood of the Lamb of God faithfully applied to the lives of sinful people saves them from spiritual death. Have you made that eternal decision? I pray that you have.

—*Thomas R. Chmura.*

Heart of the Lesson

When we read the Bible, we often forget three things. One, the people in the Bible were humans just like us; they were real people. Two, the events that we read about actually took place; we are not reading a fantasy or science fiction novel. The Bible was and is and will remain nonfiction. Three, we are only catching snapshots of their lives. We know in advance how things ended for them, but they did not. They lived their lives the same way we do: one day at a time—each day needing to trust God more than the previous day. So when the Hebrews were given the instructions for what we now call the Passover, they did not know for sure that it would bring them immediate freedom. They just knew they needed to obey.

1. Take a lamb (Exod. 12:1-10). In this portion of Scripture, the Lord gives Moses and Aaron explicit instructions. God was preparing the Hebrews for their freedom from Egypt, but He was also preparing them for their freedom from sin. The Israelites were to find a male lamb without blemish, and the blood of that lamb was to be put on the doorframes of their houses.

One of the reasons God wanted the Israelites to celebrate the Passover was that it was a kind of living prophecy about the Lamb of God who would come to take away their sin. Thousands of years later, a young man without sin would shed His blood to atone for their sin. When we trust Jesus as our Lord and Saviour, His atoning blood covers us, so that eternal death will pass over us.

2. Be ready to leave (Exod. 12:11). "And thus shall ye eat it; with your loins girded, your shoes on your feet, and your staff in your hand; and ye shall eat it in haste: it is the Lord's Passover" (vs. 11). This was not meant to be a leisurely Sabbath meal. It was meant to strengthen the people because they needed to be ready to leave. God instructed them to tuck their cloaks into their belts so that there would be nothing to make them stumble as they departed Egypt. Counter to their culture, the Israelites were to leave their shoes on while they ate. Imagine trying to get a million people, including small children, to get their shoes. Since their shoes were already on their feet, they were ready to go at a moment's notice. God is not asking us to keep our literal shoes on, but He does want us to be ready to share the hope that His eternal Passover, Jesus Christ, provides for us.

3. I will pass over you (Exod. 12:12-14). The blood on the doorposts was for the Israelites, not the Lord. The blood served as protection from the plague. This plague killed the first born of everything in Egypt that did not have the blood on the doorposts. When the Lord saw the blood, He passed over that house. The blood of the lamb was for the benefit of the people. The blood was a sign to the people. They did not have to fear. They did not have to worry. They were covered by the blood. Death would not overtake them; death would pass over them.

Jesus Christ is the Lamb of God who came to shed His blood for the forgiveness of our sins. His blood covers our sins so that we can live eternally with God. We cannot take shoes or a staff or any earthly possession into heaven with us, but we can leave earth with the assurance that Jesus has redeemed us to God.

—*Kristin Reeg.*

World Missions

Imagine the memories of the children who grew up under that first generation of freed Israelites. At the Passover celebration, they would hear a beautiful message of God's redemption and power; yet they would recall their parents complaining over leadership, whining about being hungry and thirsty, regularly crying that God was going to let them die, and pining for the good old days of slavery when they had better food.

A ceremony here and there is not enough to pass along a heritage of faith. Those coming behind us see our lives, not just our momentary celebrations. What we truly believe comes out in the choices we make in our days and years.

As the saying goes, "How you live your day is how you live your life."

When we are gone and those following behind remember us, will they recall a few church ceremonies where we extolled God's faithfulness and goodness but lived lives that showed fear or selfishness or ambition for worldly acclaim? Or will they look to a true heritage to follow—someone who did more than just come to church but actually walked with God and followed God's leading and built up treasure in heaven?

It is never too late to start living that life. Just this week I met a couple who, after retirement, bought an RV and started traveling around America. On their way to Florida for the winter, they stopped in Georgia to volunteer at Source of Light Ministries (SLM) for two weeks. It has now been over two years, and they still have not left! They are happily serving God, printing lessons that go all over the world to reach people for Christ. Florida has lost its appeal by comparison.

Stephen Yoong, who serves with SLM in Singapore, is also retired after years in civil engineering. He says, "From the biblical standpoint, there is no retirement from service for Christ. While on earth, a follower of Christ serves Christ in everything he does (Col. 3:17, 23). One's purpose in life is to bear witness for Christ by life, conduct, speech, and performance in all circumstances. . . . Since my retirement, God has opened new doors by giving me new contacts in Mongolia, Vietnam, Thailand, Malaysia, Indonesia, and Myanmar." God is using Mr. Yoong to provide lessons that help with soul winning, seminary training, and prison outreach (Source of Light International, *The Reaper Publication,* Summer 2017).

Our ceremonies are important, especially if they truly reflect our faith. We should have regular times where we tell ourselves, those around us, and the generations to come of God's faithfulness, deliverance, and redemption. Let us also add to those moments a life of faith and faithfulness. We do not want our children and grandchildren to remember that we said God would provide but were not willing to give because we did not really believe it. We do not want them to follow an example of expressing through our rituals the sentiment that God would hold us in the palm of His hand but never moving in our lives beyond what felt secure.

How wonderful if instead we led the way for the next generation to follow God with all their heart, soul, mind, and strength. Let us not whine and complain in fear, but live as the victorious, gloriously freed children God meant His people to be!

—Kimberly Rae.

The Jewish Aspect

The ultimate event in Israel's history that demonstrated God's redemptive care for them was the Exodus. The classic memorial of all, dating to that event, is the Passover. God established, "And this day shall be unto you for a memorial; and ye shall keep it a feast to the Lord throughout your generations; ye shall keep it a feast by an ordinance for ever" (Exod. 12:14). Its observance reminds the Jewish people of God's miracle of grace on their behalf.

As originally observed, Passover consisted of a relatively simple procedure (Exod. 12-13): 1. It was observed in the first month of the Jewish year; 2. On the tenth day a lamb was selected, killed on the fourteenth day, and its blood sprinkled on the doorframe and lintel; 3. It was then roasted and eaten in haste at night with bitter herbs and unleavened bread; 4. All leftovers were burned.

The Feast of Unleavened Bread began the next day, and it lasted for seven days. Although it was largely separate from Passover, the two were commonly observed together.

Fathers were instructed to teach their children Passover's significance when they questioned them about it (Exod. 12:26). From this the *Haggadah* ("explaining") developed. This is a series of instructions that includes questions for children to ask as Passover is observed.

Passover was one of three major festivals Jews were to observe each year (cf. Lev. 23). Only one observance of Passover is recorded between the Exodus and the entrance into Canaan (Num. 9:2-14). Then, just after entering the Promised Land, Joshua led Israel to observe it at Gilgal (Josh. 5:10-11).

Solomon apparently had Israel observe it, along with the other two festivals (I Kings 9:25). God decreed that He would choose the place for its permanent observance, and this place was the temple (cf. Deut. 16:5).

Hezekiah renewed the observance of Passover after it had been neglected for a long time (II Chron. 30:1-18). Josiah reinstituted it after it had again been neglected (35:1-19), and he did so in a way that "there was no Passover like to that kept in Israel from the days of Samuel the prophet; neither did all the kings of Israel keep such a passover as Josiah kept" (vs. 18). The reference to Samuel seems to indicate that the Passover had been observed in Samuel's day and perhaps prior to that.

The Jewish people observed Passover after returning from the Babylonian exile (Ezra 6:19-22). The Book of Jubilees, a second-century B.C. Jewish writing, describes Passover in detail (49:1-23). Josephus recorded that at Passover in A.D. 65, "the number of sacrifices was two hundred and fifty-six thousand five hundred; which, upon the allowance of no more than ten that feast together, amounts to two millions seven hundred thousand, and two hundred" Jews at the temple to worship (*Wars of the Jews* 6.9.3).

With the temple's destruction in A.D. 70, Passover once again became an observance in individual Jewish homes. Today's full observance of a Passover Seder in a practicing Jewish home can take four hours. Their instruction manual, the "Passover *Haggadah*," provides full information: it begins with the candle lighting, details all the cups to drink, Elijah's cup, the food to eat, questions to ask, and the Scriptures to recite. Modern Judaism, however, continues to miss the truth that the Passover was fulfilled in "Christ our passover," who was "sacrificed for us" (I Cor. 5:7).

—R. Larry Overstreet.

Guiding the Superintendent

Passover is the most important religious day on the calendar for the nation of Israel. Here is how and why it all began.

DEVOTIONAL OUTLINE

1. Regulations for Passover (Exod. 12:1-11). The Passover feast is loaded with special spiritual significance. Therefore it was very necessary that the Israelites follow the exact requirements.

It was all to begin on the tenth day of the first month. Each family was to select a lamb or goat for sacrifice. Small families could join together with other families for the celebration.

The requirements for the sacrificial animal were very specific. It was to be a male and only one year old. It could be either a lamb or goat. The selected animal was to be without blemish and was to be carefully held in readiness until the fourteenth day of the month.

At sunset on the fourteenth day, the animals were to be sacrificed and their blood put to a special use. Some of the blood was to be applied to the sides and top of the door frame of every Israelite house.

The family was to roast the animal and eat it with bitter herbs and unleavened bread. The bitter herbs were a picture of that bitter slavery experience. Also, the unleavened bread (that is, bread that did not have time to rise) symbolized the haste with which the people would leave Egypt (cf. Deut. 16:3). They were to take special care that any leftovers were destroyed in the fire.

To further remind them of their hasty departure from Egypt, the feast was to be eaten with cloaks tucked into their belts, sandals on their feet, and walking staffs in their hands.

2. Spiritual dimension of Passover (Exod. 12:12-14). The text not only explains the "how" of Passover but also the "why."

When the Lord passed through the land of Egypt, He passed over the households with the blood on the doorposts. "When I see the blood, I will pass over you, and the plague shall not be upon you to destroy you, when I smite the land of Egypt" (vs. 13).

This ritual was not just a onetime occurrence. Though God does not continue to smite the land, Passover was to be an annual memorial in order for Israel to keep this event fresh in their memories.

It would be many centuries before Israel would learn the full significance of this memorial—Christ, our Passover.

CHILDREN'S CORNER

text: **Mark 9:14-27**
title: **A Father's Faith in Jesus**

There can be nothing more hopeless than a parent with a very sick child.

In Mark 9, a very desperate father approached a group of Jesus' disciples with his demon-possessed son. The disciples were not able to help the man.

Jesus appeared and questioned the man. The man's son had been demon possessed since early childhood. The demon had left the boy deaf and mute. Many times, apparently intending to destroy the boy, the spirit would seize him, throw him to the ground, convulse him, and cause him to fall into fire or water.

Jesus rebuked the disciples' lack of faith, encouraged the father's weak faith, and then cast out the demon. After it left, the boy appeared dead, but Jesus lifted him to his feet. He told the disciples: "This kind [of healing] can come forth by nothing, but by prayer and fasting" (vs. 29).

—*Martin R. Dahlquist.*

SCRIPTURE LESSON TEXT

EXOD. 12:29 And it came to pass, that at midnight the LORD smote all the firstborn in the land of Egypt, from the firstborn of Pharaoh that sat on his throne unto the firstborn of the captive that *was* in the dungeon; and all the firstborn of cattle.

30 And Pharaoh rose up in the night, he, and all his servants, and all the Egyptians; and there was a great cry in Egypt; for *there was* not a house where *there was* not one dead.

31 And he called for Moses and Aaron by night, and said, Rise up, *and* get you forth from among my people, both ye and the children of Israel; and go, serve the LORD, as ye have said.

32 Also take your flocks and your herds, as ye have said, and be gone; and bless me also.

33 And the Egyptians were urgent upon the people, that they might send them out of the land in haste; for they said, We *be* all dead *men.*

34 And the people took their dough before it was leavened, their kneadingtroughs being bound up in their clothes upon their shoulders.

35 And the children of Israel did according to the word of Moses; and they borrowed of the Egyptians jewels of silver, and jewels of gold, and raiment:

36 And the LORD gave the people favour in the sight of the Egyptians, so that they lent unto them *such things as they required.* And they spoiled the Egyptians.

37 And the children of Israel journeyed from Rameses to Succoth, about six hundred thousand on foot *that were* men, beside children.

38 And a mixed multitude went up also with them; and flocks, and herds, *even* very much cattle.

39 And they baked unleavened cakes of the dough which they brought forth out of Egypt, for it was not leavened; because they were thrust out of Egypt, and could not tarry, neither had they prepared for themselves any victual.

40 Now the sojourning of the children of Israel, who dwelt in Egypt, *was* four hundred and thirty years.

41 And it came to pass at the end of the four hundred and thirty years, even the selfsame day it came to pass, that all the hosts of the LORD went out from the land of Egypt.

42 It *is* a night to be much observed unto the LORD for bringing them out from the land of Egypt: this *is* that night of the LORD to be observed of all the children of Israel in their generations.

NOTES

130

Out of Egypt

Lesson Text: Exodus 12:29-42

Related Scriptures: Numbers 3:11-13, 40-51;
Psalm 105:36-39; Romans 8:28-32

TIME: 1445 B.C.   PLACE: Egypt

GOLDEN TEXT—"Now the sojourning of the children of Israel, who dwelt in Egypt, was four hundred and thirty years. And it came to pass at the end of the four hundred and thirty years, . . . that all the hosts of the Lord went out from the land of Egypt" (Exodus 12:40-41).

Introduction

"Good things come to those who wait." This old adage promotes the virtue of being patient. Many of us can think back to instances when this certainly proved to be the case. In fact, seldom do we get what we really want immediately.

But why do we so often have to wait for things that seemingly would benefit us right now? It seems that the answer in many instances lies in the fact that God wants to teach us things as we patiently wait for Him to answer our prayers.

Had the Lord immediately freed the Israelites from slavery, their understanding of God would have been greatly limited. When Israel's deliverance finally came, no one could confuse the true God with the powerless false gods. Indeed, without seeing God's judgment in the plagues on Egypt, neither the Israelites nor we could fully appreciate our God.

LESSON OUTLINE

I. JUDGMENT ON EGYPT—
   Exod. 12:29-36

II. DELIVERANCE FOR ISRAEL—
   Exod. 12:37-42

Exposition: Verse by Verse

JUDGMENT ON EGYPT

EXOD. 12:29 And it came to pass, that at midnight the LORD smote all the firstborn in the land of Egypt, from the firstborn of Pharaoh that sat on his throne unto the firstborn of the captive that was in the dungeon; and all the firstborn of cattle.

30 And Pharaoh rose up in the night, he, and all his servants, and all the Egyptians; and there was a great cry in Egypt; for there was not a house where there was not one dead.

31 And he called for Moses and Aaron by night, and said, Rise up, and get you forth from among my people, both ye and the children of Israel; and go, serve the Lord, as ye have said.

32 Also take your flocks and your herds, as ye have said, and be gone; and bless me also.

33 And the Egyptians were urgent upon the people, that they might send them out of the land in haste; for they said, We be all dead men.

34 And the people took their dough before it was leavened, their kneadingtroughs being bound up in their clothes upon their shoulders.

35 And the children of Israel did according to the word of Moses; and they borrowed of the Egyptians jewels of silver, and jewels of gold, and raiment:

36 And the Lord gave the people favour in the sight of the Egyptians, so that they lent unto them such things as they required. And they spoiled the Egyptians.

Death of the firstborn (Exod. 12:29-30). The first nine plagues God brought upon Egypt probably covered a period of several months. They had brought much discomfort to Egypt but had not yet brought the hard-hearted Pharaoh to submit to the Lord's demand to free the Israelites. The Lord assured Moses, however, that one final plague would move the Egyptian king to release the captive people (11:1).

Moses informed his people that their deliverance would come as a result of the Lord passing through the land and killing all the firstborn in the land of Egypt. Only the homes of the Israelites, marked by blood, would be spared the Lord's judgment (12:12-13, 23).

At midnight the plague came: "the Lord smote all the firstborn in the land of Egypt" (vs. 29). Many people speak of a "death angel" carrying out this judgment, but the Bible simply says the Lord passed through the land and killed the firstborn (cf. vs. 23).

The tenth plague excluded no one but the protected Israelites. Every first-born male in Egypt, whether human or animal, died (12:29; cf. 11:5). Even Pharaoh's firstborn son died. This is significant, again, with regard to Egyptian religion. The Lord promised that in this final plague He would execute judgment against all the gods of Egypt (cf. 12:12). Pharaoh, who himself was considered a god, was unable to prevent the plague of death. His own firstborn son died. This was the one who would normally have succeeded him on the throne and who also was believed to be divine by the Egyptians.

We might wonder why Pharaoh himself, Amenhotep II, did not die since under normal circumstances he would be a firstborn son. His very survival, however, proves he was not the legal firstborn son of his father, Thutmose III, because Moses had been adopted as the firstborn son, and Egyptian historical records seem to agree with this (Petrovich, "Amenhotep II and the Historicity of the Exodus Pharaoh," Associates for Biblical Research). Likewise, there is evidence in a later Egyptian inscription that Amenhotep II was not succeeded by a firstborn son, which, of course, would have been impossible since his firstborn son died in the tenth plague (Davis, *Moses and the Gods of Egypt,* Baker).

The death of the firstborn was the final blow to Egyptian pride and religion. The God of the lowly, captive Israelites thoroughly humiliated the great Egyptian empire, its king, and its gods. Every Egyptian household was affected by death, and there was a "great cry in Egypt" (Exod. 12:30).

Decision of Pharaoh (Exod. 12:31-32). Pharaoh's stubborn will was finally broken. He called for Moses and Aaron that very night and told them and their people to leave Egypt. There was no attempted negotiation now. He gave in completely to the Lord's demands, allowing the people, along with their flocks and herds, to leave and serve the Lord as they had requested.

Ironically, Pharaoh, who was presumed to be a god, asked these two Hebrew men to bless him. His desire seemed to be for "a farewell blessing, instead of the curse which had been clinging to Egypt" (Cole, *Exodus: An Introduction and Commentary,* Inter-Varsity). This proud man was thoroughly humbled—at least for now.

There is perhaps no greater example of pride and its destructiveness than this pharaoh. His stubborn pride in his power and authority cost him and his people dearly. His nation was devastated, and many of his people, including his own son, died because he was too proud to acknowledge the Lord. Let us not wait for God to humble us; let us humble ourselves before Him now.

Concurrence of the Egyptians (Exod. 12:33-34). The Egyptian people concurred fully with Pharaoh's decision. Interestingly, the word translated "urgent" here is the same word used for the hardening of Pharaoh's heart. It means they were resolute, determined to see the Israelites leave their land. They realized the plagues were the judgment of Israel's God upon them, and they feared that they would all die if the Israelites did not depart.

Even before the first plague struck the land, the Lord had told Moses, "The Egyptians shall know that I am the Lord, when I stretch forth mine hand upon Egypt, and bring out the children of Israel from among them" (7:5). This purpose of the plagues was now achieved. No doubt this is one reason Israel's deliverance did not come immediately. It took ten plagues to convince the Egyptians of the supremacy of the Lord and the powerlessness of their gods.

The Egyptians were insistent that the Israelites leave immediately. As a result, they left hastily without time to mix leaven into their bread dough and let it rise. Therefore, they simply wrapped their fresh dough in their garments and carried the kneading bowls on their shoulders as they left.

Favor on Israel (Exod. 12:35-36). In accordance with Moses' earlier instructions (11:2-3), the Israelites asked the Egyptians for certain items that would aid them in their journey. "Borrowed" (12:35) can be translated "asked" here and should be understood in this sense. "Lent" in verse 36 is the same Hebrew word. The idea is that the Israelites asked for these things, and the Lord gave them favor with the Egyptians so that they readily complied with their requests. The Israelites received clothing, as well as silver and gold, which would allow them to buy provisions from traders. The silver and gold also would be used in the later construction of the tabernacle.

The Egyptians' favorable response to the Israelites was not because they were afraid of what might happen if they refused, but because the Lord gave the Israelites favor with the Egyptians. Exodus 11:3 also indicates that the people of Egypt were in awe of Moses, and this seemed to motivate them to supply the Israelites.

Exodus describes this whole transaction as a spoiling, or plundering, of the Egyptians. This is a military image of a victorious army taking possession of the goods of a defeated enemy. In essence, the Israelites had been in a war with their captors, but their only job was to collect the spoils. The Lord alone fought on behalf of His people and gained the victory. All this was in accord with the Lord's words to Abraham centuries earlier (Gen. 15:14; cf. Exod. 3:21-22).

DELIVERANCE FOR ISRAEL

37 And the children of Israel journeyed from Rameses to Succoth, about six hundred thousand on foot that were men, beside children.

38 And a mixed multitude went up also with them; and flocks, and herds, even very much cattle.

39 And they baked unleavened cakes of the dough which they brought forth out of Egypt, for it was not leavened; because they were thrust out of Egypt, and could not tarry, neither had they prepared for themselves any victual.

40 Now the sojourning of the children of Israel, who dwelt in Egypt, was four hundred and thirty years.

41 And it came to pass at the end of the four hundred and thirty years, even the selfsame day it came to pass, that all the hosts of the Lord went out from the land of Egypt.

42 It is a night to be much observed unto the Lord for bringing them out from the land of Egypt: this is that night of the Lord to be observed of all the children of Israel in their generations.

Departure from Egypt (Exod. 12:37-39). With their freedom granted, the Israelites began their journey, leaving from the city of Rameses and traveling first to Succoth. Moses' original readers would have been familiar with these places, but today we do not know their exact locations. Rameses was probably in the Delta region of Egypt with Succoth about forty miles to the southeast.

Exodus tells us that about six hundred thousand men departed Egypt. This seems to refer to men twenty years old and older (cf. Num. 1:45-46). In addition to these were women and children. Thus, the total number could have easily exceeded two million. This was a massive number of people to set out into the Sinai wilderness. The survival of this nation and their entrance into the Promised Land forty years later only adds to the supernatural aspect of the Exodus. Only God could have accomplished all this.

Among the people who left Egypt were a "mixed multitude" (Exod. 12:38).

This probably refers to non-Israelites. These would have included other enslaved people and possibly even some Egyptians. Perhaps some were outcasts while others had been attracted to the Israelites' God because of the plagues. They became a source of problems for Moses (cf. Num. 11:4), though they certainly cannot be blamed for all the troubles and rebellion that arose among the Israelites in the wilderness.

The departing people took with them "flocks, and herds, even very much cattle" (Exod. 12:38). The Israelites took the livestock that Pharaoh had at one point insisted must be left behind (10:24-26). The animals "are mentioned here . . . not merely because their presence among the departing Israelites indicated total victory over Pharaoh but as indication that the exodus constituted a complete emigration from Egypt of an entire people and their economic assets" (Stuart, *New American Commentary: Exodus,* Holman). These animals would provide food for the nation, as well as sacrifices in the worship of the Lord.

Exodus 12:39 picks up the thought of verse 34. Since the people left Egypt in a hurry, their bread dough remained unleavened. Bread was the main food for the Israelites and most ancient peoples. For now, their diet would consist primarily of the unleavened bread they brought with them.

Reminder of suffering (Exod. 12:40-41). The author, Moses, now inserted a brief notation concerning the length of time the Israelites were in Egypt. He stated that they were there for a total of 430 years; at the end of this period they "went out from the land of Egypt." Elsewhere, the Bible states that the period of Israel's oppression in Egypt was 400 years (Gen. 15:13; Acts 7:6). This is probably a round number, while the 430-year figure in Exodus is more specific.

This mention of Israel's lengthy time in Egypt was a reminder of their seemingly unending suffering in that land. These people had known nothing but enslavement, but now they were free. This in itself must have been daunting. They were leaving a place where they had suffered greatly and from which they had longed to be free, but they were also embarking on a journey into the unknown. Thus, they were stepping out in faith. They would soon learn that their faith would be constantly challenged.

Those who went out from Egypt are referred to here as the "hosts of the Lord" (Exod. 12:41). Again, military imagery is used. "Hosts" refers to an organized army. Though these people could hardly be considered a fighting force comparable to Egypt's own powerful army, they were already a victorious army and would see many military victories in the future, not because of their own might, but because they were led by the Almighty God.

It is significant too that the long years of oppression in Egypt did not separate God from His people. All along, they remained His people. He identified with them, felt compassion for them, and eventually acted to deliver them. We who are followers of Jesus Christ need to remember this truth when we are enduring difficult times. Our trials should not separate us from God, but draw us to Him. He is still present, still claims us as His own, and is at work ultimately for our good and His glory.

Reminder of deliverance (Exod. 12:42). Another note inserted here into the account of Israel's deliverance from Egypt concerns the remembrance of it. Throughout chapters 12 and 13 we see the text shift back and forth from the historical narrative of events (12:1-13, 21-23, 28-41, 50-51; 13:17-22) to instructions for future observances (12:14-20, 24-27, 42-49; 13:1-16). This points out that these events were extremely important for the Israelites. Exodus 12:42-49 reminded Israel to remember their deliverance from Egypt and introduced further instructions with regard to how the Passover was to be observed.

The Lord's mighty deliverance of Israel from Egypt fully demonstrated His compassion, power, and holiness. It clearly set Him apart as the one true God, who deserves exclusive worship.

The nation of Israel still exists, but as a whole the nation does not follow their true Messiah, the Lord Jesus. We who do follow Him should take heed. Only as we continually remind ourselves of the character of our God and of the work of salvation He has done in our lives will we remain faithful to Him and pass on our faith to the next generation.

—Jarl K. Waggoner.

QUESTIONS

1. Who died in the final plague?
2. How did the plague demonstrate the powerlessness of the Egyptian gods?
3. How did Pharaoh respond to the final plague?
4. How did the Egyptian people respond?
5. With what did the Egyptians supply the Israelites? How did this come about?
6. What image does Exodus use to describe the Israelites' receiving goods from the Egyptians?
7. Who were also included among the people who left Egypt?
8. How long had the Israelites lived in Egypt before their exodus?
9. What does "hosts of the Lord" (Exod. 12:41) mean?
10. How was Israel's deliverance to be remembered? Why was it so important for them to remember it?

—Jarl K. Waggoner.

Preparing to Teach the Lesson

This quarter, we have seen the Lord God of Israel's glorious, sovereign supremacy over all the so-called gods in Egypt. All the gods on whom Egypt relied for protection, subsistence, and prosperity had been unmasked as impotent idols whose powers resided only in the Egyptians' imaginations. Now the most illustrious gods of Egypt (Pharaoh and his son) would feel the full wrath of Him who alone can claim the title of Almighty.

TODAY'S AIM

Facts: to learn that God's final plague on Egypt secured the liberty of the Hebrews.

Principle: to realize that resisting God's will is futile and self-destructive.

Application: to submit humbly to God's revealed will in the Bible as He guides you into His truth.

INTRODUCING THE LESSON

Exodus chapter 11 is a prophetic preview of this last plague on Egypt. The Lord apparently had Moses notify Pharaoh of the exact details of this plague and also its unavoidable consequences (cf. vss. 4-8). How tragic that Pharaoh yet again ignored and scoffed at the warning that his son would die that night!

DEVELOPING THE LESSON

1. Death and deliverance (Exod. 12:29-32). As the last demonstration of the Lord's supremacy over the gods of Egypt, the Lord Himself passed through the entire land and struck the firstborn of every household from Pharaoh's firstborn to the firstborn of the lowliest prisoner. Pharaoh and his son were considered the two mightiest gods in the kingdom since they were

visibly alive and had unconditional power over every aspect of their subjects' lives.

Since the text makes the literal claim that "there was not a house where there was not one dead" (vs. 30), we should interpret the meaning of "firstborn" in a nonliteral sense. Clarke observes, "It is evident that it means the *chief, most excellent, best beloved, most distinguished, . . .* the most eminent person in every family in Egypt" (*Commentary on the Bible,* Abingdon). This would imply that even in a household with no children, someone died.

The plague was a rude awakening, literally, for Pharaoh, his palace servants, and all the people of Egypt. They awoke in the dead of night to a universal cry of grief and sorrow that could be heard throughout the land. Clarke notes, "No people in the universe were more remarkable for their mournings than the Egyptians, especially in matters of religion; they whipped, beat, tore themselves, and howled in all the excess of grief."

Brokenhearted, Pharaoh at last realized he was overmatched. The foolishness of his resistance against the Lord was now too painful to deny. That very night he begged the Israelites to leave Egypt as quickly as possible, taking everything. He even requested that Moses and Aaron bless him (vs. 32).

2. Exodus express (Exod. 12:33-39). Now that the Egyptians had tasted the full bitterness of the fruit of opposing the true God of Israel, they could not wait for the Hebrews to leave! There is certainly an irony here. Now that the Lord had no further plans to afflict them, they were so afraid of what He might do next that they could not get rid of the Hebrews fast enough! Clarke observes, "They felt much, they feared more; and therefore wished to get immediately rid of a people on whose account they found they were smitten with so many and such dreadful plagues." They were in such a rush to be rid of the Hebrews that they would not even give them time to leaven their dough. They had already been made to pack up the possessions that they could carry on their backs.

Moses had instructed them to take advantage of the Egyptians' generosity (cf. 11:2-3). The Lord enhanced the esteem of Moses in the eyes of the Egyptians so that they were doubly generous in bestowing parting gifts upon their soon-to-be ex-neighbors. The text actually describes this as a spoiling, or plundering, of Egypt (12:36). How utterly the Lord had defeated and humbled the most powerful empire on the face of the planet! Not only had He delivered them by thoroughly devastating their tormentors, He also had bestowed so much plunder on them that they had more than they could carry.

What a scene it must have been on that day! The Israelite men alone numbered about six hundred thousand. This is not counting women, children, or livestock. This mass of cattle and humanity must have numbered more than one million (perhaps three million)! Clarke rightly sees this as undisputable proof of both the divinely empowered mission of Moses as well as the infallible inspiration of the Scriptures; he writes, "This single circumstance . . . is an ample demonstration of the Divine mission of Moses, and of the authenticity and Divine inspiration of the Pentateuch."

3. Exodus legacy (Exod. 12:40-42). The Hebrew exodus from Egypt occurred precisely 430 years from the time of the divine prophecy to Abra-ham (Gen. 15:13; cf. Gal. 3:17). This is yet another proof of the infallibility of Scripture.

No wonder the observance of Passover is such a paramount day of celebration among all the generations of the Jewish people. Clarke observes that it is "a night to be held in everlasting remembrance, because of the peculiar display of the power and goodness of God . . . while the Jewish nation should continue."

ILLUSTRATING THE LESSON

The illustration shows that the final plague was so devastating that Pharaoh finally relented and let Israel go.

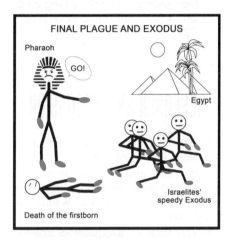

FINAL PLAGUE AND EXODUS

Pharaoh

GO!

Egypt

Israelites' speedy Exodus

Death of the firstborn

CONCLUDING THE LESSON

Hebrews 10:31 pointedly warns, "It is a fearful thing to fall into the hands of the living God." Pharaoh finally felt the full meaning of that warning and dejectedly gave in to God's demands to let His people go.

ANTICIPATING THE NEXT LESSON

In next week's lesson, we will see that Pharaoh's submission to the hand of God was short-lived.

—*John M. Lody.*

PRACTICAL POINTS

1. Judgment is terrible for those who defy God (Exod. 12:29).
2. Persistent defiance to the will of God will result in great personal loss (vs. 30).
3. No one is powerful enough to stand against the power of God (vss. 31-33).
4. We should be ready to move when God tells us to move (vs. 34).
5. God can use anyone to make sure that His people have everything that they need (vss. 35-39).
6. Deliverance can take a long time, but it is worth the wait (vss. 40-42).

—Valante M. Grant.

RESEARCH AND DISCUSSION

1. Why do you think God wants us to leave judgment to Him?
2. Is there ever a time when you should take vengeance into your own hands instead of waiting on God?
3. Was Pharaoh's request for a blessing from Moses sincere (Exod. 12:32)? What blessing could he have received by this point?
4. How can you be sure that God will provide everything that you will need for your journey with Him (vs. 36)?
5. How does God want us to treat people who persecute believers? Should we seek to plunder them?
6. What do you think is the key to remaining faithful for the duration of your journey with God?

—Valante M. Grant.

ILLUSTRATED HIGH POINTS

Be gone; and bless me also

The "Little Red Hen" found a few seeds on the ground and asked her farmyard friends to help her plant them. The lazy dog, sleepy cat, and noisy yellow duck each said, "Not I."

The wheat grew high, and she asked her friends to help her harvest. They all said, "Not I." They also refused to help her bake the bread.

When the bread was baked, they each wanted to eat bread, but the hen ate the bread alone.

As Pharaoh sent the Israelites on their way, he requested a blessing. However, the best blessing God can give is the blessing of knowing Him. You must make your own spiritual investment. Repent, seek His face, worship, and be blessed.

Send them out . . . We be all dead men

The cheerful puppy went to visit a place called "The House of a Thousand Mirrors." He bounded up the porch stairs and peeked in the front door. *Wow,* he thought. *This place is full of puppies like me.* Then he spent the day with his newfound chums.

Hoping to cheer up a grumpy older dog, the pup told him about this wonderful place. So, he went to check it out. However, he saw nothing but a house full of other grumpy dogs.

The Bible teaches us that the Word of God is a mirror (cf. Jas. 1:23-24). It shows us who we are and what we really look like to God. Christians, when they demonstrate God's Word (cf. II Cor. 3:2-3), are also mirrors of the soul. When God reveals His glory through our faith and obedience to Him, it highlights people's sin and makes them feel uncomfortable. They may run or push away, but judgement will come.

—Therese Greenberg.

Golden Text Illuminated

"Now the sojourning of the children of Israel, who dwelt in Egypt, was four hundred and thirty years. And it came to pass at the end of the four hundred and thirty years, . . . that all the hosts of the Lord went out from the land of Egypt" (Exodus 12:40-41).

This week's golden text introduces the third and final unit in this quarter's study. In our previous weeks, we have considered God's call to deliverance and God's preparations for the deliverance of His people. In our final unit, we will consider the accomplished deliverance of God's people and their repeated confrontations with Pharaoh and his pursuing army.

God fulfilled His promise to bring a plague of death upon all the Egyptian firstborn sons. At the first Passover, God brought a comprehensive plague of death that caused terrible distress among Egyptian households (cf. Exod. 12:29-30). Pharaoh then summoned Moses and Aaron and permitted a comprehensive departure of God's people.

The plague of death was so devastating that the Egyptian population encouraged God's people to leave them alone (vss. 31-33). Years later, the psalmist commented on the Egyptian response to the Israelite departure, stating, "Egypt was glad when they departed: for the fear of them fell upon them" (Ps. 105:38). The Hebrew term for "glad" suggests that the countenances of the Egyptian population brightened with joy and relief as they watched the Israelites leave their country.

Over six hundred thousand adult male Israelites, along with their wives, children, flocks, herds, and livestock, departed speedily from the land of Egypt (Exod. 12:37-38). God's people were also accompanied by a "mixed multitude," which probably refers to Egyptians from the lower classes of society and foreign individuals who took advantage of the Israelite exodus to escape the oppressive conditions in Egypt.

The golden text declares that at the time of Israel's departure, they had been living in Egypt for a period of 430 years, much of that time under harsh conditions of servitude. Their lengthy and difficult Egyptian sojourn ended 430 years to the day after their arrival in that land. Even more striking, not a single individual was left behind.

Let us remember that the long, cruel Egyptian bondage of God's people was divinely designed. God had told Abraham that His people would experience a lengthy season of affliction (cf. Gen. 15:13-14).

God also divinely designed Israel's bondage as a preparation for their return to Canaan. In many ways God's people had flourished in Egypt, and in subsequent times of hardship, many even longed to return to Egypt's seeming security (cf. Exod. 16:3; Num. 11:4-6). God had to awaken in His people a sanctified desire to move toward the Land of Promise. Despite Israel's troublesome memory lapses, God accomplished this by allowing them to experience the cruel and severe Egyptian suffering.

God's ultimate, predetermined purpose for His children is to conform them into the image of His Son, Jesus Christ. God will accomplish this purpose, even if He must permit seasons of difficulty and struggle. Do not be discouraged; deliverance is coming!

—*Thomas R. Chmura.*

Heart of the Lesson

Life is a journey. Some days we are making progress; some days we are waiting for something to change. The Israelites had been waiting for hundreds of years for God to deliver them. They must have had many days when they wondered if that day of deliverance would ever come. The waiting can be wearisome to our souls, but know this—we serve the God of suddenness. When He acts, it is undeniable and for all to see.

1. A great cry in Egypt (Exod. 12:29-30). At midnight, the Lord struck down all the firstborn in Egypt from Pharaoh in the palace to the prisoner in the dungeon to the animals in the barns. Only those with a Passover lamb's blood on their doorposts were spared. "And there was a great cry in Egypt; for there was not a house where there was not one dead" (vs. 30).

How could a loving God kill all those people? God is love, but He is also just. God had been patient with the Egyptians. He had given Pharaoh chance after chance to let the Hebrews go. It was Pharaoh's choices that brought on God's judgment, that caused these calamities on his people.

God loves us, and He will give us ample opportunities to repent and change our ways. If we choose to continue following our own sinful ways, He will remove His hand of protection; then we will suffer the consequences of our choices.

2. Plundering of Egypt (Exod. 12:31-36). Those who are compassionate in nature may want to feel sorry for the Egyptians. However, let us remember that there are spiritual laws in place. We reap what we sow. The Egyptians sowed oppression, torment, and death. Through God's plagues on Egypt, this is what they reaped.

Full of heartache and fearful for their own lives, the Egyptians urged the Israelites to leave quickly. Moses had commanded the people to ask the Egyptians for silver, gold, and clothes. The Egyptians handed over their possessions without protest. Thus, the Israelites plundered Egypt. When God moves on our behalf to deliver us from our troubles, we will move on with greater blessings. God will cause our troubles to bless us as we emerge from their shadows.

3. And it came to pass (Exod. 12:37-42). The Israelites had been waiting many years for freedom from their oppressors. When Moses returned to Egypt and told Pharaoh to let the Hebrews go, mixed emotions must have risen up in the hearts of God's people. The work got harder, but they now had renewed hope that God would deliver them. With each plague, the Israelites witnessed the power of their God. At some point, they must have believed that their deliverance was coming.

Hope is a powerful force. It is like gasoline on a smoldering spark. Together, faith and hope are an unstoppable combination that empowers us to press through even the worst of troubles.

"And it came to pass at the end of the four hundred and thirty years, even the selfsame day it came to pass, that all the hosts of the Lord went out from the land of Egypt" (vs. 41). The Lord kept watch to ensure that the Israelites got out of Egypt. God brought His people to a place of freedom from the Egyptians.

Just when we think that God has forgotten about us and our hearts believe that God has forsaken us, God will show up. He will deliver us from our troubles. We, too, will say, "The Lord is good."

—Kristin Reeg.

World Missions

For many years, it must have seemed to the Israelites that God had abandoned them, that He did not care, and that deliverance would never come. Yet those who remembered the promises given to Abraham would have known that bondage was going to be part of their history and that God had a plan for the deliverance of His people.

When thinking of our world today, no place seems more abandoned by God than North Korea. Citizens are given no freedom of speech or freedom of religion. Since 1948, they are required to worship and sing hymns to the unholy trinity of founding revolutionary Kim Il-Sung, his son and successor Kim Jong-il, and his grandson and successor Kim Jong-un. Even hearing the gospel is life-threatening. To trust in Christ means great danger; to live for Christ means almost certain persecution or worse. Some believing parents do not even share with their children that they are followers of Christ because of the pressure in the school system for students to report their parents.

How can any hope survive in such darkness?

Though it looked like Israel had been left to their slavery and oppression, God had a plan. He knew to the year and even the day when they would be delivered. None of His children are forgotten, not even in the darkest places of earth. Not even in North Korea.

The Voice of the Martyrs seeks to send encouragement to believers in North Korea and to send the salvation message to the lost. They pack gospel literature into bundles that they send across the border with balloons. Sometimes, a brave soul comes to investigate them.

"It was 10 p.m. as their car drove slowly down a dirt road. . . . The driver, a VOM field worker, had turned off the headlights to reduce the possibility of being spotted by Chinese or North Korean border guards. . . . After [they arrived] at a small house . . . they stepped inside, their eyes . . . immediately drawn to a young man sitting in front of a small television watching the *JESUS* film. He was a North Korean who had crossed the river into China for discipleship training. As soon as he was finished . . . he would be making the dangerous journey back home to North Korea.

"To avoid further endangering the young man and the home owners, the visitors left after a brief meeting, returning the same way they had come. As they drove back, . . . one of the visitors prayed fervently for the young man who would be making the risky trip back home with his new knowledge of the gospel. Anyone caught leaving North Korea illegally, or without successfully bribing officials, is arrested or shot."

To help these courageous workers who are risking their lives, go to: etools.vomusa.org/b/201703-04-mt.html (*Voice of the Martyrs Newsletter,* March 2017, used with permission.)

VOM's radio broadcast site (persecution.com/radio/default.aspx?pdid=6485) shares that many would say North Korea is "the worst place in the world to be a Christian." Yet despite the darkness, God has not abandoned His people. He has a plan. Perhaps our generation will see the doors to North Korea open. Many of us remember when the Berlin Wall fell and when the USSR became open. God can do anything and free any country's people to seek Him openly, without fear. Let us pray for North Korean believers to remain steadfast and that the lost of North Korea would be saved.

—*Kimberly Rae.*

The Jewish Aspect

Pharaoh resisted God's commands concerning Israel for about nine months. After the death of his firstborn son, though, everything changed. He called for Moses and Aaron and said the Jews could all leave, with all their possessions. He then added, "and bless me also" (Exod. 12:32). Pharaoh was considered a god by the Egyptians, and yet he now submitted entirely to the Lord of the Israelites.

The Hebrew word for "bless" (*barak*) occurs around 330 times in the Old Testament. When used of God's blessing, it emphasizes the granting of His prosperity and well-being to something or someone. In its first use, on the fifth day of creation, God blessed the sea creatures and birds, "saying, Be fruitful, and multiply, and fill the waters in the seas, and let fowl multiply in the earth" (Gen. 1:22). He also blessed His first created male and female (vs. 28).

God further "blessed the seventh day, and sanctified it" (2:3), meaning that He consecrated it by setting it apart for Himself. God is the source of all blessings. Pharaoh professed, at least for a brief time, to accept that. For the Jews, a climactic blessing was when God blessed Abraham by making a covenant with him (12:2-3).

When used of people, the word "bless" has the idea of either declaring or desiring God's favor and goodness to be upon others. It is a wish for God to give people success and prosperity, for them to enjoy a long and fruitful life.

Rebekah's family blessed her by wishing for her to have many descendants (Gen. 24:60). Isaac blessed Jacob with his prophetic declaration that he would be the heir of the Abrahamic covenant (27:27-29). The Aaronic blessing for the nation of Israel is well known (Num. 6:22-27). This desire for God's favor and goodness is what Pharaoh manifested when he asked Moses to "bless me also."

For the Jews, the concept of blessing was often paired with cursing. God would give His blessings, His favor and goodness, to them as they obeyed. In contrast, He would pronounce His curses when they disobeyed (Deut. 27:11-30:20).

Jews also knew that they could bless God. This did not mean that they wished for His prosperity but that they gratefully praised and worshipped Him for who He is and what He graciously bestows.

Observant Jews today identify blessing as a part of their normal prayer ritual in the synagogues and in personal prayers. They use the Hebrew word *berakhot* to express it.

Jewish tradition dictates that a practicing Jew should speak one hundred *berakhot* each day. By doing this, Jews consistently affirm that all blessings of life come from the hand of God. "This is not as difficult as it sounds. Repeating the *Shemoneh Esrei* three times a day (as all observant Jews do) covers 57 *berakhot* all by itself, and there are dozens of everyday occurrences that require *berakhot*" ("Prayers and Blessings," (www.jewfaq.org).

Jews recognize three kinds of *berakhot*. The first is a blessing said when enjoying any type of physical pleasure, such as eating, drinking, or clothing. Second are those said when obeying a religious duty. These can include washing hands and lighting candles. The third are those said at special occasions. These can include praising God for seeing a rainbow, meeting a dignitary, or even receiving bad news. The conscious awareness of God in the Jewish *berakhot* is a reminder to Christians to keep the Lord ever before us.

—*R. Larry Overstreet.*

Guiding the Superintendent

It took over four hundred years to happen, but when God started to move, it did not take much for Israel to escape centuries of Egyptian slavery. God is very patient, but when His planned time comes, He accomplishes His purpose quickly and decisively (cf. II Pet. 3:9-10).

DEVOTIONAL OUTLINE

1. God's power (Exod. 12:29-30). In accordance with the commands of Moses, the Israelites gathered in their homes with the sacrificial blood on the door frames (vss. 21-28). As promised, at the stroke of midnight the Lord went throughout the land and caused to die all the firstborn of Egypt, from the palace to the prison. When the Egyptians discovered this, great wailing could be heard from every household. But because of the sacrificial blood, all the Israelites homes were untouched and all the firstborn spared.

2. God's deliverance (Exod. 12:31-36). In the middle of the night, Pharaoh conceded. He summoned Moses and ordered him to get the Israelites out of Egypt. He let them leave with no conditions—they could take their families and their animals.

The Egyptians now were only too glad to see their former slaves leave. They gave the Israelites much gold, silver, and clothing. This would all be needed in the future to build their nation's economy and worship structure.

Because this all happened with such haste, the slaves did not even have time for their bread dough to rise; they had to carry their kneading troughs.

3. God's promises (Exod. 12:37-42). With their families and herds, the Israelites marched out of Egypt toward the first stop on their way, Succoth. This was truly a large crowd. It included six hundred thousand men. Including women and children, there were probably more than two million Israelites that left Egypt that night.

All that God had promised to Abraham came true 430 years later to the day (Exod. 12:41; cf. Gen. 15:12-14). God's promises are always sure, and His timing is always correct.

CHILDREN'S CORNER
text: **Luke 7:1-10**
title: **An Army Capitan's Faith**

As Jesus traveled around Galilee, He approached Capernaum. A Roman officer heard that He was coming and sent a delegation to Jesus to beg Him to heal a well-loved servant.

In spite of the fact that he was a Gentile member of the hated occupying army, the officer loved the Jewish people so much that he had helped build a synagogue for the local Jews.

However, he did not consider himself worthy to even meet Jesus. He sent a second delegation with this explanation: As a Roman officer, he was a person who had authority and told people what to do. He recognized that Jesus also was a person of authority. He confessed that Jesus needed only to say the word, and the beloved servant would be healed at a distance.

When Jesus heard this reflection of his confident faith, "he marvelled at him" (vs. 9). Here was a Gentile, a Roman officer and pagan, who had more faith than anyone in the religious Jewish nation. By the time the delegation returned to the officer's home, the servant was healed.

The key to faith that amazes Jesus is not related to gender or nationality, but to our knowledge of and confidence in Him.

—*Martin R. Dahlquist.*

SCRIPTURE LESSON TEXT

EXOD. 13:17 And it came to pass, when Pharaoh had let the people go, that God led them not *through* the way of the land of the Philistines, although that *was* near; for God said, Lest peradventure the people repent when they see war, and they return to Egypt:

18 But God led the people about, *through* the way of the wilderness of the Red sea: and the children of Israel went up harnessed out of the land of Egypt.

19 And Moses took the bones of Joseph with him: for he had straitly sworn the children of Israel, saying, God will surely visit you; and ye shall carry up my bones away hence with you.

20 And they took their journey from Succoth, and encamped in Etham, in the edge of the wilderness.

21 And the LORD went before them by day in a pillar of a cloud, to lead them the way; and by night in a pillar of fire, to give them light; to go by day and night:

22 He took not away the pillar of the cloud by day, nor the pillar of fire by night, *from* before the people.

14:1 And the LORD spake unto Moses, saying,

2 Speak unto the children of Israel, that they turn and encamp before Pi-hahiroth, between Migdol and the sea, over against Baal-zephon: before it shall ye encamp by the sea.

3 For Pharaoh will say of the children of Israel, They are entangled in the land, the wilderness hath shut them in.

4 And I will harden Pharaoh's heart, that he shall follow after them; and I will be honoured upon Pharaoh, and upon all his host; that the Egyptians may know that I *am* the LORD. And they did so.

5 And it was told the king of Egypt that the people fled: and the heart of Pharaoh and of his servants was turned against the people, and they said, Why have we done this, that we have let Israel go from serving us?

6 And he made ready his chariot, and took his people with him:

7 And he took six hundred chosen chariots, and all the chariots of Egypt, and captains over every one of them.

8 And the LORD hardened the heart of Pharaoh king of Egypt, and he pursued after the children of Israel: and the children of Israel went out with an high hand.

9 But the Egyptians pursued after them, all the horses *and* chariots of Pharaoh, and his horsemen, and his army, and overtook them encamping by the sea, beside Pi-hahiroth, before Baal-zephon.

NOTES

144

Pursuit of the Slaves

Lesson Text: Exodus 13:17—14:9

Related Scriptures: Exodus 13:1-16; Numbers 9:15-23;
I Corinthians 10:1-4

TIME: 1445 B.C.   PLACE: by the Red Sea

GOLDEN TEXT—"The children of Israel went out with an high hand. But the Egyptians pursued after them, all the horses and chariots of Pharaoh, and his horsemen, and his army, and overtook them" (Exodus 14:8-9).

Introduction

A woman in Arizona was arrested for leaving her two children inside her car while she interviewed for a job.

When the plight of the young, unemployed single mother became known, there was an outpouring of compassion for her. Job offers came her way, and someone raised over one hundred thousand dollars for her and her children.

Sadly, the woman showed no interest in the job opportunities and stole the money from her children to spend on herself.

This woman's sad story reminds us that for most needy people acts of compassion alone are not enough. They need purpose and guidance to make sure the compassion shown them ultimately leads to change and blessing.

God's compassionate deliverance of His people from Egyptian bondage was followed by His equally compassionate guidance. The Lord left no doubt that He had a plan for His people and He would faithfully guide them in the way they should go.

LESSON OUTLINE

I. DIVINE DIRECTION—Exod. 13:17-22

II. DIVINE PLAN—Exod. 14:1-9

Exposition: Verse by Verse

DIVINE DIRECTION

EXOD. 13:17 And it came to pass, when Pharaoh had let the people go, that God led them not through the way of the land of the Philistines, although that was near; for God said, Lest peradventure the people repent when they see war, and they return to Egypt:

18 But God led the people about, through the way of the wilderness of the Red sea: and the children of Israel went up harnessed out of the land of Egypt.

19 And Moses took the bones of

Joseph with him: for he had straitly sworn the children of Israel, saying, God will surely visit you; and ye shall carry up my bones away hence with you.

20 And they took their journey from Succoth, and encamped in Etham, in the edge of the wilderness.

21 And the LORD went before them by day in a pillar of a cloud, to lead them the way; and by night in a pillar of fire, to give them light; to go by day and night:

22 He took not away the pillar of the cloud by day, nor the pillar of fire by night, from before the people.

Following God's leading (Exod. 13:17-18). When the Israelites left Egypt, they did not take a direct route to the land of Canaan. The people knew this was their ultimate destination and the land promised to them. However, Moses knew he must first take the people to Mount Sinai, according to God's plan (cf. 3:12).

One reason for the detour to Mount Sinai was that the more direct route presented some unique dangers to the people. This route, known as "the way of the land of the Philistines" (13:17), ran along the Mediterranean coast. It was lined with Egyptian fortresses, and "the former slaves to Pharaoh were in no condition to wage full-scale warfare, which would have been unavoidable had the route of the exodus followed the coastal road" (Pfeiffer and Vos, *The Wycliffe Historical Geography of Bible Lands,* Moody).

The Lord understood that military resistance would discourage the people and cause them to want to return to Egypt, so He prevented them from taking this route. Indeed, the Lord knew these people, for when various trials arose along the way, they voiced their preference for returning to slavery in Egypt.

Instead of leading them on any of the common routes out of Egypt, God led the people "through the way of the wilderness of the Red sea" (vs. 18). The exact route is still not known, but it took them southeast into the Sinai peninsula.

The Bible describes the people as "harnessed" (vs. 18), which literally means organized by fives. It is a term for a military formation, and some have understood it as meaning the Israelites were armed for battle. However, it appears they were not armed at all. "Formed up for battle they may have been—after a fashion. Trained for battle, however, they were not" (Stuart, *New American Commentary: Exodus,* Holman). Yet, they were God's army— an army that could not be defeated as long as they trusted and followed their heavenly Captain.

Honoring an ancient promise (Exod. 13:19). More than four hundred years earlier, Joseph had spoken with prophetic foresight, saying, "God will surely visit you, and ye shall carry up my bones from hence" (cf. Gen. 50:25). The family of Jacob had sworn to do so at the time. Now Moses saw to it that their promise to Joseph was fulfilled. Joseph's embalmed body was taken from its coffin in Egypt (cf. vs. 26) to be transported to the land of Canaan.

Joseph's desire for burial in the Promised Land was a testimony to his own faith in God's promise that the land would belong to Jacob's descendants according to the covenantal promise of God to Abraham (Gen. 12:1-3, 7; 13:14-17; 15:13-21). Taking the bones of Joseph with them as they left Egypt also was a reminder to all the Israelites that God's plan for them had not been forgotten. Just as Joseph had believed God's ancient promise to his ancestors, so could they.

Receiving visible guidance (Exod. 13:20-22). A geographical note is inserted in verse 20, telling us the Israelite nation traveled from Succoth to

Etham. Succoth was the first stop on their journey (cf. 12:37). Continuing on a southeasterly path, the people came to Etham. Etham's precise location is uncertain, but it is described as "the edge of the wilderness" (13:20). This suggests that they were about to enter the largely uninhabited desert region of Sinai.

At this point, Moses (the author) described God's means of leading the people. Yes, they needed the Lord's appointed human leader, but their travels through the desert would be directed by divine means. The Lord Himself went before them "by day in a pillar of a cloud . . . and by night in a pillar of fire" (vs. 21). The cloud would direct their movements by day, and the fire would light their way at night. Exodus 13:22 emphasizes that it was continually present. Indeed, it continued to lead the nation throughout their time in the wilderness.

The pillar was a visible manifestation of God's presence and glory. In Exodus 14:19 it is called the "angel of God." It is also called "the glory of the Lord" (40:34). It has also been called the Shekinah-glory, from the Hebrew word meaning "to dwell" (cf. vs. 35). The pillar was a clear demonstration of God's continual presence among the people and His personal guidance of them. There could be no doubt among the Israelites that God was the One leading them on this journey.

The presence of the pillar of cloud and fire meant that any complaint about their circumstances was a direct complaint about God's leading. This is something we should all remember. God directs us by His Word, His Spirit, and His providential workings. When we complain or despair over the circumstances we face as a result of faithfully following the Lord, we are actually calling into question the wisdom of His guidance. Consequently, we forfeit the opportunity to grow stronger in our faith through the trials He brings our way.

DIVINE PLAN

14:1 And the Lord spake unto Moses, saying,

2 Speak unto the children of Israel, that they turn and encamp before Pi-hahiroth, between Migdol and the sea, over against Baal-zephon: before it shall ye encamp by the sea.

3 For Pharaoh will say of the children of Israel, They are entangled in the land, the wilderness hath shut them in.

4 And I will harden Pharaoh's heart, that he shall follow after them; and I will be honoured upon Pharaoh, and upon all his host; that the Egyptians may know that I am the Lord. And they did so.

5 And it was told the king of Egypt that the people fled: and the heart of Pharaoh and of his servants was turned against the people, and they said, Why have we done this, that we have let Israel go from serving us?

6 And he made ready his chariot, and took his people with him:

7 And he took six hundred chosen chariots, and all the chariots of Egypt, and captains over every one of them.

8 And the Lord hardened the heart of Pharaoh king of Egypt, and he pursued after the children of Israel: and the children of Israel went out with an high hand.

9 But the Egyptians pursued after them, all the horses and chariots of Pharaoh, and his horsemen, and his army, and overtook them encamping by the sea, beside Pi-hahiroth, before Baal-zephon.

God's instructions (Exod. 14:1-2). Not only did Israel have the pillar of cloud and fire to direct them, but they also had God's chosen leader, Moses, to whom the Lord gave specific directions. The Lord gave Moses instructions about exactly where the people were to encamp after leaving Etham. Pi-hahiroth was near the Red Sea, west of the sea and east of a place called Migdol.

Again, the precise locations are uncertain, but they lend historical, geographic details to the Lord's instructions and would have been known to travelers of that time. What is clear from the description, however, is that they encamped west of the sea, placing them between the sea to the east and Egypt to the west.

The sea in Exodus 14:2 is the "Red sea" mentioned in 13:18. The Hebrew literally means "Sea of Reeds." Some have sought to downplay the miraculous crossing of this sea by arguing that a sea of reeds must have simply been a shallow marsh. The biblical description of the miracle makes such an assumption impossible, however.

The sea Exodus refers to is undoubtedly the Gulf of Suez, which is an extension of the Red Sea. It is also quite possible that the crossing was a little farther north at the Bitter Lakes, which in Moses' time was connected to the gulf.

God's purpose (Exod. 14:3-4). From a military standpoint, Israel was in a very vulnerable position. If attacked from the west, they would be trapped against the sea with no place to retreat. With his Egyptian training, Moses must have realized this, so the Lord explained His purpose in having the people camp at this location.

First, the Lord explained the thinking of Pharaoh. The Israelites were still under the observation of the Egyptians, and when Pharaoh heard where the people were, he would conclude that they were wandering aimlessly and had foolishly placed themselves in an indefensible location. Indeed, the Lord said He would harden Pharaoh's heart so that he would come after the Israelites. The reason the Lord was orchestrating all this was so that He would be honored and that "the Egyptians [could] know that [He is] the Lord" (vs. 4).

The Lord's purpose was to once again demonstrate His sovereignty and power.

But why was this necessary after the plagues had already humbled Pharaoh and his people? The Egyptian gods "were arbitrary and capricious, quick to change their actions and attitudes . . . not omnipresent but manifesting themselves at given locations and then leaving those locations unpredictably" (Stuart). With this theological background, Pharaoh perhaps concluded that the apparently erratic wandering of the Israelites meant their god had left them. Also, another divine deliverance of the Israelites would reinforce for the Egyptians the truth that Israel's God was the one, true Lord. It would also encourage Israel and prepare them for the military engagements that lay ahead for them.

It is also significant that the Lord informed Moses of exactly what He was going to do. Moses presumably told the people this as well (vs. 2). They could expect the Egyptians to attack, and yet they could also expect the Lord to again demonstrate His power in delivering them.

Pharaoh's change of mind (Exod. 14:5). It appears that soon after Israel's departure, Pharaoh and his servants started having regrets about allowing them to leave. The impact of the Israelites' absence began to take a toll on them, and they started asking themselves why they had let them go.

The Israelites' vulnerability from being encamped by the sea presented an excellent opportunity for Pharaoh to crush their rebellion and regain some of Egypt's glory. It appears the memory of the plagues and the suffering they brought on Egypt had faded quickly. But when people are filled with hatred and rage, reason is often set aside. Of course, in this case the Lord was once again hardening Pharaoh's heart in order to accomplish His own purposes.

Preparations for war (Exod. 14:6-7). Pharaoh prepared his own chariot and "six hundred chosen chariots."

Pharaoh's chariot force was led by well-trained officers.

It is unclear whether the goal was to bring the Israelites back to Egypt to again serve the Egyptians as slaves or simply to annihilate them. In either case, under normal conditions this formidable Egyptian force would have been more than adequate to fulfill either mission.

A hardened heart (Exod. 14:8a). Here we are reminded that all that was taking place was part of the Lord's plan. While Pharaoh and his people made their decision to go after the Israelites, the Lord assured them that this would indeed happen because He would harden the heart of Pharaoh. God was not through with Pharaoh, Egypt, or Israel.

A determined pursuit (Exod. 14:8b-9). The Egyptian king, along with his army, set out in pursuit of their former slaves. Verse 8 mentions that "the children of Israel went out with an high hand." The expression "with a high hand" usually refers to arrogance or pride. To the humiliated Egyptians, the Israelites' joyous departure probably seemed to be marked by arrogance. Now the Egyptians were seeking to bring such arrogance to an end. All Pharaoh's forces pursued the Israelites.

While the Israelites had left Egypt some days before, the chariot army soon overtook the plodding multitude encamped by the sea. The location of Israel's camp is given again (Exod. 14:9; cf. vs. 2), reminding us that their backs were to the sea and there was no way for them to escape the Egyptian army.

Even such a seemingly small detail as where the Israelites set up their camp was directed by the Lord. The Lord used this detail to encourage Pharaoh to attack and thus provide Himself one more opportunity to demonstrate His great power and receive the glory He deserves. God graciously told Moses what he was going to do and why. He did not explain *how*.

This passage of Scripture records history. But it is more than just a recounting of events. It presents truths about God and His purposes. He moves people and history according to His pleasure to accomplish His purposes, and He grants us the ability to learn from it. However, we see only events and people's actions. We do not always see that God is using certain events and actions to accomplish His purposes. We must walk by faith, trusting God to be always present with us and to accomplish His glorious purposes for us, even when we cannot see that He is doing so.

—Jarl K. Waggoner.

QUESTIONS

1. Why did the Israelites not go directly to Canaan?
2. Why did Moses take the bones of Joseph with him? Of what should this have reminded Israel?
3. What means of guidance did the Lord provide?
4. What did the pillar demonstrate?
5. Where did the Lord tell Moses the people were to encamp?
6. What was the Lord's purpose in having the people set up their camp there?
7. Why would Pharaoh pursue the Israelites after all Egypt had suffered in the plagues?
8. What could the Israelites rightly expect regarding their confrontation with the Egyptians?
9. What preparations did Pharaoh make to overtake the Israelites? What was his goal?
10. What does Israel's leaving with a "high hand" mean (Exod. 14:8)?

—Jarl K. Waggoner.

Preparing to Teach the Lesson

The Exodus of the Israelites from Egyptian slavery was finally accomplished as we saw in last week's lesson. Pharaoh seemed utterly defeated, despairing over the death of his firstborn prince, the heir apparent to his lofty throne. In this lowly state of mind, he had given the order to free the Israelites, in effect allowing God's people to spoil and plunder the world's greatest empire!

TODAY'S AIM

Facts: to see that the Lord once again hardened Pharaoh's heart against the Hebrews only to more dramatically display His power to deliver them.

Principle: to understand that the Lord often intensifies opposition to His people to more greatly display His power to save.

Application: to remember that when opposition seems insurmountable, that is when the Lord will most dramatically intercede to deliver us.

INTRODUCING THE LESSON

All was not yet well with the freed Hebrews. Their Almighty Lord, Yahweh, had one more point to prove in making an example of Egypt; He would bring about the utter defeat of their illustrious army.

DEVELOPING THE LESSON

1. The Lord's guiding presence (Exod. 13:17-22). The Lord is wise, caring, and realistic in His dealings with His people. He did not want to have His newly freed people journey through the lands of the Philistines since it would almost certainly mean war, even though that way would have made for a shorter journey and even though He would have been well able to deliver them from defeat. So instead, He led them south, through the wilderness toward the Red Sea. Verse 18 makes the interesting observation that they traveled "harnessed," a word indicating that the Israelites were arrayed for battle. Even though they were armed for conflict, the Lord knew that they were not warriors, but former slaves. He did not want to see them lose their courage at their first sight of a formidable Philistine army and slink back to Egypt.

Note that Moses remembered the vow made by the sons of Jacob to their brother Joseph that they would carry his bones back to the Promised Land once the Lord's deliverance was accomplished (cf. Gen. 50:25). Joseph had prophesied Israel's deliverance by God's hand (vs. 24). Adam Clarke adds, "the Israelites carried with them the bones . . . of *all the twelve sons of Jacob,* each tribe taking care of the bones of its own patriarch, while Moses took care of the bones of Joseph. St. Stephen expressly says, Acts vii. 15, 16, that not only Jacob, but the fathers were carried from Egypt into Sychem" (*Commentary on the Bible,* Abingdon).

Note also that this is the first mention of the Lord manifesting Himself as the pillar of fire and the pillar of cloud. Clarke elucidates, "This was the *Shechinah* or Divine dwelling place, and was the continual proof of the presence and protection of GOD. It was necessary that they should have a guide to direct them through the wilderness . . . of which they knew nothing but just as the luminous pillar pointed out the way!" This glory of the pillar of cloud by day and of fire by night was constantly before them as a reminder that the Lord was with them in a miraculous way.

From a New Testament perspective, Clarke says, "That by *the* Lord here is meant the Lord Jesus, we have the authority of St. Paul to believe, 1 Cor. x. 9: it was he whose Spirit they tempted in the wilderness, for it was he who led them through the desert to the promised rest."

2. Pharaoh's outraged pursuit (Exod. 14:1-9). The people must have felt that their troubles with the Egyptians were over, but the Lord now warns Moses that Pharaoh's heart will be hardened one last time against them. Therefore, the Lord directed Moses to encamp the people between Pi-hahiroth (the name perhaps signifying "the mouth or bay of Hiroth") on the shore of the Red Sea and Migdol (a fortified tower). They camped against a temple-fortress of an idol called Baal-zephon, which means "master of the watch." This location was purposely selected by the Lord because it afforded the people no escape once the Egyptian army arrived. All the Egyptians would need to do to corner them would be to station themselves at the mouth of the valley between these two fortified positions.

In verse 3, the Lord reveals His plan: this was done to bait Pharaoh into thinking that the Hebrews had lost their way in the wilderness and had become hopelessly confused. Once again, the Lord was deliberately giving His people's enemies an overwhelming advantage for the purpose of showing His own supreme power; He would deliver the Israelites from yet another seemingly hopeless predicament.

Back in Egypt, Pharaoh received the report that all the Hebrews indeed had fled Egypt (vs. 5). This report aroused him to the indignant realization that Moses and the Israelites had made a fool out of him. He asked rhetorically, "Why have we done this, that we have let Israel go from serving us?"

Therefore, Pharaoh readied his personal chariot, six hundred select chariots, and all the remaining chariots of Egypt at his disposal. With these he set out to pursue his insubordinate slaves in order to punish their rebellion against him and compel them to return to their bondage in Egypt.

ILLUSTRATING THE LESSON

The illustration shows that the Lord hardened Pharaoh's heart once again to glorify Himself.

PHARAOH CHANGES HIS MIND

Pride, indignation, and outrage
Pharaoh gives in
Go!
Go get them!
Pharaoh hardens his heart again!

CONCLUDING THE LESSON

Although Pharaoh had been humbled by the last plague, which killed his own son as well as the best and brightest of every Egyptian household, the Lord had not yet finished displaying His supreme power and might against this most exalted kingdom on earth. Once again we are aptly reminded of the message of Hebrews 10:31: "It is a fearful thing to fall into the hands of the living God."

ANTICIPATING THE NEXT LESSON

In next week's lesson, we will see the Lord glorify Himself by the miracle of the Red Sea crossing.

—*John M. Lody.*

PRACTICAL POINTS

1. If you follow God, He will lead you in the direction that is best for you (Exod. 13:17-18).
2. It is important to be faithful in the details when serving God (vs. 19).
3. God will not leave us lost and alone. His presence is always with us if we are His (vss. 20-22).
4. Our enemies are under God's control. They can only do what He allows them to do (14:1-4).
5. We do not have to be fearful or run from our enemies (vss. 5-9).

—*Valante M. Grant.*

RESEARCH AND DISCUSSION

1. Why was it important to carry out Joseph's request after so many hundreds of years (Exod. 13:19)?
2. Why do you think that the enemy pursues God's people with such persistence (14:5-6)?
3. If the enemy is controlled by God, why does God allow them to attack His people (Exod. 14:8; cf. Jas. 1:2-4, 13-14; Rom. 5:3-4; II Cor. 1:3-5)?
4. How can you hold fast to your faith in God when the enemy is advancing toward you?
5. Think of a time when the enemy came against you. What did you do? What should you have done?
6. What is the difference between God's sovereignty and His providence? Why is it important to consider both together?

—*Valante M. Grant.*

ILLUSTRATED HIGH POINTS

Repent when they see war

Sam Houston, commander of the Texas revolutionary army, arrived in Gonzales to begin his newly appointed charge over 374 ragtag, ill-equipped men. Almost immediately, Houston learned that Mexican general Santa Anna was leading his army of more than 1,000 troops directly toward Gonzales. The men wanted to fight, but Houston chose to retreat.

In retreat, Houston took the time to train his newly formed army. Now they were ready! After a month, he turned his army back around and marched them south to face the enemy. With the famous cry, "Remember the Alamo," they attacked and defeated Santa Anna's army.

Newly saved believers, like the newly delivered Israelites, are not ready to wage war with the enemy without being properly equipped. We must take time to retreat into the Word and prayer.

To go by day and night

Very young puppies are attached to their owners and can be trained to follow them without a leash. Eventually they will keep a constant eye on their master's every move. Beginning in the house, the owner will move out and walk quickly, causing the pup to hustle to keep up. If the pup slows down, the owner speeds up. If the pup runs ahead, the owner slows way down, stops, or turns around and walks in the other direction. Eventually, he learns to never lose sight of his master. But this training is effective only in the first four and a half months of the puppy's life; after that, if he has not been trained to follow, he will go his own way.

From the beginning of their deliverance, God began training the Israelites day and night to follow Him.

—*Therese Greenberg.*

Golden Text Illuminated

"The children of Israel went out with an high hand. But the Egyptians pursued after them, all the horses and chariots of Pharaoh, and his horsemen, and his army, and overtook them" (Exodus 14:8-9).

The term "deliverance" implies a rescue and freedom from bondage. When a successful deliverance is accomplished, the presence and power of the thing that was responsible for the bondage is completely removed. In fact, brand-new circumstances often accompany a successful deliverance. That is what makes a second chance so desirable and gratifying.

My sanctified imagination leads me to believe that the accomplished deliverance of God's people from Egyptian bondage led them to believe they had been completely released from all Egyptian influences. Their deliverance surely was accompanied by massive sighs of relief and the belief that they would see the Egyptians no more. Freedom was theirs to enjoy; there would be no more looking back.

Yet when God delivers His oppressed people, there is deliverance of sorts for the slaveholder as well as for the slave. The slaveholder endures some form of divine judgment, but he is delivered from the spiritually perilous position of trying to maintain absolute control over another human being. Whether he benefits from that deliverance depends on his response to it. The slave experiences a liberation from oppression and servitude, resulting in genuine freedom and joy.

I believe both these factors were in play as God sovereignly accomplished the deliverance of His people from Egyptian bondage. A hint of this twofold dynamic is seen in this week's golden text.

Pharaoh had decided to let God's people leave Egypt; he had finally released them from his control. But he had not changed his attitude toward them; he did not respond well to his own deliverance. He saw a chance to regain control when he perceived that the Israelites seemed to be aimlessly wandering in the desert (Exod. 14:3). God would bring glory to Himself and bring judgment upon Pharaoh (vs. 4).

Pharaoh now regretted his decision to let the Israelites leave Egypt, so he prepared to pursue them and return them to servitude (vss. 5-7). The Lord was continuing the process of hardening Pharaoh's heart, allowing him and his powerful army to overtake and entrap God's people at their seaside encampment (vss. 8-9).

The golden text offers a hint that God's people may have left Egypt with a haughty attitude. The phrase "with an high hand" speaks of a confident boldness, but it might also suggest that Israel departed Egypt with a sense of sinful pride. It is possible that they somehow believed their accomplished deliverance was the result of their own strategies and schemes. They needed to recognize their dependence on the Lord.

God was at work in both the slaveholder (Pharaoh) and the slave (God's people). His deliverance would result in profound changes in both parties; the result was that God alone would receive the glory rightfully due Him. God had both parties exactly where He wanted them. The stage was set for the final acts of deliverance.

Does God desire to accomplish a divine deliverance in your life? If so, don't resist His work!

—*Thomas R. Chmura.*

Heart of the Lesson

Lasting life lessons are rarely learned quickly or easily. There are no short-cuts. The journey is often filled with detours, obstacles, and dead ends. God knew there was a shorter route to get to the Promised Land. But He also knew the shorter route is not always the best route.

1. The longest route (Exod. 13:17-22). Imagine the Israelites' excitement as they left Egypt with all the spoils from the Egyptians! They were free! They were rich! But where were they going? God was leading them toward the Red Sea.

God knew there was a shorter route, but He also knew the hearts of His people. Even though they cried and begged for freedom from Egypt, the Lord knew that if the Israelites faced war, they would want to return to the safety of Egypt. So God led the people with a cloud by day and a pillar of fire by night around the hostile territory. Regardless of the time of day, the Israelites could move forward in complete confidence that God was with them.

2. God's encouragement to Moses (Exod. 14:1-4). When there are undeniable signs, like a cloud by day and fire by night to lead the way, it would be difficult to get off course. However, even in the midst of much evidence, we can still feel insecure about the future.

God spoke to Moses as the Israelites were following God's miraculous pillar. The Lord informed him of what would happen. God did not allow the Egyptians to attack Israel by surprise. Instead, He spoke to Moses to comfort him and let him know that He was allowing His plans to unfold. God always has a greater purpose than we can see. Our God is the Creator of the heavens and the earth and everything in it. Our God is greater than any of the gods that the Egyptians worshipped. He wanted the Egyptians to know that He alone was the Lord of all.

3. Pharaoh's regret (Exod. 14:5-9). When Pharaoh heard that the Israelites had left Egypt, he immediately regretted his decision to let them go. "And it was told the king of Egypt that the people fled: and the heart of Pharaoh and of his servants was turned against the people, and they said, Why have we done this, that we have let Israel go from serving us?" (vs. 5).

How many times have we made a decision that we have regretted? In the moment, our choice may have seemed like a good idea; however, once we realized the consequences, we quickly changed our minds. For some decisions in life, it is better to simply make the best of the inevitable consequences rather than break our word and cast shame on our personal integrity. Ultimately, it would have been in Pharaoh's best interest to let God's people go. But Pharaoh was a proud man, and he did not want to seem weak to neighboring nations by allowing all his slave labor to slip through his fingers.

The king of Egypt gathered his army, including six hundred of his best chariots, and pursued the Israelites. He was determined to regain what he had lost. Most of us already know the rest of the story. Pharaoh lost his army, and his soldiers lost their lives. Maybe it would be wise for us to learn a lesson from Pharaoh. When we make a decision that results in our loss, let us count the cost before going back on our word. The king of Egypt pursued the Israelites to overtake and recover all. Instead, he lost it all.

—*Kristin Reeg.*

World Missions

What looked like abandonment by God—even death—was God's plan for a full defeat of the Egyptian army and an unforgettable display of His power to deliver His people.

This is a good lesson to remember when thinking of God's current work around the world. In the Summer 2017 edition of Source of Light's publication, *The Reaper,* director Ron Barnes Jr. shares this account:

"I just returned from India where once again I have seen firsthand the trials Christians are facing there. I receive weekly updates of atrocities happening to pastors and Christians. One week a man our team knows well was passing out literature and Bibles. He was abused verbally and eventually physically by radical Hindus and found himself in the hospital partially paralyzed. A few weeks later he died from his injuries.

"Then I received a video of women being forcibly removed from a new convert's house because the villagers didn't want her to be discipled. Last week I received pictures of a pastor and his wife stripped naked outside of his church so that all the village [would] see the treatment converts can expect to receive."

"So, when meeting with these valuable partners in ministry in India, did they discuss contingency plans for how to get away if danger came? Did they create a backup plan on what to do if things got difficult?

"When we sat and prayed with our team in India just a few short weeks ago, we asked for His will to be done in each of our lives. That we would be faithful to the task He has given each of us. We asked the Lord to make us strong in trial, show love and compassion in the face of being humiliated, be longsuffering with persecution."

It may sometimes look like "the wilderness hath shut them in" (Exod. 14:3), as Pharaoh believed regarding the Israelites, but God's children are moving forward. They are pursued and sometimes overtaken, but the work goes on.

Ron Barnes Jr. says of Source of Light, "Our tabernacle project in India attracts visitors among unbelievers of every faith and as they make their way through the tent, the Gospel is clearly presented, in some of the most hostile territories in Asia. Recently thousands made their way through and many made decisions or agreed to allow our missionaries to follow up. In spite of death threats and danger our missionaries go, so that others may hear."

He goes on to say, "'Foreign soil' isn't the only place still needing a 'preacher,'" and shares a letter recently received from a man named Ivan, who had been on Death Row in prison for ten years. He was set for execution in a few weeks and wrote to thank SLM for the lessons and to ask for their prayers. He was able to face death with hope because he had salvation.

"At some point, someone at SLM, through the printed Word, reached into the prison. . . . he [Ivan] couldn't just have stumbled on us."

People desperately need the Lord. The work to reach them may be fraught with danger and hardship, but those who go follow the call, for as Paul challenges us, "How shall they hear without a preacher?" (Rom. 10:14).

Oh, that God would send more laborers to the harvest, for it is great!

—*Kimberly Rae.*

The Jewish Aspect

God introduced the idea of redemption to Moses in Exodus 6:6; "I will redeem you with a stretched out arm, and with great judgments." Exodus stresses God's plan for the redemption of the firstborn. Since the firstborn of Egyptian animals and men died in the tenth plague on Egypt (4:23; 12:29), "the event was to be perpetually commemorated in Israel by the consecration of all the firstborn of man and beast to the Lord (Ex 13:12)" (*Theological Wordbook of the Old Testament,* Moody). That emphasis in Exodus 13 was renewed at Sinai when God said that "the firstborn of thy sons shalt thou give unto me" (22:29).

About a year later, Moses numbered the people. At that time God ordained that the Levites would be substitutes for "all the firstborn among the children of Israel, and the cattle of the Levites instead of their cattle; and the Levites shall be mine" (Num. 3:45). God chose the tribe of Levi. They had stood with Moses as he dealt with Israel's sin concerning the golden calf (Exod. 32:26; cf. Num. 8:14-19).

Contemporary Jews know all these details concerning firstborn sons. "However, even though their place has been taken by the Levites, the firstborn still retain a certain degree of sanctity, and for this reason, they must be redeemed" ("Pidyon ha-Ben: Redemption of the First Born," www.jewfaq.org).

Observant Jews set apart a firstborn son at the age of thirty-one days. If that day falls on a Sabbath, it is delayed for a day. The son is redeemed by paying an amount of money. In the Old Testament this was five shekels; modern Jews typically pay five silver dollars.

The money is paid to a *kohein*, a physical descendant of Aaron, who may or may not be a priest. Since the temple was destroyed two thousand years ago, with its genealogical records, how do observant Jews identify those who are *kohanim*? There are two ways.

First, through the centuries Jews have endeavored to maintain records of the *kohanim*. Second, "DNA research supports their claims: a study published in Nature in June 1997 shows that self-identified kohanim in three countries have common elements in the Y-chromosome, indicating that they all have a common male ancestor" ("Rabbis, Priests, and Other Religious Functionaries," www.jewfaq.org).

Redemption of the firstborn in modern Judaism involves a small number of children. Only firstborn boys are involved. If a girl should be born first, she is not considered for the ceremony. In addition, none of the children that are born after her are considered, even if a boy is born later. Further, boys must be born by natural childbirth; any boy born by Caesarean section is not considered, nor are any boys born after him, even if they are born naturally. If a mother's first conception of a child terminates in a miscarriage after a term of more than forty days, then no following son is considered for the ceremony. The identity of the firstborn is determined by the mother, not the father. A woman may have a firstborn son by one father, and then he may die. If she has another son by a second husband, that son is not regarded as a firstborn, even if he is that father's first son. Anyone identified as being in the tribe of Levi is also excluded, since God chose them to substitute for all firstborn.

Many Jews look for their coming Messiah, their great redeemer (cf. Isa. 59:20). That Redeemer came in the person of Jesus, the Son of God (cf. Rom. 11:26).

—*R. Larry Overstreet.*

Guiding the Superintendent

Getting Israel out of Egypt proved to be much easier than getting Egypt out of Israel. God had a much more important task than leading Israel to the Promised Land. What happens next was all designed to get Israel to follow and believe God.

DEVOTIONAL OUTLINE

1. Israel's journey begins (Exod. 13:17-22). Nothing takes God by surprise. Everything that happens to us and for us is all part of His plan for us, even when that plan may not make sense to us.

When the Israelites left Egypt, they did not follow the shortest route to Canaan, which would have only taken a few days. The shortest way was too well guarded and would have led Israel right into Philistine territory (currently Gaza), a well-armed nation. Israel was not yet ready for war. Instead, God led His people toward the Red Sea.

God encouraged the faith of Israel with a couple of visible signs—a coffin, a pillar of cloud and of fire. Perhaps one of the strangest sights was the coffin. Before Joseph died, he had made his brothers promise to take his bones with them when they returned to Canaan (Gen. 50:24-25; cf. Heb. 11:22). That coffin made the entire journey and was eventually buried in Canaan (Josh. 24:32)! Every time the Israelites saw this strange sight, they were reminded of their ultimate destination.

God also encouraged the people with a direct sign of His leading. He guided them with a pillar of cloud by day and a pillar of fire by night; this sign accompanied the Israelites during their entire desert journey and led them in the correct direction. When God calls us, He also directs us.

2. Pharaoh pursues Israel (Exod. 14:1-9). God next led His people right into an impossible situation. He had Israel turn back and "encamp by the sea" opposite Baal-zephon (vs. 2). This looked like a tactical mistake on Israel's part, and it emboldened Pharaoh. To him, this meant Israel had been wandering aimlessly in the desert and now was hopelessly trapped.

In reality, this was all part of God's plan to draw out the Egyptian army and trap them. Pharaoh ordered his chariot forces to pursue the "hopeless" nation.

What a great lesson on God's leading: while His leading might not always be clear or logical, we can still trust that what He does is always for our best.

CHILDREN'S CORNER
text: **Mark 10:46-52**
title: **A Blind Man's Faith**

Word was spreading quickly. The Prophet from Nazareth was coming through town today. For one particular man, this event would change his life.

The crowds were very large and probably pressing all around Jesus as He made His way to Jerusalem. Suddenly, out of the crowd a loud voice called: "Jesus thou son of David, have mercy on me" (vs. 47).

Jesus stopped and called the person to him. The crowd told the man, who was blind, to get up and go to Jesus.

Jesus said to him: "What wilt thou that I should do unto thee?" (vs. 51). The poor man begged for his sight. Jesus responded to the man's confident faith and gave him his sight.

Here is another example of an unexpected follower of Christ. This man was literally blind, but he expressed faith in Jesus, and Jesus responded by opening his eyes.

—*Martin R. Dahlquist.*

SCRIPTURE LESSON TEXT

EXOD. 14:10 And when Pharaoh drew nigh, the children of Israel lifted up their eyes, and, behold, the Egyptians marched after them; and they were sore afraid: and the children of Israel cried out unto the LORD.

11 And they said unto Moses, Because *there were* no graves in Egypt, hast thou taken us away to die in the wilderness? wherefore hast thou dealt thus with us, to carry us forth out of Egypt?

12 *Is* not this the word that we did tell thee in Egypt, saying, Let us alone, that we may serve the Egyptians? For *it had been* better for us to serve the Egyptians, than that we should die in the wilderness.

13 And Moses said unto the people, Fear ye not, stand still, and see the salvation of the LORD, which he will shew to you to day: for the Egyptians whom ye have seen to day, ye shall see them again no more for ever.

14 The LORD shall fight for you, and ye shall hold your peace.

15 And the LORD said unto Moses, Wherefore criest thou unto me? speak unto the children of Israel, that they go forward:

16 But lift thou up thy rod, and stretch out thine hand over the sea, and divide it: and the children of Israel shall go on dry *ground* through the midst of the sea.

17 And I, behold, I will harden the hearts of the Egyptians, and they shall follow them: and I will get me honour upon Pharaoh, and upon all his host, upon his chariots, and upon his horsemen.

18 And the Egyptians shall know that I *am* the LORD, when I have gotten me honour upon Pharaoh, upon his chariots, and upon his horsemen.

19 And the angel of God, which went before the camp of Israel, removed and went behind them; and the pillar of the cloud went from before their face, and stood behind them:

20 And it came between the camp of the Egyptians and the camp of Israel; and it was a cloud and darkness *to them,* but it gave light by night *to these:* so that the one came not near the other all the night.

21 And Moses stretched out his hand over the sea; and the LORD caused the sea to go *back* by a strong east wind all that night, and made the sea dry *land,* and the waters were divided.

22 And the children of Israel went into the midst of the sea upon the dry *ground:* and the waters *were* a wall unto them on their right hand, and on their left.

NOTES

Crossing the Red Sea

Lesson Text: Exodus 14:10-22

Related Scriptures: Psalm 106:7-9; Isaiah 63:7-14

TIME: 1445 B.C.   PLACE: Red Sea

GOLDEN TEXT—"And Moses stretched out his hand over the sea; and the Lord caused the sea to go back by a strong east wind all that night, and made the sea dry land, and the waters were divided" (Exodus 14:21).

Introduction

My late grandfather was a veteran of the First World War and was involved in one of the largest campaigns of that war. My father quoted my grandfather as saying that anyone who claimed he was not scared in the midst of battle was either a liar or a fool. It is hard to argue with that statement.

But consider this: What if a person marching into battle somehow knew with absolute assurance he would survive the engagement? Would he still experience fear?

As followers of the Lord, however, we can have full assurance of God's sovereign rule in our lives and can entrust ourselves to His gracious plan for us. This certainly should have a great bearing on how we respond to danger and trials.

Still, as the Israelites demonstrated from their experience, it is easy for our faith to be overwhelmed when we look at the circumstances instead of the One who controls those circumstances.

LESSON OUTLINE

I. **THE RESPONSE TO DANGER**— Exod. 14:10-14

II. **THE PLAN FOR DELIVERANCE**—Exod. 14:15-18

III. **THE WORKS OF THE LORD**— Exod. 14:19-22

Exposition: Verse by Verse

THE RESPONSE TO DANGER

EXOD. 14:10 And when Pharaoh drew nigh, the children of Israel lifted up their eyes, and, behold, the Egyptians marched after them; and they were sore afraid: and the children of Israel cried out unto the LORD.

11 And they said unto Moses,

Because there were no graves in Egypt, hast thou taken us away to die in the wilderness? wherefore hast thou dealt thus with us, to carry us forth out of Egypt?

12 Is not this the word that we did tell thee in Egypt, saying, Let us alone, that we may serve the Egyptians? For it had been better for us to serve the Egyptians, than that we should die in the wilderness.

13 And Moses said unto the people, Fear ye not, stand still, and see the salvation of the Lord, which he will shew to you to day: for the Egyptians whom ye have seen to day, ye shall see them again no more for ever.

14 The Lord shall fight for you, and ye shall hold your peace.

Response of the people (Exod. 14:10-12). Pharaoh's great chariot force came upon the Israelites as they were camped by the Red Sea. The people of Israel immediately realized the hopeless position they found themselves in. They were essentially unarmed, had no chariots of their own, and were trapped against the sea with no route of escape.

The fear that engulfed the Israelites seemed to push from their minds the promise of God that the Egyptians would be unsuccessful (cf. vss. 1-4). The approaching Egyptian army was all they could see, and it produced overwhelming fear in the people.

Exodus 14:10 tells us they "cried out unto the Lord." This was certainly a proper response, at least on the surface, for only the Lord could save them from the impending attack. However, they then turned on Moses, and "their words against Moses were a rebuke and disloyal, showing a lack of faith and understanding" (Ross, *Studies in Exodus,* Christian Leadership Center).

The people sarcastically accused Moses of bringing them out of Egypt just so they could die in the wilderness. They even claimed that they had begged Moses to leave them alone to serve the Egyptians rather than bring them out of the land and into the wilderness to die there. If anyone had actually said this back in Egypt, it certainly was not the prevailing attitude of the people, especially after the plagues

began. In fact, the Israelites had been happy to leave Egypt and did not have to be coerced to do so.

The complaint also was wrongly directed. Moses had not brought them out of Egypt; God had. Their complaint should have been—and actually was—against the Lord, but of course it was much easier to make it seem like they were blaming Moses. The remedy for a complaining spirit is giving thanks in everything (I Thess. 5:18). Yet the gratitude of the people was absent.

It is amazing, though maybe not so surprising, that their complaint followed so soon after their deliverance and the instruction concerning the observance of Passover. One writer makes an important observation here: "The reaction of the Hebrews is quite typical of those whose spiritual perspectives are those which are conditioned by the present alone. Without a historical consciousness of what God has done and a deep-rooted faith in what God will do, one is easily moved by the emotion of a given situation. The shallow responses of the Hebrews should be a warning to all of those who put all their emphasis on the present" (Davis, *Moses and the Gods of Egypt,* Baker).

Response of Moses (Exod. 14:13-14). Moses' reaction to the situation stands in marked contrast to that of the multitude. He urged the people to not be afraid, and then calmly and confidently announced the Lord's deliverance.

Apparently, the Lord had not told Moses the specific means by which He would deliver the people, but Moses had complete confidence that the Lord would do so. The Lord was the one who had directed His people to this place, and He would not abandon them there. He had promised to bring them into the land of Canaan, and that is what He would do.

God would bring their "salvation" (vs

3), or deliverance. The people were simply to "stand still" and see what He would do. To "stand still" here means to stand firm, without fleeing. The instruction in verse 14 to "hold your peace," or be quiet, is to be struck dumb with amazement. The Israelites had been fidgeting and complaining, and God had had enough of it. The Egyptians they saw as such a great threat that day would never be seen alive again, for the Lord would fight for His people, and the Egyptians would meet their doom.

It is interesting to contrast the attitudes of Moses and the people. Moses had been fearful and lacking in faith (cf. Exod. 4:1; 5:21-23). But he grew in faith as He served the Lord. Now he called upon his people to stand still and to be amazed into silence by the sight of God's mighty deliverance of them.

The people, however, reflected the attitude of those who are weak in faith. Such people often blame God for the uncomfortable situations in their lives. They are shortsighted and cannot look beyond the present, and they take God's blessings for granted. Indeed, the Israelites probably expected an easy journey when they left Egypt. God's way is not normally the easy way, but a difficult path that develops faith in Him.

THE PLAN FOR DELIVERANCE

15 And the Lord said unto Moses, Wherefore criest thou unto me? speak unto the children of Israel, that they go forward:

16 But lift thou up thy rod, and stretch out thine hand over the sea, and divide it: and the children of Israel shall go on dry ground through the midst of the sea.

17 And I, behold, I will harden the hearts of the Egyptians, and they shall follow them: and I will get me honour upon Pharaoh, and upon all his host, upon his chariots, and upon his horsemen.

18 And the Egyptians shall know that I am the Lord, when I have gotten me honour upon Pharaoh, upon his chariots, and upon his horsemen.

The Israelites' role (Exod. 14:15). We do not know exactly what Moses was praying for, but it seems to have been for clear direction on what to do. The Lord told him it was now time to stop praying and follow His clear directions.

First, the Lord told Moses to tell the people to "go forward" (vs. 15). They were to move forward in faith, trusting that the Lord was about to make a way for them to be delivered from the troubles they were so afraid of. They had assumed there was no place to go, but the Lord had a unique route for them to take, one they could not have anticipated. They were to gather their belongings and animals and prepare to move on.

Moses' role (Exod. 14:16). The Lord's role for Moses in the deliverance was to lift his rod over the sea and divide it. Moses' rod, or staff, symbolized "God's power and presence and reminding all concerned that it was not Moses but God who performed the supernatural" (Stuart, *New American Commentary: Exodus,* Holman). The rod had been employed in the first two plagues (7:19-20; 8:5-6), both of which had involved water. Now it would be used as God divided the water (14:16). The Israelites would then go through the midst of the sea on dry ground (vs. 16). This revealed God's miraculous means of deliverance to Moses and the people. God Himself would make the way of escape from a seemingly impossible situation.

The Lord's role (Exod. 14:17-18). The Lord also would harden the hearts of the Egyptian army so that they would follow the Israelites into the sea. This would be necessary, for as we can imagine, the Egyptians would be struck by fear and awe at the sight of the miracle being enacted before them and be naturally hesitant to pursue the Hebrews through the channel in the sea.

The result of their following the fleeing Israelites through the sea would be the destruction of Pharaoh's chariot army. The Lord did not specify how this destruction would take place, though it might be implied. But as a result of overthrowing Pharaoh and the Egyptians, the Lord would gain glory for Himself, and the Egyptians would know that He is the true Lord and God of all.

The Egyptian people and their gods had been humiliated by the plagues and forced to let the Hebrew slaves go free. The mighty Egyptian army, however, was still intact. Their defeat by supernatural means would be the final blow. It would force Egypt to acknowledge the Lord as the omnipotent, eternal God of all the universe.

The divine plan for Israel's deliverance would affirm Moses as God's chosen leader of the people. No doubt this is part of the reason Moses was to raise his staff over the water. The plan would also demonstrate that God alone was their deliverer. They would not be saved by military might or human schemes. Finally, the plan would remind the people that the work was God's; they needed only to move forward in faith.

THE WORKS OF THE LORD

19 And the angel of God, which went before the camp of Israel, removed and went behind them; and the pillar of the cloud went from before their face, and stood behind them:

20 And it came between the camp of the Egyptians and the camp of Israel; and it was a cloud and darkness to them, but it gave light by night to these: so that the one came not near the other all the night.

21 And Moses stretched out his hand over the sea; and the LORD caused the sea to go back by a strong east wind all that night, and

made the sea dry land, and the waters were divided.

22 And the children of Israel went into the midst of the sea upon the dry ground: and the waters were a wall unto them on their right hand and on their left.

Moving the cloud (Exod. 14:19-20). The intervention of God became immediately evident when the pillar of cloud moved to a place between the Israelites and the Egyptian army. The pillar is identified here with the "angel of God." This evidently is another reference to the physical manifestation of God's presence (cf. 3:2). The Lord is now seen as not only being Israel's guide but also her protector.

The pillar kept the Egyptians at bay and in darkness throughout the night as the side of the pillar that faced them was dark. However, the side facing the people of Israel gave light to them throughout the night.

Parting the water (Exod. 14:21-22). As instructed by the Lord, "Moses stretched out his hand over the sea. We can, of course, be sure he held forth his staff as he did so (vs. 16). This action provided "a visible motion to reassure him and those watching that the power of an invisible God was at work" (Stuart). Though Moses obeyed God's instruction, it was the Lord who caused the sea to divide. He did this through a strong east wind that blew all night, dividing the waters and making the exposed seabed dry.

We should not think that there was anything natural about this wind. No natural wind could accomplish this marvel described in the Bible. This was a special wind sent by God that divided the waters and dried the bottom of the sea so the people could cross through the sea to the other side. All naturalistic explanations of this miracle are futile and usually require the reader to imagine a shallow marsh dried up by a strong wind. This does not match the biblical description and certainly does not give the Lord the kind of honor he deserves for the genuine miracle He displayed.

That this wind was supernatural is further evident in that the seabed was immediately dried. This would have been necessary for the entire multitude to make the crossing in a single night (cf. vs. 24); they only had about eight hours to walk the entire distance.

Exodus 14:22 tells us that the "children of Israel went into the midst of the sea upon the dry ground." It also describes the waters standing as walls on the left and right. Thus a channel through the sea was opened. This was no narrow channel, however. For some two million people or more to cross during the nighttime hours would have required a very broad path.

The waters to each side of the channel are described as walls of water. They must have towered over the people, for they were pushed back quite some distance and were deep enough to drown the Egyptian charioteers. The poetic description in Exodus 15:8 speaks of the waters standing upright as a "heap" and being "congealed." "Congealed" means to be thickened; this word paints a picture of the waters as a firm mass.

The moving of the cloud to protect the Israelites and light their way through the night and the parting of the sea were two undeniable miracles. For the people of Israel, there could be no doubt that the Lord was once again working on their behalf to finalize their freedom from Egypt. For the Egyptians, there could be no doubt that the God of the Hebrews was again working in miraculous ways that their own gods could not match. They had little choice but to acknowledge Him as the all-powerful God.

There are lessons we can learn from these verses in Exodus 14. First, the passage illustrates once again that God does not lead His people into situations that are hopeless. He was the One who had clearly led the Israelites to the place by the sea. From all outward appearances, there was no way to escape the oncoming Egyptians. But with God there is always a way. Like the Israelites, we need only trust God and remain faithful to Him.

Second, we are reminded that God's blessings do not guarantee faithfulness. Israel experienced multiple blessings and witnessed God's miracles, yet their faith was weak and easily smothered by circumstances. We must never take God's blessings for granted.

Finally, we should note that God's purpose for us and in everything we experience is His glory and honor.
—Jarl K. Waggoner.

QUESTIONS

1. How did the Israelites react when they saw the Egyptians?

2. With what did the people charge Moses?

3. Of what did Moses assure the people?

4. What did Moses tell the people to do?

5. What is meant by the Lord's instruction to the people to go forward (Exod. 14:15)?

6. What role did the Lord assign to Moses in the deliverance?

7. Why did the Egyptians follow the Israelites into the sea? What happened to the army?

8. What was the pillar of cloud, and with what was it identified?

9. What role did the pillar play in Israel's deliverance?

10. What means did the Lord use to part the water?
—Jarl K. Waggoner.

Preparing to Teach the Lesson

In John Bunyan's *Pilgrim's Progress,* Christian reaches the summit of Difficulty Hill, where he meets two travelers—Timorous and Mistrust. They tell Christian there are lions just up ahead! Because of this, they have decided to give up their pilgrimage and return home. It is obvious by their fickle behavior that they see no value in a salvation that entails personal danger. How similar Timorous and Mistrust are to the Israelites in our lesson for this week!

TODAY'S AIM

Facts: to note that the Israelites quickly lost faith in Moses and the Lord at the first sight of danger, even though the Lord's presence was guiding them in the miraculous manifestation of the pillar of cloud and of fire.

Principle: to understand that even when supported by obvious miracles, people by nature are prone to lose faith when faced with fearsome threats.

Application: to remember that in the midst of the most fearful experiences in our lives, we must hold on to our faith in the Lord's constant presence with us and His ability to guide and protect us.

INTRODUCING THE LESSON

What a bold start the Israelites have made! They packed in extreme haste, laden with the precious plunder of Egypt. But soon adversity and danger would arise, putting their faith to the test.

DEVELOPING THE LESSON

1. Fear and grumbling (Exod. 14:10-12). Our passage speaks volumes about the shallow faith of the Israelites. Despite all they had witnessed of God's glory and the very visible pillar of the Lord's Shekinah-glory guiding them, when they first saw the Egyptians pursuing them, they lost faith and began to complain.

Verses 10-12 would make a hilarious parody if it were not such a tragic indication of the Israelites' fickleness. For all their panic, they lost none of their ability to speak sarcastically to the Lord and Moses: "Because there were no graves in Egypt, hast thou taken us away to die in the wilderness?" (vs. 11).

They went on to question why Moses had ever brought them out of Egypt in the first place. Their elation at having been freed from slavery was forgotten. They now began to wax nostalgic about the good old days of hard servitude: "Better for us to serve the Egyptians, than that we should die in the wilderness" (vs. 12).

2. Protection and escape (Exod. 14:13-22). For all his famous humility and patience, there seems to be more than a hint of aggravation in Moses' response to the people's grumbling—and rightfully so. This was only the first of many such episodes of sarcasm and complaining on the part of the newly liberated Hebrews that he would have to deal with.

Because his faith in the Lord was still strong, Moses did not need to consult Him about how to respond; he knew what to say to them in their cowering unbelief. The people needed to stop being afraid, stop murmuring, and stop fidgeting around aimlessly. If they would just be quiet, they would see the Lord's salvation soon enough. Also, he told them that they should take a good look at the Egyptian army since it would not be long before they would be gone, never to be seen again. The Lord God of Israel was going to fight for them, and until then they should just be quiet!

In verses 15-18, the Lord Himself speaks to Moses at length about the situation. Instead of standing around fretting, Moses was to get the people to move forward, presumably toward the Red Sea. Moses would soon stretch out his staff over its waters and divide them so the people would have a safe, dry path across the sea.

The Lord was going to harden the hearts of Pharaoh and his army one last, fatal time. They would foolishly follow the Israelites into the parted waters as if the divided sea were merely a natural phenomenon they were free to take advantage of in the same way the Israelites had. Pharaoh still stubbornly resisted any thought that the God of Israel was against him and his army. His stubbornness would cost him dearly, and the Lord would once and for all be honored and glorified. Pharaoh would learn the hard way that the Lord alone is the true and living God—the God of all gods.

In verse 19, the presence of the Lord in His Shekinah-glory of cloud and fire moves so as to position itself between the people and the Egyptian army, thus blocking any attack. Moreover, the pillar behaved differently toward the Egyptians than toward the Hebrews; it gave light to the Israelites but kept the Egyptians in a confusion of darkness. This situation would prevail throughout the night while Israel made their escape through the parted sea. It was then that Moses stretched out his hand and, by God's absolute power over the universe, parted the Red Sea. The text vividly describes the sea as forming two walls of water with a dry path between them, stretching to the far shore.

Picture, if you will, the overwhelm-ingly spectacular nature of the scene: the Egyptians held at bay in darkness and confusion by the flaming pillar of the Lord's glory, millions of Israelites amassed on the seashore safe from Pharaoh's forces, and Moses stretching forth his staff over the divided sea while the Lord's mighty wind from the east blows a dry path that allows the Hebrews to escape to the far shore.

ILLUSTRATING THE LESSON

The illustration shows that the Lord defended the Israelites from Pharaoh's army and created a way of escape for them.

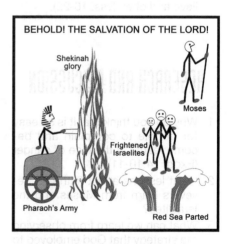

BEHOLD! THE SALVATION OF THE LORD!

Shekinah glory

Moses

Frightened Israelites

Pharaoh's Army

Red Sea Parted

CONCLUDING THE LESSON

Our lesson shows an awesome demonstration of God's mighty power to defend and deliver His covenant people. Nothing is impossible for our Almighty God and Saviour!

ANTICIPATING THE NEXT LESSON

Next week, we will see the stunning conclusion to the Lord's miraculous parting of the Red Sea on behalf of His covenant people.

—John M. Lody.

PRACTICAL POINTS

1. Fear is a natural response to danger, but faith is the spiritual solution (Exod. 14:10-11).
2. The enemy will try to convince you that you were better off in bondage (vs. 12).
3. If we are believers, there is no reason to cower in fear. God will fight for us (vss. 13-14).
4. God equips us with the tools we need and empowers us to use them (vs. 15).
5. God's instructions are clear and thorough. All we have to do is believe and obey (vss. 16-22).
   —*Valante M. Grant.*

RESEARCH AND DISCUSSION

1. Why do you think that it is so easy for people to complain and become fearful in the face of danger (Exod. 14:10-11)?
2. What lessons about faith can believers learn from Moses and the Israelites?
3. What can we learn from observing the strategy that God employed to deliver the children of Israel (vss. 17-18)?
4. Imagine you are one of the children of Israel at the Red Sea. How would you feel? What would you do?
5. Even if we never have an experience like Israel's at the Red Sea, how can we still see God's power at work in our lives?
6. How can God still be working on our behalf even when he allows us to suffer?
   —*Valante M. Grant.*

ILLUSTRATED HIGH POINTS

Better for us to serve the Egyptians

The Jews were not prepared to struggle for freedom. In contrast, the slaves who escaped captivity via the Underground Railroad understood it would be a treacherous journey. They would be leaving a roof over their heads and regular meals only to travel great distances with very little food and no protection. Their owners pursued them.

The saying, "Freedom Is Not Free" is engraved on the Korean War Veterans Memorial in Washington, D.C. It means someone has paid for our freedom. As believers, we know that our freedom from sin's bondage came at great price to Jesus Christ. However, although our freedom is already bought, the old slave masters (sin, the world, and the devil) will not let go easily. They will pursue with a vengeance. We must be strong, and we must never turn back.

Removed and went behind them

As a teen, Richard chose a path of crime. One day, after being pulled over, he told the officer, "You got me. Man, I've been running from the law for six years. I'm tired of running."

In jail, God began to lead Richard to Himself. The young man started praying, reading the Bible, and finding hope. His journey forward had begun, but (like Pharaoh's army) the bondage of his past was chasing him hard and fast.

Sentenced to prison, he asked his mother to pray. Two days later he was released. He knew it was God! Still the past was chasing him, and he soon succumbed to the temptation to indulge in his old drug habit. Then at church, Richard went down to the altar and prayed, and God delivered him.

God had been leading Richard, but He also fought his past.
   —*Therese Greenberg.*

Golden Text Illuminated

"And Moses stretched out his hand over the sea; and the Lord caused the sea to go back by a strong east wind all that night, and made the sea dry land, and the waters were divided" (Exodus 14:21).

One of the great Bible texts that reveals God's passion for His own glory is Isaiah 48:9-11: "For my name's sake will I defer mine anger, and for my praise will I refrain for thee, that I cut thee not off. Behold, I have refined thee, but not with silver; I have chosen thee in the furnace of affliction. For mine own sake, even for mine own sake, will I do it: for how should my name be polluted? and I will not give my glory unto another."

God's ultimate purpose is to proclaim His glory to His creation. No one is more passionate regarding this purpose than God Himself. God created us for His glory (Isa. 43:6-7). God called Israel for His glory (Isa. 49:3; Jer. 13:11). God raised up Pharaoh to demonstrate His power and bring glory to His name (Rom. 9:17). God delivered Israel from Egyptian bondage to glorify His name (Ps. 106:7-8). Everything that happens in God's providence ultimately results in His glory (Rom. 11:36).

As God fulfills His purpose of bringing glory to Himself, He sometimes uses miraculous acts that demonstrate His awesome power. In the New Testament era, God used signs and wonders to bring certain people to faith in Him (cf. Acts 4:29-30; 9:34-35, 40-42). As a result, many who were dead in trespasses and sins experienced deliverance from spiritual death, along with forgiveness and a life that never ends.

This week's golden text highlights God's miraculous act of dividing the Red Sea so that Israel could cross on dry land to the other side, thus finally escaping their Egyptian oppressors. As a result, God's people experienced complete and final deliverance, and God received all the glory and honor.

A commentary on Israel's crossing of the Red Sea is found in Psalm 106:7-9. These verses highlight Israel's need for changed hearts, emphasizing their sinful rebellion and lack of understanding of what God was doing in their lives. God's people neither understood nor remembered His wonders and kindnesses toward them in Egypt. Instead, they rebelled against Him as He was about to finally deliver them from bondage.

The psalmist reveals that God overlooked the rebellion of His people and delivered them "for his name's sake, that he might make his mighty power to be known" (vs. 8). God led His people to safety through a dry abyss as the waters parted and made a way of escape possible.

The golden text states that Moses obediently lifted the rod in his hand (cf. Exod. 14:16), and the Lord divided the waters of the Red Sea. The Lord also used a "a strong east wind" to completely separate the waters of the Red Sea. As a result, God delivered His people, thus glorifying His name and making His power known to all.

Do you have a sense that God is using you to bring glory to His marvelous name? If so, continue to make yourself available to Him as His servant. If not, would you repent and humbly offer yourself to the Lord in obedient service? I promise that you will never regret it.

—*Thomas R. Chmura.*

Heart of the Lesson

Freedom from oppression does not come easy. If we were being held captive and were able to escape, most oppressors would still chase us. They would not let us go without a fight. When the Egyptians realized that the Israelites had fled Egypt, they decided to pursue them.

1. The Israelites cry out (Exod. 14:10-12). Just when the Israelites thought they were free, they saw the Egyptian army pursuing them. Fear and despair had to have gripped their souls. Have you ever been there? Have you ever thought you were finally free of a situation, only to have it show up again unexpectedly? The Israelites knew all about the strength of Pharaoh's army. They must have felt doomed. They would have rather remained slaves in Egypt than ended up dead in the desert.

Even though those moments of despair are difficult, we must trust God's care and power on our behalf. In their despair, the Israelites blamed God for their predicament. When the enemy is breathing down our necks and the uncertainty of the future threatens to melt our resolve, this is the moment that we need to remember that God is all-powerful and cares about us personally. Regardless of how things feel, regardless of how things look, God is in control.

2. You will not see your enemies again (Exod. 14:13-18). Moses told the fearful and grumbling people, "Fear ye not, stand still, and see the salvation of the Lord, which he will shew to you to day: for the Egyptians whom ye have seen to day, ye shall see them again no more for ever" (vs. 13). Moses wanted the people to be quiet and watch God fight for them. Then God told Moses to position the people on the shore of the Red Sea.

God was fighting for His people. The enemies they saw, they would never see again. But how often do we flail and panic when we should stand still and be quiet, trusting in our Lord? It is important to always trust the Lord for wisdom and direction. Once again, God gave Moses specific instructions that would result in a favorable outcome for the Israelites.

3. Crossing the Red Sea (Exod. 14:19-22). As we have studied the deliverance of the Israelites, we have seen that God has continued to work dramatically on their behalf. He has not kept silent but has displayed His power and glory for all to see. But now His people are seemingly trapped, with the sea before them and the Egyptians pursuing them.

Once again God undeniably fights on behalf of His people. The cloud that had been leading the people forward moved behind the Israelites, creating a protective wall between them and the Egyptians. The cloud created darkness for the Egyptians but gave light to the Israelites. The Egyptians did not try to pursue God's people. Then Moses did as the Lord had commanded. He stretched out his hand over the sea. "And the children of Israel went into the midst of the sea upon the dry ground: and the waters were a wall unto them on their right hand, and on their left" (vs. 22).

The Israelites thought the Lord was leading them to their death when the Egyptians pursued. They believed their time as free people was over, but in fact, their journey was just beginning. God was leading them to a place where they would never have to fear the Egyptians again.

—*Kristin Reeg.*

World Missions

Did great acts of God only happen back in early Bible times? Why does God not do something great in our day to show the world who He is? Why does He not go into every corner of darkness and emblazon it with light? Does He not care about those who have never heard?

He does, very much. Perhaps the problem is not upward, but outward—right here where we are. What if God did make a wondrous master plan to reach the world with His marvelous gift of salvation? What if He gave full instructions on how to carry out that plan with the promise to supply all the resources needed?

What if the master plan was us?

We have been assigned by Jesus Christ, the One who died for us, to take His message into all the world (Mark 16:15). God has enough servants to reach around the globe, and He promises to supply all their needs according to His riches, which are endless (Phil. 4:19).

Why, then, is the whole world not reached?

Ron Barnes Jr., director of Source of Light International, wrote in the Summer 2017 edition of *The Reaper* that he was on a college campus recently when he was taken ill. "I feel miserable, and someone is to blame. At some point, I came into contact with someone who couldn't help but 'share' the bug . . . the flu is infectious. . . . The Gospel is even more infectious and I dare say has been proven to spread even more quickly than any virus. But someone has to carry it . . . it won't spread without a carrier, a preacher.

"And imagine if Christians around the globe would just be the preacher that the rest of the world needs instead of 'hiding it under a bushel,' how quickly the Gospel could spread. The solution to the Great Commission doesn't lie in those few faithful full-time missionaries and pastors around the globe, but in great commission laborers addressing the problem of laboring in the part of the world God has provided for them. In fact, I am of the persuasion that if believers would take on this responsibility we wouldn't need 'mission agencies.'"

The truth of the matter is that we love ourselves and our lives. No one naturally wants to take up a cross and follow a carpenter who says that if we want to save our lives, we have to give them up (Luke 9:24) or the God who asks us to offer ourselves as living sacrifices (Rom. 12:1).

Yet that is exactly what our Saviour and King demands of us. Few go. Few pray. Few give. Those who do are often looked at with pity by those who stand back from the commitment and the sacrifices required to make it. But as missionary martyr Nate Saint once said, "People who do not know the Lord ask why in the world we waste our lives as missionaries. They forget that they too are expending their lives . . . and when the bubble has burst they will have nothing of eternal significance to show for the years they have wasted."

He was speaking of unbelievers, but how many of God's people are the same way? How sad that so many Christians will end their lives having attained much in the way of success or wealth or perhaps even great achievement, but when it comes to eternity, their hands will be empty of anything that matters.

God does care about the lost of the world. He has made a way for them to hear. That way is through us.

—*Kimberly Rae.*

The Jewish Aspect

God miraculously opened the waters of the Red Sea so that Israel crossed in safety (Exod. 14:21-22). The KJV consistently translates the name of this body of water as "Red Sea." Sometimes, other sources refer to it as the "Sea of Reeds." This correlates with the view that the Jews did not actually cross the Red Sea proper, but some other smaller lake. No consensus exists on what that lake would be.

Jewish scholars at the turn of the twentieth century asserted that the term "Red Sea" referred to "the present Gulf of Suez, which at that time extended considerably farther north" ("Red Sea," www.jewishencyclopedia.com). Modern Jews are less certain. One source translates Exodus 10:19 as "Sea of Reeds," with this footnote: "Traditionally, but incorrectly, 'Red Sea'" (*The Jewish Study Bible,* Oxford). The Hebrew term for Red Sea is *yam suph*, and it occurs in around twenty-five references. The crossing is also referred to in numerous texts simply by the word "sea."

What evidence does the Old Testament give concerning this question of the specific body of water that was crossed? The term "Red Sea" was used in ancient times to refer to the actual Red Sea and also to its two arms, the Gulf of Suez and the Gulf of Aqaba.

The first time "Red Sea" occurs is in Exodus 10:19 where, after the plague of locusts, God cast all these insects into the water. The locust plague devoured every green tree and plant in all of Egypt (vs. 15). The cultivated land of Egypt stretched alongside the Nile River for three hundred miles from the Mediterranean southward. The "west wind" (vs. 19) God sent to blow them into the Red Sea, therefore, had to remove millions of locusts. And only the actual Red Sea could have been involved, since only it parallels that great distance.

Numbers 33:8-11 records that the Jews camped alongside the same Red Sea they had crossed miraculously five days earlier. This shows that the Red Sea was long enough to parallel five days of journeying. This indicates that the Jews crossed the Gulf of Suez, then journeyed south along its side. Israel crossing a small lake in Egypt seems at odds with the biblical record.

The name Red Sea also applied to the Gulf of Aqaba. For example, Solomon built a fleet of ships at Ezion-geber, "on the shore of the Red sea, in the land of Edom" (I Kings 9:26). Ezion-geber is located on the northern tip of the Gulf of Aqaba.

Other ancient writers confirm that the term Red Sea could apply to today's Red Sea or its two arms. The Greek historian Herodotus (485-425 B.C.) wrote that Pharaoh Neco (or Necho) II tried to build a canal to connect the Mediterranean with the Gulf of Suez, the Red Sea (*The Persian Wars* 2.158). The Greek geographer Strabo (64 B.C.-A.D. 24) specifically stated that the Red Sea had two heads, what we call the Gulf of Suez and the Gulf of Aqaba (*The Geography of Strabo* 16.2.30).

The Greek translation of the Old Testament (the Septuagint), carried out by Jews living in Alexandria, Egypt, clearly translated *yam suph* with the Greek words for "Red Sea" (*eruthre thalassa*). Josephus likewise identified the Gulf of Aqaba, the Red Sea, as being where Ezion-geber was located (*Antiquities of the Jews* 8.6.4).

The Jews actually crossed the western arm of the Red Sea, known as the Gulf of Suez. God miraculously delivered His people.

—R. Larry Overstreet.

Guiding the Superintendent

Israel had spent only a few days in the wilderness and already they had forgotten God's miraculous deliverance from their horrible slavery experience. They panicked. How soon one forgets the past!

God loves to work in hopeless situations. Quite near the start of their journey, God ordered the nation to turn toward the sea (Exod. 14:2). The ex-slave nation was caught between the sea and an attacking army.

DEVOTIONAL OUTLINE

1. Israel miscalculates God's plan (Exod. 14:10-14). The sight of Pharaoh's chariots struck fear into Israel.

Like many people in stressful situations, the nation reacted very irrationally. They forgot that God had just recently delivered them. Instead of trusting their Deliverer they turned on Moses and blamed him for their current situation. They claimed they had never wanted to leave Egypt and preferred servitude in Egypt to death in the desert.

Moses remained calm and told the people not to fear. He told them that the Lord was about to deliver them. Never again would they see the Egyptians.

2. Pharaoh miscalculates God's plan (Exod. 14:15-22). God had never intended for Israel to die in the desert. They had completely misread God's plan. Pharaoh did not think that God had a plan and thought that Israel was trapped and he could destroy them.

God told Moses to raise his staff and stretch out his hand over the waters to divide them; God would give Israel a way through the sea. Every step of God's plan was purposeful; God would be glorified before the Egyptians (vss. 17-18).

The Angel of God (the pillar of cloud) then moved from the front of the Israelites to the rear and protected them from Pharaoh's army. As night fell, it gave light to Israel but enveloped the Egyptians in darkness. The nation of former slaves then moved through the parted waters with the Egyptians still in confusion.

CHILDREN'S CORNER

text: **John 4:5-14, 25-26**
title: **A Samaritan Woman's Faith**

It was seemingly only a chance encounter that day that changed the Samaritan woman's life forever. She had gone to get water, no doubt a daily ritual. However, she left with living water that would last forever.

Jesus was the master of using the ordinary to explain the supernatural. In His encounter with the woman from Samaria, He used the concepts of water and thirst to teach her that He is the Messiah.

Jesus sat down by an ancient well, and a woman from the village approached. Jesus asked her a question: Could you give Me a drink of water?

She was quick to respond with her own, racially loaded, question: Why would a Jew ever ask a Samaritan for a drink? He told her that if she really knew who she was talking to, she would ask for God's gift of living water.

Still thinking in terms of the physical, she inquired about how He, with no bucket or jug, would be able to give her any water at all.

Jesus returned to the subject of living water and encouraged her to drink of the water that would cause her to never be thirsty again. From there the conversation led to Jesus' disclosure that she was talking to none other than the Messiah: "I that speak unto thee am he" (vs. 26).

Here is a great example of Jesus' patience and persistence in helping people come to faith in Him.

—Martin R. Dahlquist.

SCRIPTURE LESSON TEXT

EXOD. 14:23 And the Egyptians pursued, and went in after them to the midst of the sea, *even* all Pharaoh's horses, his chariots, and his horsemen.

24 And it came to pass, that in the morning watch the LORD looked unto the host of the Egyptians through the pillar of fire and of the cloud, and troubled the host of the Egyptians,

25 And took off their chariot wheels, that they drave them heavily: so that the Egyptians said, Let us flee from the face of Israel; for the LORD fighteth for them against the Egyptians.

26 And the LORD said unto Moses, Stretch out thine hand over the sea, that the waters may come again upon the Egyptians, upon their chariots, and upon their horsemen.

27 And Moses stretched forth his hand over the sea, and the sea returned to his strength when the morning appeared; and the Egyptians fled against it; and the LORD overthrew the Egyptians in the midst of the sea.

28 And the waters returned, and covered the chariots, and the horsemen, *and* all the host of Pharaoh that came into the sea after them; there remained not so much as one of them.

29 But the children of Israel walked upon dry *land* in the midst of the sea; and the waters *were* a wall unto them on their right hand, and on their left.

30 Thus the LORD saved Israel that day out of the hand of the Egyptians; and Israel saw the Egyptians dead upon the sea shore.

31 And Israel saw that great work which the Lord did upon the Egyptians: and the people feared the LORD, and believed the LORD, and his servant Moses.

NOTES

172

Deliverance from Pharaoh's Army

Lesson Text: Exodus 14:23-31

Related Scriptures: Psalms 78:51-54; 106:10-12;
Joshua 3:14-17; 4:18-24

TIME: 1445 B.C.   PLACE: Red Sea

GOLDEN TEXT—"Thus the Lord saved Israel that day out of the hand of the Egyptians; and Israel saw the Egyptians dead upon the sea shore" (Exodus 14:30).

Introduction

The Old Testament records much destruction, warfare, and violent death. Such, sadly, is the norm for human society in every age. Human sin, which began with Adam and Eve, guarantees that such horrors will continue till the Lord Jesus returns to this earth.

Yet we must acknowledge that the Lord Himself brought about death and destruction as well. Unlike most human violence, however, the divine judgments of the Lord are wholly just.

While God's wrath is often seen in Scripture, thankfully also is His grace. While wrath rests upon those who reject Christ (John 3:36), through Jesus

Christ, God has provided the means of escaping divine wrath (Rom. 5:9).

The destruction of the Egyptian army was an act of divine judgment. For the Hebrews who witnessed it, it was also a demonstration of God's power and glory.

LESSON OUTLINE

I. THE EGYPTIANS' PURSUIT—
Exod. 14:23

II. THE EGYPTIANS' DEMISE—
Exod. 14:24-29

III. THE LORD'S GLORY—
Exod. 14:30-31

Exposition: Verse by Verse

THE EGYPTIANS' PURSUIT

EXOD. 14:23 And the Egyptians pursued, and went in after them to the midst of the sea, even all Pharaoh's horses, his chariots, and his horsemen.

The Lord had miraculously parted the waters of the sea and dried the exposed seabed, creating a wide channel through the very midst of the sea. The Israelites, who had been trapped between the sea and the Egyptian force, were given a way of escape, and throughout the night they made their way through the sea to the other side.

The Egyptians had been held back by the pillar of cloud, unable to approach the fleeing Israelites (Exod. 14:19-20). At some point in the early morning hours, however, it appears the pillar moved from its place and allowed the Egyptians to move toward the sea. Israel had been on the move all night and by now all were either safely to the other side or nearly there.

With the hindrance to their advance removed, the Egyptians pursued the Israelites into the midst of the Red Sea. One would think they might stop to consider the miracle that stood before them in the form of the walls of water bordering the path through the sea and be hesitant to continue their pursuit. But it appears they simply plowed ahead, determined to carry out Pharaoh's orders.

Perhaps seeing the path the Israelites had taken, the Egyptians decided they could surely follow the same trail. However, we know that ultimately the Lord was leading them to their destruction in the sea, and He hardened their hearts to assure that would happen (vs. 17).

THE EGYPTIANS' DEMISE

24 And it came to pass, that in the morning watch the Lord looked unto the host of the Egyptians through the pillar of fire and of the cloud, and troubled the host of the Egyptians,

25 And took off their chariot wheels, that they drave them heavily: so that the Egyptians said, Let us flee from the face of Israel; for the Lord fighteth for them against the Egyptians.

26 And the Lord said unto Moses, Stretch out thine hand over the sea, that the waters may come again upon the Egyptians, upon their chariots, and upon their horsemen.

27 And Moses stretched forth his hand over the sea, and the sea returned to his strength when the morning appeared; and the Egyptians fled against it; and the Lord overthrew the Egyptians in the midst of the sea.

28 And the waters returned, and covered the chariots, and the horsemen, and all the host of Pharaoh that came into the sea after them; there remained not so much as one of them.

29 But the children of Israel walked upon dry land in the midst of the sea; and the waters were a wall unto them on their right hand, and on their left.

The Lord confuses the army (Exod. 14:24-25). The Egyptian chariot army entered the road through the sea sometime during the morning watch. The morning watch was from about three o' clock to six o' clock. It was also during this time that the Lord took action against the Egyptian force.

With the Egyptians already in the midst of the sea, the Lord looked down upon them from the vantage point of the pillar of fire and cloud (cf. vs. 24). Again, God's visible presence is associated with the pillar (cf. vs. 19). The Lord was still present, overseeing the Israelites' flight through the sea and at the same time luring the Egyptians to their doom.

The Lord then "troubled" (vs. 24) the Egyptians. The Hebrew word here means to harass or throw into confusion. It is used in Joshua 10:10 and Judges 4:15 of the panic of an army that is overwhelmed on the battlefield.

Specifically, the trouble involved the failure of the Egyptian chariots (Exod. 14:25). The Hebrew expression "took off their chariot wheels" can mean either to cause to swerve or to be removed. They apparently lost control of their chariots, which may well have caused them to lose their wheels. The obvious result was great difficulty in driving them. As we learn from Psalm 77:17-19, there was a sudden rainstorm that also might have made the ground below them muddy, causing further difficulty for the chariots.

There were probably two purposes for this divine work. First, the trouble experienced by the Egyptian chariot drivers prevented them from catching up to the Israelites before they all had emerged safely from the seabed to the other side. Second, as the text indicates, it made the panicked Egyptians realize that the all-powerful Lord was once again fighting against them on behalf of Israel.

Moses had assured the people, "The Lord shall fight for you" (Exod. 14:14). That was now apparent even to the Egyptian soldiers. "God's purpose of revealing himself not merely to Israel but to Egypt as well had in fact been accomplished. The army, all of whom had experienced the plagues, now knew who Yahweh [The Lord] was, even if prior to the plagues his name would have meant nothing to them" (Stuart, *New American Commentary: Exodus,* Holman).

The Egyptians saw no hope at this point. They decided to flee, but their way back to shore would soon disappear.

The Lord addresses Moses (Exod. 14:26-27a). By this time, all the Israelites had arrived on the other side of the sea. While the Egyptians down in the sea were in complete confusion and unable to continue the pursuit, the Lord spoke to Moses. He told Moses to again stretch out his hand over the sea. This, He said, would return the divided waters to their original place, bringing them down upon the Egyptians and their chariots. The miracle enacted when Moses first stretched out his staff over the sea to deliver Israel would be reversed, drowning the Egyptians.

Moses followed the Lord's command, and as the Lord had promised, the walls of water collapsed upon the Egyptian army as the sea returned to its normal state. This occurred in the early morning light so that the Israelites could clearly see the Lord's victory.

The Lord destroys the army (Exod. 14:27b-29). The Egyptians saw the water collapsing upon them and instinctively sought to flee, but there was no place to go. They were far from the shore in the middle of the sea with no hope of escape.

The text says, "The Lord overthrew the Egyptians" (vs. 27). Though Moses had a prominent role, it was clear to all that the Lord was the one responsible for the destruction of Egypt's chariot force.

Not one of the men, chariots, or horses of Pharaoh that entered the sea survived the onslaught of the waters. The complete annihilation of an elite chariot force was a devastating blow to Egypt. However, there is no indication this incident destroyed the entire Egyptian army, leaving the empire defenseless. Historical records do not support this assumption.

Of course, the historical records of Egypt make no mention of this incident. This was typical of ancient pagan nations, however, and "the Egyptians were the last people to record their misfortunes" (Unger, *Archeology and the Old Testament*, Zondervan). Their records proclaim the glories of their kings and conquests but never mention their defeats.

Another issue related to the loss of the Egyptian army concerns the pharaoh. Did he die along with his army? Many cite Psalm 136:15 as evidence that he did die in the sea with his soldiers. However, the wording there does not clearly state that Pharaoh drowned with his army, and Exodus 14:28 does not mention him at all among those killed in the sea. In fact, the last time Pharaoh is mentioned as being present is in verse 10. The text does not say he accompanied his chariot army into the sea.

The importance of this question becomes evident when we consider the biblical dating of this event. While a complicated issue, certain chronological markers in the Bible (cf. Exod. 12:40; I Kings 6:1) indicate the Exodus occurred around 1445 B.C. Comparing this to Egyptian history, we find that Amenhotep II would have been the pharaoh of the Exodus, and we know he did not die in the sea. In fact, "he lived twenty-two years after this, and his mummy has been found in the Valley of the Tombs of the Kings along with those of the many other Pharaohs buried there" (Wood, *A Survey of Israel's History,* Zondervan).

If this chronology is accurate—and it appears that it is—the pharaoh did not drown in the sea but lived to rule in Egypt, yet he had to have been greatly humbled trying to explain the loss of his army. His humiliation in losing his chariot force as well as the Hebrew slaves must have weighed on his mind till the day he died, for he could not deny the power of Israel's God and the impotence of the gods of Egypt, including himself. Truly the Lord gained honor through Pharaoh (Exod. 14:17) so that the Egyptians knew that He was the Lord (vs. 18).

Exodus 14:29, which follows the description of the destruction of the Egyptians, might appear to be saying that the Israelites were still in the sea when the Egyptians were drowned but were in an area where the water did not return to its place. However, the verse seems to merely give a summary statement that contrasts the fate of the Egyptians in the sea with the safe passage of the Israelites through the sea. It probably does not follow the previous verse chronologically.

We are reminded that the waters that engulfed and killed the Egyptian soldiers

had stood as walls on both sides of the Israelites, providing a way of escape for them. The sea was a means of deliverance as well as a means of judgment.

When there seems to be no way out of the trials of this life and the wicked seem to act without fear of judgment, we need to remember what happened at the sea so long ago. Our God is all-powerful. He can and will provide a way of escape, and He will enable us to bear up under the pressures we face as long as necessary (cf. I Cor. 10:13). And the judgment of the wicked is certain, even if the timing of that judgment is unknown.

THE LORD'S GLORY

30 Thus the Lord saved Israel that day out of the hand of the Egyptians; and Israel saw the Egyptians dead upon the sea shore.

31 And Israel saw that great work which the Lord did upon the Egyptians: and the people feared the Lord, and believed the Lord, and his servant Moses.

Another summary statement is given in Exodus 14:30: "The Lord saved Israel that day out of the hand of the Egyptians." Again, Moses emphasizes the fact that it was the Lord's work. Nothing Moses or his people could have done would have accomplished anything like what Israel saw that day. Indeed, apart from the Lord's intervention, they would have been doomed.

In the aftermath of the miracle, the people of Israel saw the bodies of the Egyptian soldiers on the seashore. "This is a very graphic touch, an eyewitness account. The drowned Egyptian soldiers stand for an old way of life in slavery, now gone forever. . . . the sight of those dead bodies was the concrete sign that salvation and a new life for Israel were now assured" (Cole, *Exodus: An Introduction and Commentary,* InterVarsity).

The ancient Jewish historian Josephus records the tradition that the sea also washed to shore the weapons of the Egyptians, which the Israelites then collected to arm themselves for future encounters (*Josephus: Complete Works,* Kregel). While this is not stated in the Bible, it may well have been the case.

All the people "saw that great work which the Lord did upon the Egyptians" (vs. 31). "Work" is literally "hand," which speaks figuratively of power. Israel saw God's deliverance, God's judgment of the ungodly, and a very clear demonstration of God's limitless power.

What the people saw, however, was not as important as what resulted from what they saw. As a result of witnessing the miraculous work of God, the people of Israel "feared the Lord, and believed the Lord, and his servant Moses" (vs. 31).

Fear of God goes hand in hand with faith and obedience (cf. Deut. 17:19; II Kings 17:36). Yes, it means respect and awe, but also fear of the consequences of disobedience. The Israelites had new respect for God and realized the need to be loyal to Him.

Having seen the Lord's work, they also believed in the Lord. They were willing to put their trust in Him and in His chosen servant Moses to lead them. Subsequent events would reveal how weak and unsettled their faith was, but they had made a definite break with their past and were now looking to the Lord to lead them.

It is significant that Moses is here called the Lord's "servant" (Exod. 14:31). "This is the highest title a mortal can have in the Old Testament—the servant of Yahweh. It signifies more than a believer; it describes the individual as acting on behalf of God" (Ross, *Studies in Exodus,* Christian Leadership Center).

God indeed received glory through the deliverance at the Red Sea. But that would not have happened if He had not first led His people into a seemingly dangerous place, trapped between the mighty Egyptian army and the imposing and impassable sea.

Like the ancient people of Israel, we are often quick to complain about our circumstances, our leaders, and even God. Yet our purpose in life is to bring glory to God (cf. I Cor. 10:31). In order that He might receive great glory, God often leads us into very uncomfortable situations—situations in which He alone can sustain and use us and from which He alone can deliver us. Rather than complain about our circumstances, let us be grateful for the unique opportunities to serve and honor Him.

—*Jarl K. Waggoner.*

QUESTIONS

1. What permitted the Egyptians to pursue the Israelites into the sea?
2. How did the Lord trouble the Egyptians, and why did He do it?
3. What instruction did the Lord give to Moses?
4. What happened to the Egyptian army, and who was responsible for it?
5. Why do Egyptian historical records not mention this event?
6. What evidence is there that Pharaoh did not die in the sea?
7. How did the author contrast the fate of the Egyptians with that of the Israelites?
8. What did the Israelites see in the aftermath of the miraculous destruction of the Egyptians?
9. What effect did witnessing the miracle have on the Israelites?
10. What title is given to Moses here?

—*Jarl K. Waggoner.*

Preparing to Teach the Lesson

In Victor Hugo's classic novel *Les Miserables,* the protagonist Jean Valjean, an escaped convict who has become the wealthy, respected mayor of his small town, is fanatically pursued by Inspector Javert, who is obsessed with Valjean's recapture.

The story reaches its climax when Javert finds himself at the mercy of Valjean. Valjean spares Javert's life and helps him to safety. Having experienced such powerful evidence of Valjean's undeniable reformation and goodness, Javert's sense of justice will allow him neither to arrest Valjean nor live with himself; he realizes he has all along been persecuting a profoundly good-hearted man. In despair, Javert takes his own life.

Like Javert, Pharaoh obsessively pursued God's beloved covenant people to his own ultimate destruction by the same sea that had allowed the Israelites to escape from him.

TODAY'S AIM

Facts: to see that the Lord miraculously delivered His people by parting the waters of the Red Sea and then destroying the Egyptian army by closing the waters while they were stranded in the midst of the sea.

Principle: to realize that often the Lord's blessings to His people mean destruction for their enemies.

Application: to remember that the same gospel that saves those of us who believe in the Lord Jesus Christ is a message of destruction for those who reject His salvation.

INTRODUCING THE LESSON

Last week's lesson showed us how God miraculously divided the Red Sea and stood in the breach between His people and Pharaoh's army, allowing His covenant people to escape to safety. Our lesson today tells the rest of the story.

DEVELOPING THE LESSON

1. An unwise pursuit (Exod. 14:23-28). Our text does not mention it, but the Shekinah pillar must have moved aside to allow the Egyptian army to pursue the Hebrews, since its presence had kept the them at bay throughout the previous night.

Recognizing their opportunity and seeing that the Israelites were escaping into the midst of the sea, the Egyptians pursued them. But the Lord had terrors in store for the Egyptians that they could not have foreseen. The text tells us that in the morning watch (just before dawn), the Lord looked upon the army from the pillar and "troubled" them (vs. 24). The writer of Psalm 77 describes in more detail just what sort of trouble the Lord visited on them. It included heavy rain, thunder, lightning, and even earthquakes (cf. vss. 17-18).

Exodus 14:25 tells us that the Lord even took the wheels off their chariots! What a horrific predicament the Egyptians suddenly found themselves in! Surrounded by torrents of rain, lightning, thunder, and earthquakes, they called to each other in abject terror, "Let us flee!" But there was no way to flee, since their chariots no longer had wheels! And things were about to get much, much worse!

The ominous tone of verse 26 is palpable: "And the Lord said unto Moses." Never had these words been more portentous than now. By the simple act of stretching forth his hand, Moses would destroy the entire Egyptian army! Now the full meaning of the Lord's words to him in Exodus 7:1 became clear: "And the Lord said unto Moses, See, I have made thee a god to Pharaoh." Surely, Moses never appeared more godlike to Pharaoh than at this moment.

Verse 28 reports that their destruction was both swift and complete; not even one Egyptian survived the collapse and inundation caused by the motion of Moses' hand. Adam Clarke adds, "Josephus says that the army of Pharaoh consisted of *fifty thousand* horse, and *two hundred thousand* foot, of whom not one remained to carry tidings of this most extraordinary catastrophe" (*Commentary on the Bible*, Abingdon).

2. An object lesson (Exod. 14:29-31). And so, the great historic spectacle of the Lord's contention with the world's most powerful empire was complete. It was unambiguous to anyone who witnessed it that even the full might of Egypt was no match for the Israelites' God, Yahweh.

In the light of that new day, the people gazed in astonishment upon the grisly aftermath of Egypt's devastating defeat. A multitude of drowned and ruined bodies of both men and horses either lay washed up on the seashore or maybe even floated on its surface, with still more invisible beneath the waves. Clarke observes, "By their spoils the Israelites were probably furnished with *considerable riches,* and especially *clothing and arms;* which latter were essentially necessary to them in their wars."

In verse 31, we are told that the Israelites saw, feared, and believed. If there were any doubters among them before this event, there remained none after. Later, in Joshua 2:9-11, the harlot Rahab testifies that she knew that the Lord had given Israel the land because all Jericho and the surrounding lands had heard of the Lord's miraculous deliverance, "Our hearts did melt, neither did there remain any more courage in any man, because of you: for the Lord your God, he is God in heaven above, and in earth beneath."

ILLUSTRATING THE LESSON

The illustration shows that the Lord overthrew the Egyptian army by drowning them in the same sea that the Israelites had safely crossed.

THE LORD OVERTHROWS THE EGYPTIANS

Moses

Safely crossed Israelites

Pharaoh's Army Pursues

Pharaoh's Army Drowned

CONCLUDING THE LESSON

Like the parted waters of the Red Sea in this week's lesson, the gospel of Jesus Christ is both the way to salvation and abundant life for those who trust Him as Lord and Saviour, but the savor of wrath, death, and destruction for those who reject His gracious offer (cf. II Cor. 2:15-16).

ANTICIPATING THE NEXT LESSON

Next week we begin a new quarter of lessons on discipleship. The first unit of next quarter is titled "Prelude to Discipleship." Next week's lesson text is Luke 1:26-38; it focuses on the prophecy of Jesus' birth announced to Mary by the Archangel Gabriel.

—*John M. Lody.*

PRACTICAL POINTS

1. God has the power to reverse any situation to His children's favor (Exod. 14:23-24).
2. When God is working on your behalf, even your enemies will recognize His power (vs. 25).
3. The spectacular miracle at the Red Sea is heartening, but God's quiet work on our behalf is perhaps even more important to trust in (vss. 26-27).
4. God can turn our impossible situations into total victory (vss. 28-29).
5. God's awesome power reveals that He is worthy to be praised (vss. 30-31).

—*Valante M. Grant.*

RESEARCH AND DISCUSSION

1. What is the result of looking back at your enemies instead of looking forward in the direction that God is leading you?
2. What are some reasons why believers today forget God's faithfulness?
3. Could Moses take any credit for what God commanded him to do? How should believers view God's power and their actions (cf. Eccles. 5:2; Rom. 8:28)?
4. Is fear always bad? What examples of good fear and bad fear do we see in Exodus 14?
5. The Israelites should have remembered the Red Sea crossing for generations. Why had they forgotten this miracle just days later (chap. 16)?

—*Valante M. Grant.*

ILLUSTRATED HIGH POINTS

The Lord fighteth for them

Rose, a border collie, was born to protect sheep. Living in upstate New York, she had battled a few blizzards while guarding her charges, but this storm was like no other. Helplessly cut off from the barn by giant snowdrifts, the sheep would starve. Rose could hear their bleating, but she could no longer see them.

The faithful dog began digging into the half-frozen mounds. Over and over, the farmer could see her head rise for air only to dive in again. To his delight, after several hours, one sheep came back through the opening Rose had forged, then another, and then the entire flock.

We are like mere sheep, yet our Saviour fights tirelessly for us. He even laid down His life to make a way for us to get back to the Father's care.

The waters were a wall unto them

The aerial photo of Pam and Warren Adams's home is almost unbelievable. The coastal town of Gilchrist, Texas, held roughly two hundred homes, but after being blasted by 2008's Hurricane Ike, only a single yellow home was left standing tall amid absolute devastation.

The Adamses had owned an older home in Gilchrest (constructed to an earlier building code) that was destroyed three years earlier by Hurricane Rita. They determined to take greater precautions when they rebuilt. Adams decided to support the house on a foundation of fourteen-foot columns, bringing the home far above any other home on the peninsula.

The judgment of God will come suddenly like a flood. If our lives are built on a faulty foundation, they will be leveled. But if we have Christ as our foundation, we will stand unscathed.

—*Therese Greenberg.*

Golden Text Illuminated

"Thus the Lord saved Israel that day out of the hand of the Egyptians; and Israel saw the Egyptians dead upon the sea shore" (Exodus 14:30).

As we bring this quarter's lessons to a close, the ultimate fulfillment of God's accomplished deliverance of His people from cruel bondage is brought fully before our view. Specifically, we will concentrate our thoughts on God's final deliverance of Israel from Pharaoh's army and the complete destruction of that mighty force.

As we ponder this week's golden text, which declares that God delivered His people from the cruelty and control of the Egyptians, let us consider the psalmist's commentary on God's deliverance. Psalm 106 concentrates on Pharaoh's attitude toward God's people. As the singular, godlike authority of the Egyptians, Pharaoh utterly hated the Israelites (vs. 10), and his hatred prompted him to pursue them with vengeful rage.

Pharaoh had previously used and abused God's people to his imperialistic and financial advantage. His irrational hatred of the Israelites seems to have been especially inflamed by Moses and Aaron's demands as representatives of the one true, living God. These demands struck at the very core of Pharaoh's sinful heart. They also led straight to the destruction of his legacy—through the death of his firstborn son.

The plague of death that took every firstborn Egyptian son was devastating to the nation's morale, stability, and status as an economic and cultural superpower. It did not, however, immediately affect the Egyptians' military strength. To accomplish the final deliverance of His people, God would strike a demoralizing and devastating blow to Pharaoh's mighty army.

As the Israelites made their way through the midst of the Red Sea's separated waters, Pharaoh's rage appears to have escalated to total irrationality. It can only have been at his order that his army pursued the Israelites into the midst of the parted sea (Exod. 14:23). It was a suicidal mission. As Pharaoh's horses and chariots and horsemen went after Israel, God threw them into confusion and chaos (vs. 24). Finally, but too late, the military commanders sounded the rational decision to retreat (vs. 25).

God then directed Moses to once again stretch out his hand over the Red Sea (vs. 26). Moses obeyed God's command, and the Red Sea's parted waters overwhelmed Pharaoh's entire army (vs. 28). The entire Israelite nation, however, had made it through the sea on completely dry ground.

This week's golden text tersely comments on the carnage of God's judgment upon Pharaoh's army. The Israelites were given visual confirmation that the Lord had indeed annihilated their cruel oppressors.

The Apostle Paul commands believers to rely on God's almighty power as they battle against the devil's cunning and deceitful plans to destroy their lives and testimony for Christ (Eph. 6:10-11). Although Satan's evil schemes often seem overwhelming, God is well able to throw those schemes into confusion. As God's people achieve spiritual victory and deliverance over their adversary, they will ultimately see the death of Satan's attacks. Praise the Lord!

—*Thomas R. Chmura.*

Heart of the Lesson

We live in a society of speed. We can use a microwave oven and cook dinner in almost no time. We can go through a drive-thru and have a complete meal handed to us in minutes. We can search on Google and within a few seconds obtain answers to questions we may have wondered about all our lives. But often the most important things in life do not happen quickly. They are not so easy, and in many cases they are costly, as many have lost their lives fighting for them. In our lesson for today, the Israelites' freedom cost Egypt an entire army.

1. The Egyptians pursue (Exod. 14:23-25). When the Egyptian army saw that the Israelites were crossing the Red Sea, they decided to pursue them. They saw the water parted and a passage of dry ground; so they tried to cross the sea as well. The Egyptians still did not seem to realize that God was working only on the behalf of the Israelites to bring them out of Egypt and into their Promised Land. God threw the Egyptian army into confusion and caused the wheels of their chariots to fall off. While the Israelites crossed the sea in safety, the Egyptian army was stranded in no-man's-land.

2. The waters flow (Exod. 14:26-28). Then the Lord spoke to Moses and commanded him to stretch his hand out over the water again. This time the water began to close in on the dry passage that had been cleared by the Lord for His people. The Egyptians were inundated with tons of water. "And the waters returned, and covered the chariots, and the horsemen, and all the host of Pharaoh that came into the sea after them; there remained not so much as one of them" (vs. 28).

No one from Pharaoh's army survived the walls of water crashing back down. The Lord had completely annihilated the Egyptians. The Israelites would no longer have to worry about the Egyptians pursuing them ever again. Moses' words to the Israelites had been true; the enemies they had seen that day would never be seen again. The Lord glorified Himself among the Egyptians.

3. The mighty hand of the Lord (Exod. 14:29-31). Even though the waters came down on the Egyptians, the entire company of the Israelites safely crossed the Red Sea on dry ground. The water had created a wall to the right and to the left of them. The Lord saved Israel that day. They were free!

"And Israel saw that great work which the Lord did upon the Egyptians: and the people feared the Lord, and believed the Lord, and his servant Moses" (vs. 31). It is interesting to note that even after all the plagues that the Lord had sent upon Egypt, it was not until after the Israelites crossed the Red Sea that the people really believed.

What are you going through right now? What have you been crying out to the Lord for deliverance from? What act of God will it take for you to trust Him? Do you believe that God is still mighty enough to save you? Do you believe that He can deliver you?

The God who pushed back the sea and dried the ground for the Israelites to cross over is the same God who sent His Son to die on a cross to pay for your sins. Our God has not stopped fighting for His people. God is no respecter of persons. He still glorifies Himself on behalf of anyone who loves Him and trusts Him!

—*Kristin Reeg.*

World Missions

God-sized victories are not just for the Old Testament. God is still just as much at work today as ever. Reports coming in from all over the globe bring good news.

One ministry with interactive websites receives visits from millions of people in nearly every country on earth—on average more than two hundred per hour! This one ministry's indicated decisions for Christ have almost reached ten million.

One ministry to persecuted believers and the lost will operate over 1,400 projects this year.

Another group that seeks to set the captives free rescues an average of 150 victims of human trafficking each month.

The shoebox ministry has directly impacted over 135 million children. Families have been saved and churches planted. Over 7 million children have become part of a follow-up discipleship program.

As David says in Psalm 126:3, the Lord has done great things, and we are glad!

But there is sad news as well. Though there are 900 churches for every unreached people group of the world and 78,000 evangelical Christians for every unreached people group, nearly half the world is still considered unreached. Of the over 4 million full-time Christian workers, more than the majority are within the Christian world. In fact, that number is a staggering 95 percent (thetravelingteam.org/stats).

Why are we so afraid to go? We know God is at work. We know He promises to be with us (Heb. 13:5), to provide for us (Phil. 4:19), and to keep us held in His everlasting arms (Deut. 33:27).

What was true for the Israelites is true for us: if we follow Him, He may indeed lead us to fearful places. At any point along the story, had the Israelites stopped, backed out, or decided to not obey, they would have remained in the miserable "safety" of slavery, bitterly remembering how God let them down. However, because they went, even though all seemed lost, God "led them on safely, so that they feared not" (Ps. 78:53). When He shows Himself on behalf of His people, their enemies flee in terror, for "the Lord fighteth for them" (Exod. 14:25).

God loves us. If we truly believe that, we know that wherever and however He leads, He will take care of us. "Perfect love casteth out fear: because fear hath torment" (I John 4:18). Sometimes fear comes specifically because of something God has asked us to do. It might be beyond our qualifications or abilities or resources. It might require more of us than we want to give.

Yet God says he who fears is not made perfect in love. He knows we will fear and reassures us over and over in the Scriptures that we do not need to fear. The reason He says this is not because there is nothing to fear. Rather, it is because He is with us (Isa. 41:10) and loves us (I Pet. 5:7). If we can truly believe His love for us is perfect, we will not be afraid. He can take us to the fearful places and right through them—making protective walls out of the very water of our own Red Sea—and on to a great victory that builds our faith and glorifies His name.

Do we want that?

God is at work. He is doing great things. He wants us to be part of it. Today may we trust in His perfect love for us, so that when He directs, we may boldly say, "Yes!"

—*Kimberly Rae.*

The Jewish Aspect

God miraculously opened the waters of the Red Sea so that Israel crossed in safety (Exod. 14:21-22). Pharaoh's army, however, suffered a disastrous defeat: "The Lord overthrew the Egyptians in the midst of the sea. And the waters returned, and covered the chariots, and the horsemen, and all the host of Pharaoh that came into the sea after them; there remained not so much as one of them" (vss. 27-28).

The parting of the water of the Red Sea was not facilitated by any natural phenomena. The strong east wind was clearly supernatural (vs. 21). This is shown by the fact that it caused the water to rise in heaps on the right (south) and left (north) (vss. 22, 29). The waters of the Red Sea were not blown toward the west, the direction of the wind, but were divided as if by a knife.

After the waters divided, the bottom of the sea was not muddy but was "dry land," the Hebrew word stressing that it had no moisture in it. The water of the sea piled up, "stood upright as an heap," and "congealed" (15:8). All of this points to a supernatural event.

The number of Israelites involved in this crossing is a crucial matter. Moses records that there were six hundred thousand men taking part in the Exodus (12:37). To these must be added the women and children. That probably made the total number in excess of two million! For comparison, the current population of Houston is about 2.3 million.

This creates enormous difficulties with the pictures of the Exodus found in many children's Bible story books. They typically show a relatively narrow opening in the water and a long marching line of people, maybe ten or twenty abreast. Consider, however, that a "marching line of two million people, walking ten abreast with an average of five feet separating each rank, would be 190 miles long" (Wood, *A Survey of Israel's History,* Zondervan).

So after God's wind blew "all that night" (Exod. 14:21), at least two million people crossed the sea within a few hours of the night, during "the morning watch," about 3:00 to 6:00 A.M. (vs. 24). Instead of a narrow column of marching Israelities, it is more accurate to imagine them walking across one thousand abreast.

Allowing the people to have 5.28 feet of "personal space" would require an opening in the Red Sea of a full mile! With an average of five feet between each row of people, the distance from front to back would be about 10,000 feet, almost two miles. Since the Hebrews had flocks and herds with them, they probably did not march across in rigid military style. The width, therefore, must have been even greater than a mile to accommodate their large numbers.

The northern tip of the current Gulf of Suez, the Bay of Suez, is about five miles wide and from twenty to thirty feet deep. If the Israelites spread out over a mile wide, it would mean that the walls of water to their left and right were indeed held in place by the miraculous hand of God.

The great width of the sea opening would also account for the initial fearlessness of the Egyptian army in pursuing the Israelites. With such an inviting, dry, seabed before them, the fleeing Hebrews must have seemed like easy prey. God intervened again, however, and directed the waters to return to their normal place. When that occurred, the Egyptians drowned in the depths of the sea. The lesson is clear. When God directs His people, they are secure in His care.

—*R. Larry Overstreet.*

Guiding the Superintendent

What a difference a day can make! Israel was completely surrounded—mountains to the left and right, a vast body of water before them, and the attacking Egyptian army behind them. Their reaction was only too human: "They were sore afraid: and . . . cried out to the Lord" (Exod. 14:10). A day later, they stood on the other side of the water with the Egyptians totally destroyed in the sea. We are told that the Israelites then "feared the Lord, and believed the Lord" (vs. 31).

DEVOTIONAL OUTLINE

1. Destruction of the Egyptian army (Exod. 14:23-28). When the Israelites were faced with water in front and an army behind, the Lord told Moses to raise his arms and part the water for Israel. They went through on dry land (vss. 21-22).

The descendants of Abraham would soon watch as the same water that had been their means of deliverance became the means of destruction for their enemy.

Pharaoh's army mistook the parted waters for a window of opportunity. They quickly followed Israel into the seabed. Very early in the morning, however, the Lord threw the Egyptians into a panic. Psalm 77:17-18 tells us that there was heavy rain, thunder, and an earthquake that came from the Lord. The wheels of their chariots even came off. By the time the army realized that the Lord God of Israel was fighting against them, it was too late.

The Lord told Moses to stretch out his arms again. The parted waters now closed in on the army. The water that had so soon before delivered Israel destroyed Pharaoh's army.

2. Deliverance of Israel (Exod. 14:29-31). Having witnessed the great power of God, the Israelites again feared. The same word translated "sore afraid" in verse 10 is used in verse 31, but this time they feared the Lord. They believed and trusted God.

An impossible situation can easily produce fear. If one only sees the difficult circumstances, the result will be terror-filled fear. However, when one looks at the situation as part of God's plan, a new kind of fear will result. This is the type of fear that produces trust, belief, and wisdom.

CHILDREN'S CORNER

text: **Acts 16:19b, 22-34**
title: **A Jailer's Faith**

By occupation and perhaps by temperament, he was a cruel and mean individual. He was a Roman jailer stationed at Philippi. His job was simple; he was to keep Rome's prisoners confined and as uncomfortable as possible.

Unfounded charges landed Paul and Silas in this man's jail. He was ordered to keep the prisoners secure. At midnight, in spite of their horrible treatment, Paul and Silas started praying and singing praises to God.

Suddenly, a great earthquake flung all the doors of the jail open. Thinking that all the prisoners had escaped, the jailer took his sword to kill himself.

Paul was able to stop him with the assurance that not one prisoner had left. The jailer brought a light and immediately asked how he could be saved. The disciples told him to believe in the Lord Jesus Christ.

Like the Samaritan woman (lesson 12), here was a man who turned quickly from darkness to light. The proof of his salvation was the kind treatment he showed Paul and Silas. He brought them into his home and fed them both, celebrating his newfound salvation.

—*Martin R. Dahlquist.*

there are additional truths we have to keep in mind in order to avoid becoming discouraged as we wait for God to answer our prayers. The first thing to keep in mind is the truth that God is working out His plan. Our prayers must always be subject to His sovereignty.

Some of the things we are asking for require a great deal of groundwork and contingencies that God needs to work out. If we are praying, for example, for a loved one who is not walking with the Lord, just think of how many things God might have to arrange in order for that loved one to be drawn back to Christ.

God might cause that person to go through certain trials or experiences in order to soften their heart. He might send a certain person into their lives who will have just the right kind of influence. All of that takes time, wisdom, and foresight.

God may take a great deal of time to arrange everything into its perfect order to impact the person we are praying for. When we are between "ask and "receive" we must realize that God may take plenty of time to work out His plan in *His* way. Meanwhile we should continue to pray and believe with perseverance.

A second thing to keep in mind is that there is often a "school" of prayer. God has to teach us and prepare us to receive the answer to our prayers. That takes time too. God may have to draw us through certain experiences or cause us to understand certain passages of Scripture so that we have the proper mind-set to receive the answer He plans to give.

As we continue to pray, what might God be teaching us? How might He be preparing us? These are questions that we should ask as we look to the Lord to deliver us and answer our prayers. Perhaps this will help us to continue to persevere faithfully in prayer as we wait between "ask" and "receive."

Seeking God's Deliverance

JEFFERY J. VANGOETHEM

The narrative of the Exodus is one of the greatest demonstrations of God's deliverance in all of biblical history. God came in a mighty way to set His people free from Egyptian bondage. But it was not a walk in the park! As we consider that great deliverance, we recognize that Israel endured many struggles to gain that freedom; it took a good deal of time, and they learned some hard lessons.

God had to raise up a leader (Moses), He had to confront a powerful enemy (Pharaoh), and He had to challenge, teach, and change His people. Sometimes we think deliverance will be easy.

We ask ourselves, Can't God just do it?

Of course we believe that God can change our nation. He can change our churches. He can change society. He can change our families. But deliverance seldom comes without a long, prayerful struggle, accompanied by many steps of faith on the part of His people.

The promises. Let us first of all agree that God does bring deliverance. He changes lives; He renews churches; He brings revival to nations; He alters history when He chooses to do so. He can bring deliverance in many and various ways. We have some great and mighty promises that can form the basis of our prayers for deliverance.

For example, II Corinthians 2:14 says, "Now thanks be unto God, which always causeth us to triumph in Christ." God causes us to triumph. Also, I John 3:8 assures us, "the Son of God was manifested, that he might destroy the works of the devil." Sometimes we are up against satanic opposition as we move forward in ministry, yet we know that the Lord can defeat Satan and all of his hosts. With such mighty promises, we dare not settle for a state of defeat.

Let us not be satisfied with cold churches, unsaved family members, troubled marriages, and a decadent nation. Let us seek the Lord for His mighty intervention and deliverance by praying the promises of Scripture in faith.

The problem. That is not to say that we are always in a position to seek the Lord as we should. Sometimes we have wandered from God. Our minds and hearts are more in tune with the culture around us than with the things of God. God often reminds us of our spiritual poverty by seeming to withdraw His power and presence from our lives. After all, the Scripture exhorts us to "draw nigh to God, and he will draw nigh to you" (Jas. 4:8).

Our relationship with God is not always consistent. Sometimes we sense His closeness, and our prayers come easily. In other seasons, we have drifted away and it takes a fresh season of renewal, a change of pace, or a new leader to remind us to draw near and seek the Lord afresh.

We see this over and over again in the era of the Judges, during which there were many cycles of idolatry, repentance, and deliverance. For example, after Joshua's generation passed from the scene, this sad note was recorded: "And also that genera-tion were gathered unto their fathers: and there arose another generation after them, which knew not the Lord, nor yet the works which he had done for Israel" (Judg. 2:10). Yes, we can forget the mighty things that God is able to do when spiritual complancency or a sinful, unbelieving attitude sets in.

When this happens among God's people, we lose our fervency for the gospel; traditionalism and legalism can take hold of us and we can forget God and His power. Often we become satisfied with our man-made traditions, rituals, and practices; worshipful obedience to God becomes secondary. Our Leader, the Lord Jesus, stands over us, but we are no longer surrendered to Him in careful and full obedience. We are a long way from God. And deliverance cannot be found.

Let's acknowledge this problem of spiritual decline. It explains why growth, victory, and deliverance are not always constant in the life of the church and in the lives of believers.

The prospects. So what shall we do? How should we seek God's deliverance? Maybe our family needs renewal. Maybe our church needs revitalization. Maybe our nation needs revival. What should we do?

First, we must be convinced that God does grant deliverance when His people seek Him. As pointed out above, we have many promises to claim.

Second, we must also acknowledge that we are in a battle. Deliverance is not always going to come easily. The devil does not like to cede ground that he has gained. If he has enslaved us in sin, neutralized our church, poisoned our family relationships, or polluted our culture, he is proud of that and does not want to give up any of it. We are going to have to fight. But remember, we do not fight against flesh and blood (Eph. 6:2)!

Third, we have to draw near to God. We have to confess our sins, attempt to right our wrongs, and engage in fresh steps of obedience wherever it is required. We must ask ourselves, What fresh steps of obedience should I and could I take right now? That is a great place to start if we want to see things change.

And finally, we have to pray and seek the Lord afresh. Almost every occasion of biblical deliverance was preceded by the heartfelt, fervent, and persistent prayers of God's people. Remember the Lord's words to Moses: "the cry of the children of Israel is come unto me" (Exod. 3:9). Are we crying out to God? Have we persisted? Let us be people who believe in and seek deliverance.

TOPICS FOR NEXT QUARTER

PARAGRAPHS ON PLACES AND PEOPLE

HOREB

Horeb is also known as Sinai. It was here that Moses heard from God as he came to look at a burning bush that was not consumed.

Moses returned to Mount Sinai—this time not leading a flock of sheep, but the people of Israel. They arrived at Mount Sinai about three months after they left Egypt. It was at Mount Sinai that God gave the Ten Commandments and the Law to the nation of Israel.

The exact location of Mount Sinai is unknown. However, the traditional site is a mountain now called Jebel Musa. This mountain stands near the southern tip of the Sinai Peninsula.

DRY GROUND

There is difficulty determining just where the Israelites crossed the Red Sea. Several views place the crossing between the Mediterranean Sea and a lake—or through a lake. The most likely route has the Hebrews crossing a northern extension of the Red Sea.

A second problem concerns the type of body of water that the Israelites crossed. Some scholars theorize that they crossed a shallow flood plain or a marsh. Others claim they crossed over water only inches deep. These naturalistic theories miss the point.

Scripture is clear that God intervened directly in the escape of the Israelites. He could have routed the Israelites anywhere. Their safety was not dependent upon natural occurrences, but upon His intervention.

REUEL

Reuel is the name of Moses' father-in-law as given in Exodus 2:18. In other passages he is called Jethro. Perhaps he was known by different names to different tribes he encountered.

Jethro is introduced to us as a priest of Midian. Midian was a son of Abraham by Keturah (Gen. 25:2, 4). It is possible that Jethro belonged to a group of Midianites who continued to worship the God of Abraham.

Sometime later, Jethro came to visit Moses in the Israelite camp. He observed that Moses' entire day was occupied with deciding disputes. Jethro stated that this was too much for one man to bear and suggested setting up a system of judges with only the most difficult cases coming to Moses.

AARON

Aaron was the older brother of Moses and the Israelites' first high priest.

When Moses fled to Midian, Aaron remained behind in Egypt. Forty years later when Moses was sent back to Egypt, Aaron became his mouthpiece. Together they appeared before Pharaoh, calling on him to release the Israelites from slavery.

While others were also chosen to the priesthood, it was Aaron, as high priest, who once a year entered the holy of holies (Lev. 16:11-14). God attested His choice of Aaron for high priest by the budding of Aaron's rod, while rods beside it did not bud (Num. 17:2-9).

Because of his and Moses' sin at Meribah (Num. 20:12), Aaron was prohibited from entering the Promised Land. Aaron died on Mount Hor (33:38), and his son Eleazer succeeded him as high priest.

—Steven D. Pyle.

Daily Bible Readings for Home Study and Worship

(Readings are for the week previous to the lesson topics.)

1. September 1. A Long, Hard Oppression

M — Israel in Egypt. Exod. 1:1-6.
T — Another King over Egypt. Acts 7:17-19.
W — Hatred for God's People. Ps. 105:23-25.
T — The Wisdom of the World. I Cor. 3:18-20.
F — Further Growth After Persecution. Acts 4:1-4.
S — Courage Under Fire. Dan. 3:16-25.
S — Enduring Cruelty and Danger. Exod. 1:7-22.

2. September 8. The Birth of Moses

M — Moses' Family History. Exod. 6:16-20, 26-27.
T — Moses' Birth and Upbringing. Acts 7:20-22.
W — Protection in Times of Trouble. Ps. 9:8-14.
T — Protection from the Wicked. Ps. 12:5-8.
F — Drawn out of the Waters . Ps. 18:16-19.
S — Childlike Trust in God. Ps. 131:1-3.
S — Moses Saved from Pharaoh's Malice. Exod. 2:1-10.

3. September 15. A Comfortable Exile

M — Israel's Affliction Foretold. Gen. 15:13-16.
T — Moses' Sacrifice and Choice. Heb. 11:24-27.
W — Moses' Flight from Egypt. Acts 7:23-29.
T — Leadership Aspirations Rebuked. Gen. 37:5-11.
F — Jacob's Encounter at a Well. Gen. 29:1-12.
S — Hearing the Cries of the Distressed. Ps. 107:19-22.
S — Moses' Exile to Midian. Exod. 2:11-25.

4. September 22. Moses at the Burning Bush

M — Moses' Encounter with the Lord. Acts 7:30-34.
T — David Called from Shepherding. Ps. 78:70-72.
W — Joshua on Holy Ground. Josh. 5:13-15.
T — The I AM Who Calls. Exod. 3:13-18.
F — The God of the Living. Matt. 22:23-33.
S — Further Assurance to Moses. Exod. 6:2-8.
S — Moses' Call from God. Exod. 3:1-10.

5. September 29. "Let My People Go"

M — Pharaoh's Obstinance Foretold. Exod. 3:18-20.
T — Israel's Burden Increased. Exod. 5:10-18.
W — Complaints and Reassurance. Exod. 5:19-23.
T — Pagan Taunts Against God. II Chron. 32:9-15.
F — The Lord Versus Pagan Worship. II Kings 18:28-35.
S — A Pagan King Acknowledges God. Dan. 2:46-49; 4:34-37.
S — Moses Before Pharaoh. Exod. 5:1-9.

6. October 6. A Plague of Blood

M — Further Instructions to Moses. Exod. 7:1-13.
T — The Plague of Frogs. Exod. 8:1-13.
W — The Plague of Lice. Exod. 8:14-19.
T — The Plague of Flies. Exod. 8:20-24.
F — Pharaoh's Seeming Change of Heart. Exod. 8:25-32.
S — Bowl Judgments of Blood. Rev. 16:3-7.
S — The Nile Turned to Blood. Exod. 7:14-24.

7. October 13. Pharaoh's Hardening Heart

M — The Plague on Livestock. Exod. 9:1-7.
T — The Plague of Boils. Exod. 9:8-12.
W — The Plague of Hail. Exod. 9:13-26.

T — Balaam's Insincere Repentance. Num. 22:34-41.
F — Saul's Insincere Repentance. I Sam. 15:24-35.
S — Simon's Insincere Repentance. Acts 8:18-24.
S — Pharaoh's Insincere Repentance. Exod. 9:27-35.

8. October 20. Final Confrontation with Pharaoh

M — Warning of Locusts. Exod. 10:1-6.
T — Pharaoh's Vacillations. Exod. 10:7-11.
W — The Plague of Locusts. Exod. 10:12-20.
T — An Object of God's Wrath. Rom. 9:17-24.
F — A Day of Darkness. Amos 5:18-20.
S — Darkened Understanding. Eph. 4:17-24.
S — The Plague of Darkness. Exod. 10:21-29.

9. October 27. The Passover

M — Death of the Firstborn. Exod. 11:1-10.
T — Passover Instructions. Deut. 16:1-8.
W — Jesus' Final Passover. Luke 22:7-20.
T — Behold the Lamb of God. John 1:29-36.
F — Christ Our Passover. I Cor. 5:6-8.
S — Worthy Is the Lamb. Rev. 5:6-14.
S — The Passover Lamb. Exod. 12:1-14.

10. November 3. Out of Egypt

M — Firstborn of Egypt Slain. Ps. 105:36-39.
T — Israel Led Forth like Sheep. Ps. 78:51-54.
W — Brought Out by God's Strong Hand. Ps. 136:10-12.
T — Levites Instead of Firstborn. Num. 3:11-13, 40-51.
F — The Promise Endures. Gal. 3:15-18.
S — God's Firstborn Not Spared. Rom. 8:28-32.
S — Israel's Exodus from Egypt. Exod. 12:29-42.

11. November 10. Pursuit of the Slaves

M — Remember This Day. Exod. 13:1-8.
T — A Lasting Memorial. Exod. 13:9-16.
W — A Command from Joseph. Gen. 50:22-26.
T — Guided by the Cloud. Exod. 40:34-38.
F — The Cloud and the Tabernacle. Num. 9:15-23.
S — Baptized into the Cloud. I Cor. 10:1-4.
S — Israel's Road to Freedom. Exod. 13:17—14:9.

12. November 17. Crossing the Red Sea

M — The Red Sea Miracle Remembered. Neh. 9:9-12.
T — Saved Despite Rebelliousness. Ps. 106:7-9.
W — Rebellious Complaining Resumes. Exod. 17:1-7.
T — Redeemed by God's Love. Isa. 63:7-14.
F — Stand Still and See. II Chron. 20:13-17.
S — Saved from a Stormy Sea. Matt. 8:23-27.
S — Parting of the Red Sea. Exod. 14:10-22.

13. November 24. Deliverance from Pharaoh's Army

M — Israel's Enemies Overwhelmed. Ps. 78:51-54.
T — Redeemed from the Foe. Ps. 106:10-12.
W — A Second Miraculous Crossing. Josh. 3:14-17.
T — The Crossing Memorialized. Josh. 4:18-24.
F — God's Power over Enemies. Exod. 15:1-10.
S — God's Reign over All. Exod. 15:11-18.
S — Miraculous Redemption. Exod. 14:23-31.

REVIEW

What have you learned this quarter?

Can you answer these questions?

Deliverance
UNIT I: The Call to Deliverance

September 1
A Long, Hard Opression

1. What did the new king of Egypt fear?
2. What did the king initially do to address his fear?
3. What did the Egyptian king order the Hebrew midwives to do? Why?
4. How did the midwives respond to the king's order? Why?
5. What final edict did the pharaoh issue in an attempt to prevent the continued increase of the Israelites?

September 8
The Birth of Moses

1. In what context was Moses born?
2. What was the parents' plan for saving their son?
3. Who found the baby Moses?
4. What role did Pharaoh's daughter give to Jochebed?
5. How do we see God working providentially to save Moses?

September 15
A Comfortable Exile

1. How did Moses respond when he saw an Egyptian beating a Hebrew?
2. Why did he flee from Egypt?
3. What did Moses do on behalf of the seven women? What did his actions reveal about him?
4. Who was the father of the women, and what did he do for Moses?
5. What was the Israelites' situation back in Egypt?

September 22
Moses at the Burning Bush

1. What had Moses been doing during his forty years in Midian?
2. What did his work in the wilderness teach Moses?
3. Who was the "angel of the Lord" (Exod. 3:2)?
4. How did God express his concern for the Israelites?
5. What did God say He was going to do for the Israelites?

UNIT II: Preparation for Deliverance

September 29
"Let My People Go"

1. How did Moses' attitude differ from what it had been forty years earlier?
2. What message did Moses and Aaron deliver?
3. What did Pharaoh mean when he said he did not know the Lord?
4. In what sense did the conflict go beyond Moses and Pharaoh? Whom did it really involve?
5. What order did Pharaoh give in relation to the Israelites? Why?

October 6
A Plague of Blood

1. What message did God want to deliver to Pharaoh and the Egyptian people?
2. What purposes were the plagues designed to accomplish?
3. What significance did the river have to the Egyptians?
4. What resulted from this first plague on Egypt? What physical and spiritual impact did it have?
5. How did Pharaoh respond to the plague?

October 13

Pharaoh's Hardening Heart

1. What phenomena were involved in the seventh plague?
2. How did the Israelites fare during the seventh plague?
3. Did Moses believe that Pharaoh would actually release the Israelites?
4. What is the religious significance of the details regarding the destruction of crops?
5. How did Pharaoh respond to the ending of the plague?

October 20

Final Confrontation with Pharaoh

1. How did the darkness affect the Egyptians? The Israelites?
2. What made this plague so terrifying to the Egyptians?
3. What did Pharaoh offer to do?
4. Why did Moses insist the people's animals must go with them?
5. Was Moses surprised by the king's refusal to let the people go? Why?

October 27

The Passover

1. How did the Lord highlight the uniqueness of the final plague?
2. What qualifications did the sacrificial animal have to meet?
3. What did killing the lamb and putting its blood on the door symbolize?
4. How did the death of the firstborn strike a blow against Egypt's gods?
5. Why was it important for the Israelites to observe Passover annually?

UNIT III: Deliverance Accomplished

November 3

Out of Egypt

1. Who died in the final plague?
2. How did Pharaoh respond to the final plague?
3. How did the Egyptian people respond?
4. How long had the Israelites lived in Egypt before their exodus?
5. Why was it so important for the Israelites to remember the Exodus?

November 10

Pursuit of the Slaves

1 Why did the Israelites not go directly to Canaan?
2. Why did Moses take the bones of Joseph with him? Of what should this have reminded the Israelites?
3. What did the pillar demonstrate?
4. What was the Lord's purpose in having the people set up their camp in such a vulnerable place?
5. Why would Pharaoh pursue the Israelites after all Egypt had suffered?

November 17

Crossing the Red Sea

1. How did the Israelites react when they saw the Egyptian army?
2. What did Moses tell the people to do?
3. What role did the Lord assign to Moses in the deliverance?
4. Why did the Egyptians follow the Israelites into the sea? What happened to the army?

November 24

Deliverance from Pharaoh's Army

1. What permitted the Egyptians to pursue the Israelites into the sea?
2. How did the Lord trouble the Egyptians, and why did He do it?
3. What happened to the Egyptian army, and who was responsible?
4. What did the Israelites see in the aftermath of the miraculous destruction of the Egyptians?